Aura-Soma

Aura-Soma

Healing Through Color, Plant, and Crystal Energy

Irene Dalichow and Mike Booth

Translated from the German Language
by Joan M. Burnham

Hay House, Inc.
Carlsbad, CA

Published and distributed in the United States by: Hay House, Inc., P.O. Box 5100
Carlsbad, CA 92018-5100 (800) 654-5126

Edited by: Jill Kramer   Designed by: Christy Allison

Library of Congress Cataloging-in-Publication Data

Dalichow, Irene.
    [Aura-Soma. English]
      Aura-Soma : healing through color, plant, and crystal energy /
Irene Dalichow and Mike Booth : translated from the German language
by Joan M. Burnham. — 1st English-language hardcover ed.
        p.   cm.
    Includes bibliographical references.
    ISBN 1-56170-322-2. — ISBN 1-56170-291-9 (pbk.)
    1. Color—Therapeutic use.   2. Phototherapy.   3. Essences and
essential oils—Therapeutic use.   4. Chakras.   I. Booth, Mike.
II. Title.
RZ414.6.D3513   1996
615.5—dc20

                                                      95-25375
                                                      CIP

ISBN: 1-56170-322-2

00 99 98 97 96   5 4 3 2 1

First Printing, 1994, by Droemer Knaur Publishing, Munich, Germany

First English-Language Hardcover Edition, March 1996, by Hay House, Inc.
(Tradepaper edition published simultaneously)

Printed in the United States of America

The greatest teacher is in yourself.
What we offer, are just guidelines.
— Vicky Wall

C O N T E N T S

CHAPTER:

APPENDIX:

WHAT IS AURA-SOMA?

Y ou are the colors you choose. This statement, repeated so very often in connection with Aura-Soma, may at first seem quite bold. Why should colors that especially appeal to you affect your inner being? Please allow yourself to consider this concept, though. Think about the affinity that children have with color. On one particular day, they simply must wear the hot pink sweater that clashes with the red paisley pants. Mother's pleas for reason fall on deaf ears. How many tears must have been shed throughout the years over the issue of stubborn youngsters versus determined mothers? There must be a reason behind this phenomenon—that is, children creating such conflicts just for the sake of color.

Similarly, take the case of older teenagers who are going through their "black" phases. Nothing, no one, and especially not Mother, can keep them from shrouding themselves in black, to show the world what is most important to them—namely, freedom from set limits.

A certain therapy has been in existence since 1984. It is called Aura-Soma. It consists, among other things, of the use of the contents of 94 small angular glass bottles (numbered from 0 to 93), each containing two different-colored layers of liquid. Many people have come to feel a greater affinity to the unaffected, childlike part of themselves by using the contents of these bottles. They accept the offer to read from this 94-bottle "menu" and choose from it what they confidently feel will fully satisfy them. In this system, it doesn't matter how "impossible" the color combinations appear, be it pink over red, blue over green, or yellow over violet. No parent, no teacher, actually no one at all, will assume the right to interfere with this choice. Every color combination is right and good. For, as we stated, one of the principles of the Aura-Soma therapy is this: *You are the colors you choose*, and there is no doubt about it.

Why it is that we, with the help of such appealing and harmless little bottles, can come close to the lofty goal of self-knowledge, cannot be explained in a few sentences. But through the contents of this book and through contact with the bottles and their contents, you will soon be able to discover this secret for yourself.

Let's say that you have made your selection. Usually it consists of four little bottles, each with two color elements. They are wonderful to look at, and when you take off the screwed-on tops, you'll smell a wonderful fragrance coming from essential oils—ready to be massaged into your skin. What a feast for the senses!

But this tempting, sensuous aspect is not all there is to the Aura-Soma oils. There is much more. Aura-Soma is in a relationship with systems of ancient wisdom, such as the Tree of Life from the Kabbala, the Tarot, and the Chinese I Ching. The unlocking of the meanings of the colors is also related to the Hindu chakra system. And there are even more interesting references to ancient wisdom.

Another point that transcends the appealing sensuous aspect is the following: *The choice of colors you make and the sequence of this choice tells much about yourself—perhaps everything that really counts.* There is a similarity to an astrological birth chart.

The bottles present information about your attitude about life and your life goals. They reveal your current problems, what you have learned from them up to now, and what you can still learn. And finally, they tell (and quite believably so) how you will progress on your path in view of your spiritual, mental, emotional, and physical dimensions.

The fact that you have selected and are using the substances indicates that you are supporting the process of seeking out your goals and the meaning of your life, and examining your problems to find new ways of dealing with them. Little by little, you will be rid of some of the roadblocks that fate has placed in your path. Or, spiritually speaking, you will rid yourself of the blocks that you, yourself, have placed in your path. These aspects of Aura-Soma are the most important. However, the fact that the substances on the physical level have a healing effect, sometimes soft and subtle, but at times strong and penetrating, we see only as a side effect. For Aura-

Soma represents the view that there is really only one sickness, really only one dis-ease: not knowing one's place in life or the meaning of this life. This is what results in resistance, stress, and physical ailments.

When you awaken within yourself the understanding of light and color, you will understand the meaning behind your lack of wellness. You can unlock the door of your true self. And "understanding" winds its way, in this case, not only through the pathways of the brain, but is present in your whole body, in your emotions, and in your intuition.

᪥ ᪥ ᪥

But what exactly is Aura-Soma? How did this unusual system of color and fragrance and little bottles come about? Why are hearts taken by storm? What is the meaning of the words *Aura-Soma* anyway?

The word *Aura,* first of all, refers to the electromagnetic field surrounding every person, something that many psychics can see. Babies also have that ability, for parents and schools have not yet been able to wean them from their psychic abilities. The word comes from the Latin. It means: *akin to air, a slight breath, vapor, a shimmer.*

Soma is the Old-Greek word for "body." It is also a word from the Sanskrit, the Old-Indian language, which in India is still used in literary and erudite circles. In Sanskrit, *Soma* designates a mysterious drink that transports the soul into a divine ecstasy. What is contained in this drink, no one knows exactly. There has been much speculation about it, but a recipe has obviously not been found. Both concepts, *Aura* and *Soma,* have essentially more meaning inherent in them. The combination of the two words sets up a specific vibration. Similarly, the carefully chosen first name of a person is said to reveal something about his or her nature.

The name of the therapeutic system, which was discovered by Vicky Wall—a British chiropodist and pharmacist—was transmitted to her by means of prayer and meditation. And it is curious to note that the dash between *Aura* and *Soma* was transmitted in the same way.

The History of Aura-Soma

Vicky Wall grew up as the youngest daughter in a Hasidic family in

England. Her father was a master of the Kabbala, the Jewish esoteric teaching. She was the seventh child of a seventh child, as Vicky Wall wrote in her autobiography, *The Miracle of Colour Healing* (Aquarian/Thorsons, 1990). In it she described in detail how Aura-Soma came into being. Here, we shall touch only on the most important aspects of her story.

When Vicky was a little girl, she and her father would stroll through the London parks, and he would ask her, "Which disease, do you suppose, this plant can heal?" Or he might say something such as: "Look for a plant that can help the soreness in my throat." As a result, her father, in a playful manner, acquainted her with what is known in the healing arts as the "Science of Signatures" (described more fully in Chapter 3). He helped his daughter to develop her intuition in this field, which would later prove very beneficial in her healing work. However, Vicky was already exceptionally endowed with intuition; in fact, from her childhood on, she was both psychic and clairvoyant. Until her death in 1991, Vicky's great love for her father and her close bond to him always remained with her.

In 1984, Vicky, then 66 years old and blind as a result of sudden and massive eye hemorrhages, received the first formulas for the Aura-Soma substances, and she had the impression that they were transmitted to her with input from her father. At this time, however, he had already been deceased for a long time, but he most certainly had a hand in her knowledge from "beyond," along with other beings and other forces.

In light of her psychic ability, her education, and her experiences, Vicky Wall was obviously the appropriate person to transfer information from another dimension to this one, to realize and to materialize it. Everything she had experienced in this life seemed to have prepared her for this assignment.

The miraculous event happened one night. Vicky Wall gathered an abundance of various natural ingredients together in her small laboratory at her home and began her alchemical work. Her hands were guided to do it, she later reported.

All Aura-Soma ingredients belong to the mineral and plant kingdoms and, in addition, to the kingdoms of color and light. Vicky's talent for perceiving colors—including the colors of the human aura—did not diminish in spite of her blindness. To the contrary, this ability was even strengthened. In the morning following that historic night, Vicky's friend and colleague,

4

Margaret Cockbain, asked her, "What are these pretty bottles for?" Vicky had no answer. She didn't know. She guessed that they must be cosmetic oils, for the upper half of the substances in the bottles consisted of a colored oily liquid floating on a second layer of water-based liquid of another color. When shaken, for a short time a lotion of 50 percent water and 50 percent oil was produced. This proportion corresponds exactly to the consistency of asses' milk, in which Cleopatra used to bathe to retain her soft and beautiful skin.

Emulsions with these proportions of water and oil are ideally suited to penetrate the skin. Within these new substances, containing no artificial stabilizers (for only in this way would Vicky Wall form her combinations), the healing and energizing forces could do their work undisturbed. Vicky would eventually come to these realizations, but at this point in time, she had as yet no inkling of the scope or the importance of her "discovery."

Quite rapidly, Vicky began to present her "jewels," as she called the oils, in exhibitions. As a result, she and Margaret Cockbain experienced one surprise after another, for the contents of the little bottles were substantially more effective than could have been expected from mere cosmetics. They had an extraordinary healing effect on many people. Vicky reported that a woman with a feverish abscess could turn the tide of infection by applying the royal blue/magenta-colored "Rescue Oil"—to the affected area. Patients with migraine headaches and with chronic back pain experienced a lessening of pain. Oils of other colors helped in cases of impotence, heart ailments, depression, and so forth.

A particularly great surprise then occurred. For Vicky Wall it constituted definite proof that the contents of the lower half of the bottle correspond to "the true aura," as she called it, of the one purchasing the bottle. This true aura has nothing to do with the electromagnetic field and the other subtle bodies. It is a subtle domain located somewhat above the navel. In every person it has a unique marking, as individual as a fingerprint. (There will be further discussion on this subject in Chapter 4.) Vicky's thousands of clients allowed her to verify this observation over and over again. In most cases it held true, which showed her that there was still more to be known and realized about Aura-Soma. Not only the fact that the formulas were transmitted to her during her periods of prayer and meditation, but also the effect these formulas had, seemed to lie beyond the normal realm of perceptibility. They seemed to awaken in people memories of something long lost. Vicky, with her unusual psychic ability, could *see* that certain something. She could, after considering the many reports, verify it. That certain something has been lost to most people, who have been programmed by the mindset of our times, so in tune with science and materialism. But one can find it in many books of wisdom, stemming from ancient cultures. *The Tibetan Book of the Dead* is an example. *That certain something is that the essence of humans, their innermost being, is related to color!*

In the same year that the first substances came into being, Vicky Wall met Mike Booth. He had studied art and education and had worked a long time as a painter, potter, and as director of an art colony. When he met Vicky, he was a healer and was engaged in management training. He could see the scope of this newborn system. He immediately changed his future plans in order to devote his talents to the establishment of Aura-Soma.

Booth possesses similar capabilities as a healer and psychic as did Vicky. They were able to compare and confirm their perceptions—certainly a rare bit of good fortune! From then on, Mike Booth worked with Vicky and helped her in both professional and personal ways, for she had by then developed diabetes and a serious heart condition. Mike and Vicky traveled together and taught jointly.

Vicky instructed Mike in the production of the Aura-Soma substances. He was present at the birth of most of the products, now so readily available. He added his knowledge of homeopathy, natural healing, theosophy, and Buddhism. In her book, *The Miracle of Colour Healing,* Vicky Wall wrote: "Mike Booth serves as my eyes and is my constant helper. We work closely together in spiritual unity. Mike will eventually take over and continue my work."

Vicky Wall died in early 1991. Since then, Mike Booth has been leading and coordinating the whole organization, the production, and the training program. (Margaret Cockbain and Booth's wife, Claudia, are currently co-directors.) Mike also receives the new formulas, as Vicky did. To date, the assortment is not yet complete.

Aura-Soma Conquers the World

Today Aura-Soma is represented in most of the European countries, as well as in Israel, South Africa, Canada, the USA, South America, Australia, New Zealand, Japan, and India. In Germany and Switzerland, one might even say that there is an Aura-Soma boom. Altogether, since 1984, the number of people buying the substances has doubled each year. The products, starting with the oils and then the "Pomanders" and "Quintessences," are being used by people of all ages and from all strata of society. Seriously ill and comatose people, little children, animals, even sick plants can benefit from them.

People who have guarded their thoughts and kept them free from bias often attain swift and profound results—their intuition is strengthened, and they seem to be able to reach down to grasp an archetypal knowledge. Many times they find a new direction for their lives. It becomes easier for them to give up worn-out patterns of behavior and to take new paths. If the substances are selected "with the heart" (and not with the head), and if they are regularly and properly used, then there is often an improvement in physical and emotional illnesses. However, it happens again and again that at the beginning of their use, a health crisis may occur that can shatter the faith of the person. As is necessary in other systems—homeopathy, for instance—it is also imperative that this kind of crisis be overcome in Aura-Soma. The body and the soul can truly free themselves of the old, and make room for the new.

By the way, it is always advisable, in the case of special problems, to seek the professional counsel of a good physician, a health practitioner, a psychotherapist, a body worker, or others. (You will find more information on this subject at the end of Chapter 12.)

People who tend to be skeptical, something to be expected in this time of often questionable "New Age" offerings, are often not at all drawn to Aura-Soma at first. Or, if they find it appealing, they have to battle with doubts. Many who currently use the substances successfully and are convinced of it now have experienced and overcome this phase. And they have good cause for both.

One such reason for doubt is this: during the building-up period (when Aura-Soma was in its initial growth phase)—which is still ongoing—much had to be postponed. Reliable research undertaken with scientific methods regarding the effects of the substances is not yet available. Another reason is that, up to now, it has been unprecedented that a comparable system for gaining self-realization and for complete healing has been transmitted through prayer and meditation. After all, it is truly not easy to swallow the idea that formulas, exceptionally complex formulas at that, have simply fallen from heaven, and continue to do so. It is true, also, that they do not offer humankind much in the way of information, only the challenge, "Go ahead and do it!" Some people who had confidence in their intuition have actually rolled up their sleeves and "done it." And they, in the few years that have passed since the birth of Aura-Soma, have contributed ideas and reported results, without which this book could never have been written.

Yet, the process of unlocking all the secrets concerning the therapeutic and esoteric/spiritual aspects of the whole system is still in full swing. And keeping that fact in mind—that Aura-Soma is something esoteric, skeptical minds can understandably harbor doubts. Besides, Aura-Soma speaks of the contents of the bottles being "inspired," of angels and devas, of the subtle bodies of humans, and of their karmic experiences—hardly an easily digestible diet for everyone!

Nonetheless, the fact is that the substances are effective; the colors really do unlock the secrets of the vibrations of the body and harmonize them. This has a direct bearing on the total person, and works on his or her spiritual, mental, emotional, and physical level in a very gentle way. Aura-Soma is described as a "nonintrusive soul therapy." It is never obtrusive. Therapies, functioning in a similar way, are said to have been practiced in the healing temples of ancient Egypt and ancient Greece, by the Essenes[1] and other societies and cultures.

The great German poet and sage, Johann Wolfgang von Goethe, in his "color theory," fought for humans gaining understanding of the esoteric aspects of the phenomenon of color. All in vain! The scientific approach of Isaac Newton, the English physicist and mathematician, prevailed.

Goethe said that one day his theory of color would be more meaningful to humankind than his poetry. Since many of us know and appreciate his poetry, we can therefore understand the importance of his assertion.

---

[1]The community that existed from 150 B.C. until A.D. 70, and to which the historical Jesus is said to have belonged.

8

Today, there are over a million users of Aura-Soma worldwide, as well as several thousand trained practitioners. One may assume that Goethe's prognosis will prove to be correct, for so many people have opened themselves to the mysteries of color. They have done so to such an extent that they have ventured on a journey of discovery through the rainbow. But of course, not many will take the trouble to study Goethe's scholarly color theory. However, the essence of what he wanted to convey might possibly touch more people through the channel of Aura-Soma than do his masterful literary works.

❦ ❦ ❦

You are the colors you choose.

As children we stood up for our right to choose the colors we wanted in our lives, and we were ready to risk a great deal. Today, as adults at the end of the 20th century, we have the opportunity to get to the bottom of this innate desire. And we can do so without risking the wrath of our educators, and in a more refined fashion than with the help of that hot pink sweater. It is especially thrilling to know that Vicky Wall perceived Aura-Soma as an "ever-growing therapy." We can then envision that the journey through the rainbow shall lead ever higher, ever deeper, into unknown dimensions.

Fasten your seat belts, please!

❦ ❦ ❦ ❦ ❦

HEALING WITH COLOR— THE OLDEST THERAPY IN THE WORLD

In May 1987, when the renowned teacher of Tibetan Buddhism, Chögyam Trungpa, was buried, a circular rainbow appeared around the sun. Co-incidence? The 3,000 guests present did not consider it to be such, but rather, saw it as a sign. Heaven had declared that something important had happened. A great soul had been transported from this plane to another.

From the Old Testament, we know the rainbow to be a bearer of information. It heralded the end of The Flood; God sent it as a sign of reconciliation and connectedness.

When a rainbow appears, people stop in their tracks. An atmosphere of something unusual, something wonderful, surrounds it. For that reason, it is considered a symbol of good luck in many cultures.

In the meantime, the "New Age" movement, having become somewhat suspect with respect to superficiality and questionable ethics in finance, has chosen the same symbol—the rainbow. Since some of its followers think that we are still in the age of Pisces, ruled by a patriarchal system, with its ideals, institutions, and ways of the past, they believe the sun is slowly penetrating. A rainbow, with all of its wealth of symbolism, is the right sign to announce the coming of a new time.

No matter how this new era turns out, one thing is clear: the subject of color and light has already been awakening intense interest everywhere. It has been aided by photography, film, television, and computers. Their development in the last decades has progressed from black-and-white, two-dimensional images to colorful, highly realistic, three-dimensional (3-D) images. For example, we now have 3-D films, "virtual reality," and also 3-D reality in art forms. Never before have color and light been as evident as they are today. The well-known British esoteric author, Alice Bailey (1880-1949), posed the noteworthy theory that the rapid evolvement of humankind and its civilization at the end of the 19th century was due to the availability of electricity. Therefore, the result was more light in the world.

It could probably not have been predicted in the time that Alice Bailey lived, what abuse to nature and to human beings would come about through civilization. Today, people are again giving credence to ancient wisdom in order to offset the damage done. They are turning back to ancient knowledge of natural laws and rhythms and the unity of life. All this had been set aside for the euphoria about the mechanistic philosophy. Ancient knowledge about physical health is also back in good repute. Information about fragrances and aromas, herbs and crystals, and how all these magical methods and instruments of Mother Nature affect the body and the soul, are becoming more accepted. And something else is having a renaissance—namely, the oldest vibrational healing method in the world: color, as well as light, therapy.

As far back in time as the legendary sunken continent of Atlantis, physical, emotional, and spiritual illnesses were treated with color and light. In Heliopolis, an ancient Egyptian city of the sun, and the cult center of the god Atum, there existed healing temples that were infused with color and light throughout their structures. The ancient Chinese would place patients with epilepsy on violet carpets and in rooms with violet veils covering the windows. It was meant to lessen their discomfort. Patients with scarlet fever were clothed in red and were treated with red light beams. Those with disorders of the colon were painted with yellow paint, and a yellow light streamed through curtains of the same color in order to ease cramps.

Traditional color therapy also included color beams aimed at drinking water and foods that were chosen for their colors. This same therapy was and is prevalent in ancient and modern India, in ancient Greece, in Babylon, Persia, and Tibet, where it has continued to the present.

A book published in 1933 that has become a classic was written by the Indian healer Dinshah Ghadiali about vibrations of color. He stated that illness originates from the lack of color or the overabundance of specific colors in the body. (This is also the view of Aura-Soma.) The therapy of Ghadiali consists of a colored lamp light beamed over the total body or parts of it in order to dispel imbalances in the body.

Then, in the 1970s and '80s, it was scientifically proven that colored light influences people—even color-blind or sightless individuals. Blue lowers blood pressure and the activity of brain waves. Pink neutralizes aggressiveness. Consequently, jail cells are now sometimes painted pink to calm violent inmates. In the past, they were treated with medication, but now the effects of colored walls can be sufficient to cool off their emotions. And way before that? Who knows? Maybe the unruly Babylonian bandits were put to rest in prisons with pink walls. It is regrettable that historians and archeologists have up to now written mostly about battles and heroic deeds. It would be so much more interesting to discover in-depth information about daily life in times past. (However, it should be noted that in recent years, the feminist movement has sprung up among archeologists of both sexes. They follow the beliefs of the late well-known archeologist Marija Gimbutas, who had been researching the everyday life of people in ancient times, what women did, what was considered their domain, and how spirituality was expressed in daily life.)

Today, the knowledge gained about the effects of color is being applied in many hospitals. Seriously ill patients are being placed in rooms with walls painted in muted tones in order to induce calmness. Short-term patients, on the other hand, are given rooms with bright, warm colors to speed the healing process and to raise the energy level. In the treatment of jaundice in newborns, rays of blue light are used.

Specific conditions of color and light also have an impact on learning ability. This fact was discovered during studies of elementary schools in Canada by the pioneer in color research, Harry Wohlfahrt, who is German. He determined that the environment for learning and for positive moods is most favorable when the walls are painted light blue and yellow, and the rooms are lit with full-spectrum light bulbs (which simulate sunlight).

The last example can be found in a book by Jacob Liberman, which has earned the acclaim of laypersons, as well as that of the experts. In *The Healing Power of Light,* Liberman concentrates on advances in color and light therapy since 1974. In 1977, he treated his mother, who was going blind, with these methods, and she retained her eyesight. He writes that this miracle builds the foundation for his life from then on and for the work he introduces in this book.

The science of light opens the door to a new era in medicine. Liberman writes:

> In the center of this new medicine—that is, energy-medicine, stands light, a noninvasive powerful tool. In the decade of the '90s it will become clear that the foundation upon which all life is based, upon which it evolves and progresses, is light. Wise men of ancient times as well as those of the present show in their metaphysical texts that they are quite familiar with this concept. But we shall witness a new marriage of the intuitive and the rational sciences. It will be a union performed by light.

Light and color contain the essence of all that human beings want to attain through the intake of nutrients and vitamin preparations. They act as catalysts for the acceptance and utilization by the body of these nutritive substances. A human being is basically a living photocell, and the eyes do not exist only to see, so writes Liberman. Modern science ought to begin viewing the eyes as a possible gateway to the spirit. In fact, some researchers are convinced that there is a connection between the color of the eyes and one's conduct. Some of them are certain that different eye colors correspond to different areas of the brain and, therefore, influence our personalities. If that were true, one could also conclude that different areas of the brain would be affected when one looks at colors, so writes Liberman.

His view differs from that of Alice Bailey in that he sees no blessing for humankind in the prevalence of the electric light. He rather regrets that its all-pervasiveness has robbed us of the awareness of natural rhythms of light and darkness. However, the rediscovery of light therapy, color therapy, and light-and-color therapy would offset the errors of the past.

Today, there exists an abundance of different offshoot therapies regarding color or light or both. They start with counseling about color and style and clothing, of the personal environment, and of office space. All of them offer people an amelioration of well-being or promise to do so. The list goes on, from acupuncture using color, to "crystal cards." The latter are aluminum cards that are dyed with 20 different tones and etched with thousands of microscopic pyramidal crystals. This technique originates from work undertaken at the National Aeronautics and Space Administration (NASA). These cards are to be placed on the body or under the pillow for a healing effect. And then, there is Aura-Soma....

That which has belonged to the body of medicinal knowledge since the beginning of sentient human beings has been buried for a very long time. But today it is reappearing in a variety of modern guises. Little by little, it will be proven by methods of modern science that light and color, phenomena present all around us and in us, have immense power inherent to them. If purposefully applied, they can work miracles.

But what is the distinction between Aura-Soma and other color therapies offered today?

First, Aura-Soma represents a combination of color and light therapy. Just about everyone becoming acquainted with it sees that at first glance. The bottles, with their colorful substances, are normally displayed in such a way that light can shine through them. This is how the double quality of their contents is evident in brilliant, translucent, bathed-in-light soulful colors.

The second distinctive quality is that the formulas were received through prayer and meditation by Vicky Wall, a blind elderly lady. In spite of her handicap, she managed to retain her clairvoyance and her ability to perceive color—skills she had developed to perfection. But the directions for the use of the "Power-Pack," the colorful, very effective kit for healing that she received, were not transmitted clairvoyantly. They were revealed little by little, and there will be even more to discover in the future. Whoever works with it is compelled to experiment. And there we have a new point of interest. Aura-Soma "tickles" the creativity of the layperson as well as the professional.

At this point, we wish to emphasize one thing clearly: with all due respect for Vicky Wall's capabilities and her devotion to what was entrusted to her, the fact is that the manner in which she received information is not essential to the system. More important is that the substances are available and that their healing effects can unfold to the benefit of more than a million people.

We believe that here on this material plane there are certain standards of quality, even if relative, and these should be adhered to. Then, when that which is transmitted through channels from other dimensions does not conform to these criteria, one should not pay any attention to it. If, however, the quality is there, then the information deserves the same consideration as the speculative discoveries that come into existence in "natural," intellectual ways. The question arises, then, whether discoveries do not, after all, have something to do with inspiration. (The word *inspiration* originates from the Latin. It means: *enlivenment; exalting; to be breathed upon by spirit,* which points to a dimension other than the material one.) Albert Einstein, for example, admitted that his theory of relativity originated from information transmitted to him in dreams.

A third unusual characteristic that distinguishes Aura-Soma from other color therapies is the meaning of color as a means of communication. As the rainbow can be considered a multifaceted bearer of information, so also the Aura-Soma bottles contain within them individual codes for each color. One could view the facets of the rainbow as letters of a cosmic alphabet. It is in that manner that the colors of Aura-Soma speak their own language. Whoever understands this language knows why a person makes one particular choice, why he or she chooses exactly this one and not another bottle as his or her favorite. Goethe has already said that there is a language hidden in the phenomenon of color. However, he said that for him it was not the time to go deeper into the subject, but that would happen sometime later.

Color is linked with language, and it is also related to sound. There are a number of people who are engaged in finding the matching tone to each of the 94 balance bottles. This part of the system is still waiting to be explored. (There are already mantras for the seven colors with corresponding tones designated.)

Because the substances contain essential oils from plants, the sense of smell plays an important role. The sense of taste is indirectly connected with that. One reason is that the olfactory nerves and gustatory nerves are closely related. (When our nose is stuffed up during a cold, we cannot enjoy the finest of foods, for our sense of taste is also blocked.) Another reason is that just gazing at certain bottles stimulates the salivary glands, for whatever reason. Perhaps it is that the colors are reminders of blackberry juice, or certain flavors of Jello. It is by the actual use of the contents of the bottles, the massaging of the substances into the skin, that the sense of touch is also brought into play. And it is quite obvious which role the sense of sight has in Aura-Soma.

A Feast for the Senses

All five senses are called into play when one works with the substances. The sixth sense also develops noticeably. Intuition and "being in the flow" play a greater role than ever before. Deep parts of the inner self, long buried, step into consciousness and can be observed in the light. This process can also take place in dreams, in meditation, in heightened awareness, or in connection with body- or psychotherapy.

Aura-Soma works well with other subtle healing methods—homeopathy, flower essence therapy, various forms of body work, rebirthing, hypnotherapy, past-life therapy, speech therapy, shiatsu, osteopathy, chiropractics, Rolfing, Feldenkrais, reflexology, different massage methods, and even more. Aura-Soma speeds up, deepens, and supports the processes introduced by these methods.

And last but not least—Aura-Soma is a therapy for the soul. It uses no forceful persuasion and leaves the choice of the appropriate "medicine" to the patients. At one time, only priests and physicians were allowed to decide what a person needed to do or not to do for his or her physical, emotional, mental, and spiritual healing. With Aura-Soma, people may determine for themselves what to use. They can depend on their own inner voice, which will lead them to specific color combinations.

One encounters this term again and again: non-intrusive and self-selective soul therapy.

There are Aura-Soma practitioners whose knowledge and experiences can be helpful, for they can help the interested seeker decode the symbolism of the various color combinations. The information resulting from such a session is stored in the brain. Every time the contents of the bottles are applied, not only is the energy of the crystals, the active substances of the plants, and colors activated, but so is the energy of the information in the brain. In this way, the potential of the user can be stimulated. Yet, this is also possible through concentrated reading of the descriptions of the single bottles, which are found in Chapter 8.

Never before have we been so aware of color and light. All the signs point to even brighter and more colorful times in the future. Jacob Liberman predicts an age of light in our future. Not an unpleasant prospect! Let's not forget, however, that throughout history there have already been a number of cultures that practiced sun worship, and they disappeared from existence—the ancient Egyptians and the Mayans, for example. No matter why they disappeared, part of the reason no doubt had to do with the fact that certain people inflated their egos in connection with the light and then caused great harm.

The new color and light therapies, including Aura-Soma, harbor this danger. And this we must not forget in the midst of all the enthusiasm about their aesthetic value and their effectiveness.

❦ ❦ ❦ ❦ ❦

HOW AURA-SOMA IS CREATED AND HOW IT WORKS

D o you remember the fairy tale about *The Spirit in the Bottle?* It tells of somebody who opens a corked bottle from which a living being climbs out. The most exciting part of the story involves the great effort that is made to get the spirit back into the bottle.

How does one get spirits into bottles? And of what use are spirits in bottles anyhow?

Now, spirits have it in them to exert power over certain supernatural forces. They can become weightless and formless, at least formless to the eyes of those with an everyday consciousness. Bottles can bring them into form, so to speak.

To be able to carry a captured good-natured spirit in a bottle, and to be in command over its power in precarious situations—that has been a long-held dream of humankind.

Relationships with spirits do not necessarily evolve into something beneficial, though. Contact with beings from "beyond," for example, encouraged through help from certain occult techniques, can conceal a great number of risks for those who are inexperienced. But now there are spirits, and have been for a few years, who have found their home in small squared-off glass bottles. They are not only relatively safe, but they are beautiful to look at and extremely helpful. They were created to enter into a relationship with humans and, therefore, do not need to be tamed first. If they are treated with deference and respect, with gratitude, friendliness, and perhaps even with love, they evolve in quite a remarkable way.

Through them, the ancient dream of humans has been fulfilled. The possible danger that they harbor has been alluded to in the last chapter—they can be misused to inflate the ego of the user. But when someone does that, he or she alone is responsible, not the "spirits in the bottle."

There is something else, however, that can occur: Applying the Aura-Soma oils ("the spirits") to the body can result in the release of physical, emotional, mental, and spiritual blocks, which can bring up the old, the suppressed, and the unwanted. Moods, emotions, dreams, and ideas can arise, as well as certain physical reactions. These can be uncomfortable, perhaps fear-ridden. They can force you to confront things again that you supposed you'd dealt with long ago. Also, subjects can surface pertaining to the present, making it necessary to decide on matters that you really wish to avoid. The same goes for visions and future projects about which you still lack confidence. It is also possible, as mentioned above, that unwanted physical symptoms could be more evident for a short time.

During your first experiences with Aura-Soma, a healing crisis can occur. In such a situation, one of the "spirits" has an especially strong effect: the Orange/Orange Bottle, called the Shock Bottle (#26). It is capable of averting the often fatal effects of shock on various levels. But it is necessary, and in total conformance with the basic principles of homeopathy, to bring about another less intense shock, in order to heal the greater shock. (The Shock Bottle has such drastic effects that demand for it is five times greater than for any other!)

And yet, something else can happen—namely, *nothing!* It can happen that for a time no effect at all is noticeable. But, for this situation, there is also a friendly helper at hand: Bottle #11 (Clear/Pink). Here we also find a parallel to homeopathy. There are times when some method prescribed by a doctor or a health practitioner does not work, yet the expert was sure of its effectiveness. In this case, he or she gives the patient something in the interim, for example, sulphur, to clear the way. After that, the originally selected medicine can be effective. Bottle #11 has such a capability.

Since all of the above effects may result from use of Aura-Soma, these possible consequences can create resistance in people who are hesitant to take risks. However, the risk is really very small when compared to the effects of the chemicals found in the medicines and remedies we use every day, which have nothing to do with the chemistry of the human body.

Because all of the contents in the Aura-Soma bottles come from a natural source and are fully in tune with the human body, they act only as a stimulant for that which is already present in the body. In fact, it has been said of Aura-Soma that it is an aid to self-knowledge. For this reason, it is certainly worthwhile to get involved with the "spirits in the bottle." Users learn to know themselves and their life tasks.

And there's still another point worth mentioning: the use of the substances often leads to the deep insight that suffering and pain need not evoke bitterness, resignation, or despair, but rather a maturation process and growth. The products help people to break down resistances, to consider their fate as chance, to see illness as part of the path, and to accept both. Here lies the first step to change, to become whole and to be healed. In some cases, the healing of a person lies in the acceptance of his or her death.

❦ ❦ ❦

Now how do the "spirits" get into the Aura-Soma bottles? Erik Pelham answers this question for us. He was at one time a photographer who became interested in the subject of color. Over the course of many years, in his free time, he created flower essences and experimented with a great variety of combinations. Since 1985, he has been in close contact with the spirit world. Mike Booth has known Erik for a long time, and in 1992 trained him in the process of creating and energizing the oils. Erik Pelham's assignment is to create the contents of the bottles according to the required standard, which pertains to color as well as the healing energy.

Pelham describes his work not as alchemy, but as co-creation, as a cooperative endeavor of his, as well as of beings from another dimension. He considers alchemy as something egocentric, for the alchemist sees him- or herself as one who creates something.

Erik says this about his work: "I do not myself create the energies in the bottles. I do not even create the colors. Rather, I make myself into a channel for the creative act."

Beings from the spirit world, as well as Erik and everyone else in the workshop, contribute to this act.

For Erik, every work day begins with communication between himself and his inner guidance. Therefore, he knows which beings from "over there" offer their cooperation on that particular day, and he senses their presence in his astral body. He then enters into a free-flowing telepathic connection with them, and the beings give him instructions for the production process. When it comes to filling the bottles with healing energy, the beings work through him. And he is aware of this on all levels. He says, "I could not energize anything at all with my own power."

The picture, then, of the "spirits in the bottles" is really a bit too simplistic, but is basically a good analogy. In the bottles are the energies of spirit beings, combined with material ingredients. These, in turn, also have something special. They originate not only from natural sources, but also from bio-dynamic cultivation. The particular oil in which the essential oils and colors are dissolved consists of a natural plant oil. The essential oils— for example, lemon grass, are manufactured by French firms. These firms, or more accurately, these production cooperatives, work with the greatest precision and in total accord with nature and her rhythms.

The suppliers of the plant extracts—that is, the nonfragrant extracts consisting of the watery parts of the plants, are in part still the same as the ones Vicky Wall worked with. They have proven their dependability over decades. You can find these essences in the lower water-based layer of the bottles that Vicky Wall called "balance." ("Balance" is today synonymous with the 94 glass bottles with two-colored layers—in contrast with the "Pomanders" and the "Quintessences," which have an alcohol base, contain only one color, and fill small plastic bottles.)

Only a small percentage of the wonderful colors originate from the essential oils or plant extracts; they are too weak. They grow stronger and brighter in color, through colors of other plants, mostly vegetables. For example, orange, gold, and yellow tones come from carrots. The users of bottles with those colors can reap additional benefits from the ingredient, beta-carotene, which is especially kind to the skin.

The minerals—gemstones and crystals—used in the formulas have been gathered from all parts of the world. They have a single characteristic in common: their high quality and strong healing abilities, both perceived originally by Vicky Wall, and today by Mike Booth.

Now we arrive at the question that many friends of Aura-Soma are highly interested in: *By what method do the crystals get into the bottles? Are they ground? Pulverized? Are they placed in water and exposed to sun-*

light or moonlight, and then added to the substances?

None of the above is the case. The energy of the healing stones is brought into the liquids by a Kabbalistic invocation. We are obviously dealing with an esoteric method of transposing energy solely with the help of words, and that is no nonsense! Today, this input of energy can be proven by Kirlian photography.

For the production of the contents of the balance bottles, glass containers are used exclusively, because glass is one of the few neutral materials. Every container is used only one time, and must then be cleansed not only physically, but also energetically—actually a very time-consuming process.

The water used in the process is brought to an optimum standard of purity by a highly technical procedure. First, it is filtered, then energetically balanced. Finally, in order to free it from all micro-organisms, it is given a treatment with highly intensive ultraviolet rays. Similar to homeopathy, the shaking of the liquids in the bottles is of great importance. Through this procedure, the ingredients are blended with each other. Then, when the user later shakes his or her individual bottle, this phase of the production process is activated and, so to speak, brought to memory.

The Pomanders

What has, up to this point, been explained regarding the process of creation pertains mainly to the balance bottles. But there are yet other Aura-Soma products—the Pomanders, for example. Pomanders also have names and numbers.

Pomander is really the name for a fragrant bouquet, sometimes presented in a small box made of braided straw or sewn into fabric, but also in the form of a bouquet of flowers, or fruit pierced with spices. In times past, Pomanders were used for protection, for disinfection, for cleaning of the atmosphere—similar to the burning of frankincense, sage, and other herbs. While the contents of the balance bottles are applied directly to the body, the Pomanders are not. They are used by placing three drops on the left hand, spreading them by rubbing with the right hand, and distributing them around the body, keeping the hands close to the body. In this way, you support your own healing process, especially in regard to the subtle bodies, and you can protect yourself. Because the Pomanders are offered in small lightweight plastic bottles, they can be taken everywhere in the handbag or pants pocket. They can be used discreetly any time of the day, throughout the entire day, if necessary. That would not be possible with the oils. The Pomanders are created mostly for the protection of persons who are in the process of opening up. Be aware that they do not have the same effect on everyone. You have to experiment somewhat. The Pomanders can also be used for cleansing the energy in rooms (see Chapter 9).

The Aura-Soma Pomanders have a unique history. Many years ago, when Vicky Wall could still see, she collected herbs on her walks, and she preserved these herbs in alcohol. She did not really know why she did so, but she followed her own inner voice. For herself and those around her, this was a somewhat mysterious hobby to which she was devoted. When Vicky had the feeling that her collection was complete, she had 49 different herbs lying in alcohol—7 x 7—a number of significance in the Kabbala.

In 1986, Vicky once again followed her inner guidance and created the first Pomander, the white one. She was able to offer it in Denmark shortly after the reactor catastrophe in Chernobyl so that people could protect themselves from the damaging rays. Today there are 14 different-colored Pomanders containing all 49 herbs. The white one has equal doses in its contents, while the colored ones have dominating shades of color analogous to the specific herbs.

Most plants necessary for Pomanders grow in Tetford, England, in the garden of Dev-Aura, the training center of Aura-Soma. They are picked when ripe, and then they are placed in alcohol for at least a year so that they can give off their energy.

In closing, the following needs to be said about the creation of all Aura-Soma products. Previously everything, including the filling process, was done by hand, so as not to damage the subtle energies of the substances. In the future, however, since Aura-Soma is expanding so rapidly, a few processes must, by necessity, be mechanized. Much consideration will be given to the sensitivity of the mechanical equipment chosen, and people in the Aura-Soma organization will keep a careful watch on the creation and the filling of containers so that quality will always be assured.

How Does Aura-Soma Work?

In her seminars, Vicky Wall enjoyed drawing a comparison between the human body and a television set. When a television is functioning as it should, the channel is clear, the picture is sharp, and the sound is good. But if the tuning is not right, then there are problems. The apparatus cannot fulfill its task—at least not satisfactorily.

With a healthy person, it is exactly the same, so Vicky said. The individual's energies can flow freely and undisturbed—all functions can be fulfilled without error. When a disturbance, an incorrect tuning occurs, then difficulties appear. The application of the balance oils induce proper operation of the wavelengths in the body and can cause the person to function perfectly again.

At the end of the '80s, various radionics specialists analyzed the path of the Aura-Soma substances through the body. One of these specialists was David Tansley, the author of a highly recommended book on the subject. With radionics, the vibrations in the body can be detected with instruments, and areas of weakness and even specific illnesses can be diagnosed.

The experts discovered the following: after both of the layers in the balance bottles were shaken together and applied to the corresponding spots all around the body, they penetrated through to the semi-permeable membrane of the skin into the body. They then moved further into the lymph system, from there into the bloodstream, and finally into the organs of the body. This last process is now being tested by physicians with electrocardiograms. More importantly, Aura-Soma has a balancing and healing effect on all of the glands of the body, on the total hormonal system. The world of traditional medicine has, in this area, only chemically based remedies to offer.

This mystery remains the same today as it did before: How do the contents of a pill arrive at the exact area in the complex system of the body where they are needed? A similar mystery also remains unsolved—that is, why do the Aura-Soma oils unfold their beneficial and healing effects in precisely the right places?

The paths of the Pomanders and Quintessences take a similar course, but they are applied solely to the hands, or on the pulse. From there, the contents, in a more reduced dosage (compared to that of the balance oils), go through the skin into the lymph system, into the bloodstream, and to the organs. The hands, at the time of the application of the Pomanders and Quintessences, are led through the electromagnetic field. Therefore, these substances especially affect the subtle bodies.

The fact that the healing color vibrations and their concentrated energy can be directly physically applied and absorbed sets Aura-Soma apart from all previously known color therapies.

Signature and Chakra Teaching

There is a reason, above all, why the energy in Aura-Soma is so concentrated. Without knowing why at the time, Vicky Wall tuned in her creativity to the "Science of Signatures." The most important and best known representative of this was Theophrastus Bombastus von Hohenheim, known as Paracelsus (1403-1541). *Signature* means *inscription*. The Science of Signatures states that everything in nature is described or marked—that is, that the outer appearance of a plant gives clues to its characteristics. For example, when Paracelsus discovered that the seeds of the pomegranate resemble the shape of human teeth, he concluded that these fruits could heal toothaches (which proved to be true). Paracelsus considered the decoding of the essence and the healing characteristics of a plant as an art. He said that one should rely less on book-learning than one's own patience and humility, so that the signs can reveal themselves.

Vicky Wall applied this same Science of Signatures in combination with the Vedic Chakra Teaching, which divides the human body into areas of different colors. Vicky's clairvoyance enabled her to perceive a person as a "rainbow." She could also detect if something was not right in this rainbow. She was amazed when, at more than 60 years of age, she learned that her ideas coincided with the ancient Indian Chakra Teaching.

In accordance with her own perception and intuition with respect to the Chakra Teaching, she combined plants and minerals of the same color. In this fashion, the healing energies contained in them could unfold at the corresponding place in the body. For example, for the head, which, according to the Chakra Teaching, corresponds to the colors blue and violet in the human rainbow, she combined extracts and essential oils from lavender and violets, among others, and the healing vibrations of amethyst. She strengthened the effect of this mixture with matching colors of plants. (Indeed, the blue as well as the violet substances act as healing agents for headaches, sleeplessness due to nervousness, and other symptoms originating in the head.) Vicky always acted following the counsel of her inner guidance. The explanation for how it works, the background, and the logic of the whole system would come to light later, little by little. And that is still the case today.

Many people work at bringing their masculine and feminine aspects into balance, in order to fashion life on earth to be more pleasant and harmonious (again). Vicky's approach toward Aura-Soma, which is simply to accept the message of nature, sent out through color and form, results from a "feminine" thought process. The message was to make a few combinations, and in so doing, bring about an extraordinary intensification of healing energies. This is a system that is based on trusting the inner voice and having an empathy with nature. This approach can be followed by men as well as women. Perhaps up until now, the time has not been ripe. It is surprising that no one has as yet come upon this idea.

The rainbow is also a symbol of the cosmic vagina, of the fertile, form-giving feminine aspect of God. However, this concept has been discounted and dismissed for hundreds of years.

We shall close this chapter as we began it—with the "spirits in the bottles."

It does not matter whether we really think of beings from the realm of plants and minerals or newly created spirits living in bottles, or whether we favor a more abstract viewpoint. But with every application of the substances, we might consider sending out thanks for the help that we receive. It would be good if we gave some thought to the fact that not only do we receive healing, wholeness, and peace, but others do as well. Other people, animals, plants, the elements—in fact, the whole Planet Earth, can benefit. This aspect of gratitude and exchange of information has, from the beginning, been of utmost importance to Aura-Soma. *All* of us are connected with *all*. There is a social dimension to it, also. As we deal with Aura-Soma with full awareness, we are given the opportunity to be involved with the healing of our own problems—spiritual, mental, emotional, and physical— as well as healing the deficiencies of our immediate and greater environment.

❦ ❦ ❦ ❦ ❦

THE SUBTLE ANATOMY OF HUMAN BEINGS

" If you cannot speak about something, keep silent." That is a good principle, and we highly recommend it, especially when dealing with spiritual matters. To speak or write about the subtle energies of human beings is not impossible. However, for various reasons, it is very difficult. Why do we attempt to do so, anyway? And what constitutes these difficulties? That is what we wish to explain in the following pages:

1. In the matter of the subtle bodies or energy-bodies of humans, we find that only especially talented people or those specially trained can become aware of them.

2. Even what these people see and/or feel is not consistent. Healers and psychics have different opinions about what they perceive. In this field, there are no objective criteria.

3. The same can be said about the literature that is available about the subject. Perceptions and explanations vary from school to school. One could say that they even vary from author to author.

4. All of this is not exactly conducive to attracting people with a "normal" background to such subjects. They have as little success at seeing their own subtle bodies as seeing those of their fellow humans. They cannot feel them. The experts do not agree. Even the specialized literature is recognizable by its very non-uniformity.

We are obviously considering a subject about which one does not talk or write with confidence. Well, then, do we say nothing about it? Usually. Or we silence it to death. However, in the wake of a greater openness to alternative healing methods and to the connectedness between body, soul, and spirit, many people have an inkling, a vague feeling, that there is something more than just the physical body.

While chemical medicines have their effect almost entirely on the physical level, Aura-Soma does its work on the physical and subtle levels. If we profess thoroughness in our dealings with this subject, we cannot help but include the subtle energies.

In our case, we (the authors) shall limit ourselves exclusively to the viewpoint of Aura-Soma, putting aside any others. In regard to the meaning behind the colors, we shall proceed in the same way.

Should you, dear reader, have experienced or learned something other than what we are presenting here, we ask you to do the following: would you kindly set that other paradigm aside for a moment, at least for the time of this presentation? We do not assert that our viewpoint is "correct" and all others are "incorrect." We simply present the assumption that Aura-Soma offers, and the expressions used in this system. After that, you are welcome to return to your own experiences and your preferred theories and authors. Or, as we said at the beginning, you might return to silence concerning these issues that lie deep in the realm of mystery and inscrutability.

The Different Bodies of Human Beings

According to Aura-Soma, human beings consist of the following bodies:

1. The physical body.

2. The electromagnetic field that can be seen with the use of Kirlian photography. It is very near to the physical body, directly over the skin, and can stretch 4 to 5 cm (up to 2 inches) outward. In this field, the entire momentary condition of the body is pictured. This can change in a matter of a few moments.

3. The etheric body, which can extend about 20 cm (approximately 8

inches) around the physical body. (More information about this body is discussed in the next few pages.)

4. The astral body, which extends 30 to 40 cm (between 12 and 16 inches) out from and around the physical body.

The electromagnetic field and the etheric body are located within the astral body. You might envision someone wearing several thick sweaters, one over the other. The various energy bodies influence each other; they are in close relationship with each other.

There are still other subtle bodies that exist besides the electromagnetic field, the etheric body, and the astral body. Since they essentially remain untouched by the work of Aura-Soma, we shall not discuss them here.

The etheric body, in contrast to the electromagnetic field, reveals the more profound, the more constant, characteristics of the physical body. In it are stored such experiences as accidents, including those from childhood or previous lives, as well as all shocks and traumas. With Aura-Soma, the etheric body is brought into contact with the shocks, but also with dependency, co-dependency, and with the resolved state—independence.

A further connection exists between the etheric body and the second chakra, the "sacral" chakra, that mainly processes sexual energy. And there is a connection with the spleen, too. According to esoteric beliefs, the spleen transforms substances from the astral body into etheric substances. These substances take care of damage caused by shock and rips in the etheric body are covered over and mended, but they cannot close the holes permanently. When the person in question is fatigued and exhausted, then the spleen has to deal more with matters relating to the physical body rather than creating the substances mentioned. Therefore, in a condition of weakness, the effects of past shocks will become evident. The person feels worse and worse, and the medical profession is faced with a puzzle.

As we mentioned, in this case, the Shock Bottle, #26 (Orange/Orange), and sometimes #87 (Coral/Coral), can also work veritable miracles. The contents of these bottles, as unbelievable as it may seem, are capable of closing the wounds in the etheric body and healing them. This produces fast and effective relief on all levels. It is often advisable to begin work with the Aura-Soma substances by using Bottles #26 or #87 because the prerequisite for the applied substances to keep unfolding their strength is a healed and whole etheric body. An indication that someone might profit very much from the contents of these two bottles can be a special appeal or even a special aversion to the combination of Orange/Orange or Coral/Coral.

Most people ignore their etheric body, yet it is as grateful as the physical body for loving care and attention. When the pains of this body are suddenly lessened, and possibly even disappear altogether, when the etheric body experiences support and stimulation from all the other Aura-Soma substances—Pomanders and Quintessences, as well as the balance oils—it will be spurred on to a great effort to give its best. And this can lead to a new appreciation of life.

You might use any of these subjects as the basis for a meditation: shock, trauma, dependency, co-dependency, independence, and sexuality, and their connection. Perhaps it will also be possible for you to imagine the color orange during your meditation. You will most likely gain some surprising insights.

Aura-Soma refers to the body that exists independent of the other bodies as the "astral body." It leads its own life during sleep; it separates itself and travels. What you experience in your dreams is often a part of impressions that you gain on such trips. But with the "silver cord," which is separated from the physical body at the time of death, the astral body remains connected to the other subtle bodies and the physical body.

The more awake you are spiritually, the more aware you will be of the traveling of the astral body and of where it travels to. It can happen that you will recall in the morning exactly where you went during the night. This memory is clearer and less foggy that it is with respect to "normal" dreams.

If you attain an even higher consciousness, you can decide where you would like to go with your astral body. In this way, you can "visit" someone; you can heal; you can offer service in areas of crisis. When you have progressed this far, your astral body becomes an "astral double." (Please note that these terms are Aura-Soma-specific.)

The astral body is connected to the *astral world*. That is a kind of parallel world that can be accessible in some, but not all, dreams; in rituals;

32

and in some forms of meditation. It can be accessed through the help of mind-altering substances. Carlos Castaneda deals with this astral world in his books. The highest energies are at home here, but deceit and illusion are also at work, even more so than in our material world. Discrimination, clarity, and protection are even more important than on the physical plane.

At this point, we would also like to emphasize that the whole collection of Aura-Soma substances is in a close bond with the best and most beneficial of energies. It is unlikely that anything unpleasant will happen to the user, except the possible problematic situations already mentioned. These may arise from something inherent in the personality of the user.

Stored in your astral body are your visions, plans, and highest goals. It contains your total future potential, including the spiritual aspects of your life. The balance bottles from the Master Set, as well as the Quintessences—that is, all pastel-colored substances—affect the astral body. They support the goals we have set for ourselves, our visions, our plans, our highest potential, and the spiritual part of our being.

The pastel colors affect the astral body directly. From there they swing back into the etheric body, into the electromagnetic field, and then into the physical body. The latter can be seen with the help of Kirlian photography.

The colors orange and coral work directly on the etheric body, and from there the same process is active: the effects continue on into the electromagnetic field and into the physical body, then also out into the astral body. All other colors affect the physical body, and their effect proceeds outward onto the electromagnetic field, the etheric body, and the astral body.

In the Aura-Soma system, the meaning of the term *light body* is this: modern physics states that all matter—including the human body, of course—is light that varies in frequencies. The subtle bodies are also light with other frequencies. All bodies in total comprise the *light body,* but only for people who are conscious of it. In that regard, you might take particular note of Bottle #54—Serapis Bey (Clear/Clear), and begin a process in which you can come to realize that you consist of light. That realization will not only be intellectual, but also sensual and psychic. These kinds of experiences lie so far beyond all words that we cannot accurately describe them here.

❦ ❦ ❦

33

The *aura,* then, is the combination of all three subtle bodies: the electromagnetic field, the etheric body, and the astral body. The chakras are situated (to put it in the most simplistic terms), between the physical and the etheric bodies. When a chakra is overactive, a clairvoyant person perceives the corresponding color with greater intensity. For example, for the base (the first) chakra, the color red surfaces in the aura at the exact spot where it is located in the physical body—namely, in the region of the lower abdomen. If this chakra functions below the normal level, the color appears too pale. Clairvoyants can easily recognize where the imbalance exists in the body of the person. They actually see the colors of a person's aura in the manner that Aura-Soma describes them—as a rainbow.

Nothing that is offered on the market today described as "aura photography" resembles even slightly what a clairvoyant perceives. People might spend their time allowing themselves to be photographed in this manner and enjoy looking at these pictures, but it would be a mistake to draw any definite conclusions from that.

The "True Aura"

Aura-Soma does recognize the "true aura," as has been mentioned, and psychics can also see it. Allusions to it can be found in other esoteric systems, but up to the present time, only Aura-Soma has given a clear description. The true aura is a subtle domain the approximate size of a walnut, at least in the area where it is the most concentrated. From there it extends itself into a ball the size of a saucer. The center of this walnut and this ball is located about the width of two fingers above the navel and again the same distance into the body. One could say that the ball extends itself out over the physical body. Inside the true aura, similar to the case of a hologram or a three-dimensional computer diskette, is stored all important information about past existences and about the present life of the person concerned. It includes a view of the future, taking for granted that not everything is predetermined. You must act here and now in such a way as to influence your life in the future.

The true aura comes into being in this way: when the sperm of the prospective father meets the ovum of the prospective mother and unites with it, an explosion takes place. This is not only an esoteric view. This phenomenon has been shown by the use of micro-photography. The cloud created by the explosion keeps the other ova from being fertilized further by other sperm. If this process does not occur quickly enough, the result is the conception of fraternal (fertilized from two separate ova) twins.

The energy of the very first cell delineates the center of the true aura, and this energy attracts a being that would like to incarnate.

To summarize, four things occur:

1. A sperm meets an ovum.
2. An explosion occurs.
3. The kernel of a true aura comes into existence.
4. A being wishing to incarnate is attracted.

At this time, we need to mention briefly the concept of *rays*. This is a system fostered by Theosophy and embraced by Alice Bailey, among others.

The teaching about the rays (similar to astrology) aims to offer people assistance in recognizing their temperament, their talents, the main themes of their life, and their life tasks. It is known to be very difficult to evaluate one's own being, as it has evolved to the present. In that regard, a good astrological chart can aid in pinpointing present strengths and weaknesses, important needs, and in foreseeing possible hindrances and dangers. Thus, you can save yourself needless detours and can get into closer contact with your life task, with your *essence*. This is the exact aim of the teaching about the rays. In Theosophy there are seven rays, namely the rainbow colors that correspond with the colors of the chakras. In Aura-Soma, there are nine chakras, which also correspond to the colors of the rainbow. And then there are still two more, specifically belonging to Aura-Soma, connected to the colors, turquoise and magenta (more about that in the next chapter).

Each ray corresponds to certain traits and energies, as well as to certain helpers in the astral world. By carefully choosing the first bottle, the "Soul Bottle," you can find out on which ray you came into this world. As such, you discover what issues need to be worked on in this lifetime.

Where, now, is the connection between the true aura, color, and the Soul Bottle? The explosion at the time of conception has, in esoteric terms, a certain color. This color represents the personality of the being that desires to incarnate. It is attracted by the color of this explosion because it is the ray that is to match his or her personality in this life. However, it is the *soul ray* that the being brings from his or her previous incarnations. This soul ray is brought from the world in which he or she existed before this and previous incarnations. It is possible that the personality ray and the soul ray can be one and the same, but not necessarily. Correspondence is neither better nor worse than noncorrespondence.

When in the moment of, or shortly after, conception, the soul ray connects with the personality ray, it impresses the total information present in this person's being upon only one cell—namely, the first. The three-dimensional holographic "diskette" comes into being.

When you have truly found your Soul Bottle among all of the Aura-Soma bottles, the one which you feel truly represents you, then the color in the lower layer of liquid is that of your soul ray. The one in the upper layer is that of your personality ray. As we said, they can both be of the same color, but they need not be.

The very beginning of the growth process of the fetus takes place in the true aura. Later, it grows beyond it. Yet, the true aura stays in the area of the navel with the energy of the moment of conception.

When you experience a shock or trauma, the true aura wants to leave the body. It moves itself to the *etheric gap* on the left side of the body in the area of the chest. (The Shock Bottle, #26, Orange/Orange; as well as #87, Coral/Coral, can help to bring it back to its normal position.) In the same way, it can repair wounds and injuries to the etheric body caused by shock, as we have already described. Should a person die in a condition of shock, the true aura then leaves the body here. If a criminal dies, the true aura leaves the body through the anus. When a "normal" person dies a "normal death," the true aura exits through the mouth. When a highly evolved person dies, it exits through the crown chakra—in other words, through the top of the head.

So much for the subtle bodies or energy bodies as seen through the eyes and language of Aura-Soma.

❦ ❦ ❦

The two other components of the energy system of human beings are the chakras or energy centers, and the *Nadis,* or energy canals. It is through the Nadis that *prana* is guided through the subtle energy system. (*Nadi* means "tube" or "vein" in Sanskrit. *Prana,* also Sanskrit, means "absolute energy" or "life force.") The Nadis of the one energy body are connected to the Nadis of the other energy bodies through the chakras.

They take up prana from the near and far environment of a person and transform it into "digestible" frequencies, spreading it out into the physical as well as into the energy bodies. The chakras also beam energies outward, which, as we said, can be seen and felt by psychics. By no means do all clairvoyants see the same thing, though. There are no objective criteria in this domain.

The Chakra Teaching

The chakra teaching theory originated in ancient India and is older than Christianity. On the whole, Aura-Soma agrees with this theory—that is, with the color sequence beginning with the base chakra (red), ending with the crown chakra (violet), and with most of the traditional coordination of the chakras. The first essential difference lies in the fact that in Aura-Soma, there is not the emphasis on the rotating energy wheels (*chakra* is also a Sanskrit word meaning "wheel")—rather, the whole body is taken into consideration. In regard to color, too, they are not limited to the place where the chakras are. Instead, the whole body is seen as colored.

Let us begin with the feet (red), progress to the legs (red), and the base chakra (red), then slowly into coral-red and orange and pass over gold and yellow, until the area of the head is reached. There, blue turns into royal blue, and royal blue turns into violet. With Aura-Soma, when the human rainbow is mentioned, this is the exact picture that is implied. (You can refer to the colored illustration in the center section of this book.) When you view it carefully, you will notice the second difference. In the area of the genitals, there is one area that is colored pink. The explanation follows: The color red, which, according to the chakra theory is located in that area, is on the one hand linked with passion and also with aggression. With many people, their sexuality is dominated by these two characteristics. What devastating results that can have is well known. When light is brought into the color red, it turns into pink. It means that the "frequency is raised," and aggression is lessened or disappears altogether. Aggressive passion is turned to warm and gentle love—at least in ideal cases. An important goal of the pink combinations in the Aura-Soma collection is exactly this—to foster the process of transformation.

The traditional theory recognizes seven chakras, Aura-Soma, nine. The eighth chakra is above the head, outside of the body. Its designated color is magenta. (Once again, please refer to the illustrations in the center of the book.) Then there is another chakra, already recognized here and there in the literature, specifically by the Indian sage, Ramana Maharshi, who calls it the *ananda-khanda center*. It lies near and on the level of the heart chakra opposite the physical heart of a person on the right side of the body. In Aura-Soma, it is called the fourth-and-a-half chakra. Its designated color is turquoise, the color of the sea and the dolphins. There is more information to come about both of these additional chakras.

The traditional chakra theory stems from the premise that the *kundalini energy*, the serpent energy, sits in the base chakra. In most people, the serpent is rolled up and is sleeping. Every once in a while it raises itself to the second chakra that has to do with sexuality and to the solar plexus chakra, where power and intellect are at home. Not much more happens. It means that for most people, the main issues are survival, sexuality, and the use of power.

When, however, the higher chakras are also awakened, when the kundalini energy can rise unhindered, then you can awaken your full potential. You can unfold completely, and can even attain enlightenment. Now, if many alternative healing methods honestly intend to bring the chakras into balance, that means nothing other than that they are helping you achieve your complete unfoldment. And that would include unfoldment on all levels—the spiritual, the mental, the emotional, and the physical.

But, to overstimulate certain chakras and to neglect others in the process of spiritual work is foolish. Everyday issues such as eating and drinking belong to human life as much as, for example, a fulfilled sexuality, a balanced emotional life, and a spiritual awareness. To put forth great effort in the line of "higher" things such as communication, psychic abilities, or spirituality, and to neglect the "lower," is not recommended. Any spiritual teacher with a sense of responsibility will observe carefully whether his or her students are bringing a sense of order and balance into their everyday lives—no matter what path they choose.

❦ ❦ ❦

In the following pages, we will present a brief explanation of the chakras. We are limiting ourselves to what is absolutely necessary for you to work with Aura-Soma. There is an abundance of literature about this subject. We especially recommend the books of David Tansley (see Bibliography).

❦ ❦ ❦

The **base chakra** in the Aura-Soma system relates to the whole lower torso, from the feet to the lowest part of the body. It is located at the base of the spine at the coccyx. It corresponds to:

- the color red;
- to a small extent, the color pink, also;
- the spine;
- the kidneys; and
- the suprarenal glands (adrenalin production—in traditional chakra theory, as in Aura-Soma, there is a close relationship between the chakras and the glands).

The base chakra anchors the person in the physical world. It has to do with the issue of survival. When the base chakra is in balance, meaning when it is open but not overstimulated, when it functions harmoniously, then you are nurtured by an instinctive trust. Everything that you need for survival flows to you—life force, protection, food, and money.

If your base chakra is not in balance, you will have problems in all of these areas. In your thinking, you will circle around these issues in such a way that you desire to be satisfied in an egocentric manner. It will be important to you that all goes well with yourself and those close to you, but you will not be interested in much more than that. You will be inclined either to gain that which you believe you deserve by aggressive methods, or you will find that you lack the ability to persevere and to succeed.

The **second chakra** is connected to the area in which the reproductive organs are located. It lies in the area where you can feel the lowest vertebra of the spine. In coordination with it are:

- the color orange;
- the reproductive organs; and
- the gonads (ovaries, prostate, testicles).

The second chakra has to do with creativity and is connected with the reproductive organs. When it functions harmoniously, you can enjoy your sexuality with happiness and relaxation, but you do not constantly think about that subject. If you incessantly focus on sex, then you will not achieve balance in this energy center. Another sign of malfunction would be a lack of interest in sexuality.

The **solar plexus chakra** for Aura-Soma relates to the physical area of the stomach, above the navel. The literature does not agree exactly with that location. However, most of the references indicate the area about two finger-widths above the navel. In coordination with it are:

- the color yellow;
- the digestive system; and
- the pancreas (insulin-producing gland).

The solar plexus chakra in other systems is defined as the "power" chakra. Aura-Soma has deviated a little bit from this meaning. The solar plexus and the color yellow here are connected mainly with acquired knowledge. When your solar plexus chakra is in balance, then you understand how to handle your harvested knowledge constructively. You are aware of its worth, but also of its limits. When it is not balanced, you rely too much on the knowledge you have amassed. You might tend to brag about it. Or you might be inclined to feel confused; you find that you cannot depend on your knowledge, or you quickly forget what you have learned.

The **heart chakra** includes the whole chest area. In coordination with it are:

- the color green;
- the heart and lungs; and
- the thymus gland (which regulates growth, the lymph system, and strengthens the immune system).

Traditionally, the heart chakra is the center of all chakras. Its subject is "love." When it is open and works harmoniously, then you project warmth, sympathy, and understanding. You love and feel loved. If your heart chakra is not in a balanced condition, you feel yourself cut off from love, or you feel extremely dependent on other people. Perhaps it is difficult for you to accept or to give love. Or, you expect a pat on the back for every small, loving act.

The **ananda-khanda center** plays an important part in the system of Aura-Soma. It relates to the upper chest area. Its most important area is on the right side of the chest, opposite the heart. It is called in Aura-Soma the "fourth-and-a-half" chakra. It is already found here and there in the literature.

Its meaning has been discovered rather recently—within the last few years. In coordination with it are:

- the color turquoise;
- the upper chest area; and
- the thymus gland.

The ananda-khanda center is related to the field of mass communication. Through it, an individual can spread information quickly on a worldwide basis. It is a means to connect people, to bring people together. A few examples of that already exist, one of which is the benefit concerts that are broadcast at the same time throughout the entire world over the airwaves. Since these concerts can be experienced by so many people on the planet via radio and television, an indescribable feeling of universal connectedness has surfaced. The song "We Are the World" serves as a symbol of these endeavors.

A balanced ananda-khanda center gives you the capability to speak or to express yourself personally in front of a large audience. The same is true of the arts: music, dance, painting, drama, poetry, writing, journalism—all of these fields can be shared with many people. The learning and mastery of foreign languages belong in this category, also.

If the ananda-khanda center is not yet developed, or if it does not yet work harmoniously, then you might suffer from stage fright and have a fear of creative expression in public. You might have difficulty learning a foreign language, or you might be hesitant to speak it. A further sign is technophobia—the fear of handling computers, cameras, electrical household appliances, and so forth. The other side of the coin would be exclusive communication with your computer or television, as well as the addiction to being in front of the camera or on stage.

The **throat chakra** in Aura-Soma deals with the entire area of the throat. In correlation with it are:

- the color blue;
- the whole throat and neck area; and
- the thyroid gland.

The throat chakra relates to communication (not mass communication, though, for there is a marked difference between turquoise and blue). When this chakra functions well, then you are capable of expressing your thoughts, insights, and feelings in words without difficulty. When it's appropriate, you can also be silent. If this chakra is not in balance, you might suffer from stuttering, you may be afraid to speak, or you may speak endlessly about insignificant things even if you really have something of substance to say. Or, you may just talk too much in general.

The **third eye** is related to the middle of the head. It is in coordination with:

- the color royal blue (indigo in other systems);
- the face and all the sense organs in the head; and
- the pituitary gland (which is also called the "master" gland because it guides the functions of all the other glands).

The theme of the third eye is intuition. When it functions harmoniously, which at the present time only seldom happens, you have the ability to combine the insights attained by the intellect with those gained by intuition in order for them to bear fruit in your experience. You can perceive the greater picture and create an understandable whole from various fragments. If your third eye is not in balance, it could be that you depend entirely on the intellect, or only on your intuition. You might be inclined to rely on fantasy.

The **crown chakra** in Aura-Soma relates to the area of the top of the head and is located in the uppermost part of the head. It correlates to:

- the color violet;
- the brain; and
- the pineal gland, whose function is scientifically not yet clear (for the ancient Greeks, it was the seat of the soul).

For most people, the crown chakra is considered inactive as yet. When it begins to open, you will experience moments of total unity with everything.

The **eighth chakra,** as such, plays a role only in Aura-Soma. It is located above the head outside of the body. It correlates to:

- the color magenta.

Because it is located outside of the body, there is no physical connection to the glands. Also, the eighth chakra is developed only by very few people. It has to do with love for the little, everyday things, as well as with love that serves others, and the love that is linked with warmth. Again, because it is located outside of the body, it is not subject to duality; it has no negative aspect. It can evolve only more or less.

You will find more information regarding Aura-Soma's point of view about the chakras in relation to color in Chapter 6. The descriptions of the bottles will supply you with more details, telling you the way in which the substances function, or better said, how they affect the physical and subtle bodies on which you put them.

A Few Thoughts on the Subject of Meditation

Many interpretations and misunderstandings exist concerning the meaning of *meditation.* For example, a favorite assertion is that only specially trained, highly evolved persons can meditate, or those who are able to let go of stress easily. It is also said that meditation is limited to particularly "sacred" situations and special circumstances.

This is not the case at all. The word *meditate* originated in Latin and means nothing more than "to go into the center." And that is something that everyone can do, whether young, old, well educated, or not. When someone who is experiencing tension knowingly goes "into the center," this person will find that stress diminishes considerably.

Meditation can be practiced in many ways. A person can retreat into silence for a week and do nothing for a number of days but sit on a pillow with closed eyes. This practice can result in profound experiences that strengthen the individual with respect to the functions of daily life.

Meditation can also take place in prayer, in ritual, in a group situation, or by listening to a song, a favorite passage of text, or a piece of instrumental music. However, it is also possible to build meditation into a purely normal day. You can stop briefly to contemplate the idea that there is more to life than what you are doing at the present and that you are bonded to a Higher Power. You can say a short prayer, acknowledging that everything in life—even the smallest detail—is meaningful, even if, perhaps, you do not understand it. You can be cognizant of the fact that your goal is self-knowledge—to be alert, to be awake, even if the world around you is not presently in a position to aid you.

This reflection can manifest itself through a brief thought, for example, while you are appreciating beauty, perhaps as you become aware of a tree, an animal, the blue sky, or another person. It can happen through the experience of friendliness, by giving it or by receiving it. You can also display small mementos in your home or workplace, such as a picture, a note tacked on the bathroom mirror, a symbol...you can even set the alarm clock and stop for a while when it rings. Such moments of "being awake" and "being in the center" have a place in every life, no matter how plagued with stress it is. The effort expended amounts to nothing more than a bit of concentration. That slight effort is richly rewarded in at least three ways: by establishing a relationship with the unseen worlds surrounding us all, from which we can obtain strength, and to which we can give strength in return; through inner growth and fulfillment; and by the acquisition of a treasure that nothing or no one can ever take away.

Of course, it is recommended that you take a little more time for your personal meditation. Perhaps it can be in the evening for 10 or 15 minutes when you simply go into the silence or when you allow the integration of specific issues to take effect. For example, as has been suggested, you can focus on concepts such as shock, trauma, dependency, interdependency, and sexuality, together with the color orange, and allow this to have its effect on you. Or you can simply center yourself just before going to sleep, and in the morning just as you awaken. (At these times, you are especially connected with the other worlds.) However, the first and easiest step is the experience of "awake" moments in everyday life.

With the Aura-Soma substances, you have wonderful helpers that can assist you in bringing this meditative quality into your life. For example, the balance bottles lend themselves beautifully to being placed on your nightstand, or on your desk, or in your bathroom. Their superior brilliance and beauty can remind you of the light, of the Highest Being, and of the All-in-All—to an even greater degree when you shake the oil and the watery layer together and apply the mixture to your body. Use the time spent in the process of shaking and rubbing the substances into your skin for a moment of connecting with your innermost being.

Whenever you use the Pomanders or the Quintessences, you can then, too, create a special moment of this kind for yourself.

ℱ ℱ ℱ

Through Aura-Soma, you will become more open and more sensitive. This is a beautiful thing for you and for all those with whom you come in contact. To be sure, it does not bring only advantages; you do not get more sensitive to pleasant and positive things alone, but also to everything else. It can happen that some people may show aggression toward you, for they sense that you are connected with a great source of strength. You will possibly encounter challenges unfamiliar to you up to now, such as jealousy, envy, and even insanity. Do not allow anything to deter you! Remember that you can be threatened only by that to which you give your attention. Indifference is the best antidote against these energies. And be sure to make it a habit to protect yourself regularly. For this purpose, you can take most of the Pomanders (see Chapter 9). Experiment to find out which Pomander affords you the best protection. And, there is also an effective visualization and meditation for that purpose to be found in the text of that chapter.

If you desire a short version of the part in the visualization referring to personal protection, you can do the following:

> Imagine that you are sitting in a shining sapphire blue sphere or bubble, "blue as the sky without clouds." You can allow people or things or situations that are close to your heart to be there, too. It can be your husband

or wife, your friend, your children, your car, your home, the project you're working on, the test you're confronting....Imagine that this blue sphere will protect you for the whole day and that it provides complete protection. However, it will allow positive influences to enter, for that is a specific attribute of blue. If you get into the habit, directly upon awakening, of practicing this exercise—it takes less than a minute—then you can create the best assurance for a good day.

As for children, they love little exercises like this one. Present them like beautiful little secrets, or create a story in connection with this protective color blue. Children today are burdened with a lot of stress from their outer world. Allowing them to visualize that the color blue is something in which they can wrap themselves in the morning can alleviate many of these stress factors.

❦ ❦ ❦

The great teacher of Tibetan Buddhism, Chöygam Trungpa, mentioned in Chapter 2, had this to say about meditation: "Meditation has nothing to do with attaining ecstasy, spiritual delight, or rest—neither has it to do with becoming a better person. Meditation means simply to create a place in which we are able to unmask and dissolve our neurotic games, our self-deceit, our hidden fears and hopes."

❦ ❦ ❦ ❦ ❦

ANCIENT WISDOM

To see the ancient wisdom systems of the world condensed into a few pages would certainly be unacceptable to one person or another. For, descriptions, interpretations, and commentaries of these systems do indeed fill up entire libraries. Would it even be at all possible to attempt to be concise on this subject? Besides, the wisdom systems contain much fuel for controversy.

On the one hand, the secrets of creation, more or less hidden, are contained therein, including those of the creative powers of human beings—and therefore, they are dangerous. The directives for co-creation can be used for destructive, as well as for constructive, purposes. On the other hand, much of what is said in the ancient wisdom systems does not fit into the specific compartments of structured religion. Consequently, records—even entire libraries—were burned in order to keep these "heretical" ideas in oblivion forever. This subject is addressed by the Italian author, Umberto Eco, in his novel, *The Name of the Rose*.

A rather delicate matter, our chapter on the wisdom systems! But not to deal with this subject would be a sin of omission, for Aura-Soma definitely has something to do with them.

In the various cultures of the world there exist different systems, adapted in accordance with their mentality and their history. Although they lead to the same goal, it is recommended that you stay with your own traditions. For, these paths into the archetypal knowledge of human beings are locked in your genes. After involving yourselves in these domains for some time, it can happen that certain channels open, and you are suddenly able to access information that is stored in the collective unconscious of your society.

The "Tree of Life" from the Kabbala and the Tarot[2] are probably the most important Western paths to archetypal knowledge. Each presents a system of its own, and each is useful in its own way in its approach to that which is true for all people. Both are models of the cosmic creative hierarchy and the objective truth existing within. They look at this truth from different points of view, but there are similarities.

One can combine the Tarot and the Kabbala. In the 19th century, the French occultist, Eliphas Levi, was the first to determine the connection. There are overlappings between the Kabbala and the Tarot, but also between the I Ching (the ancient Chinese wisdom system),[3] astrology, the Enneagram, and others. All these different facets are connected to objective truth. Regrettably, how much of this truth will be reflected upon depends on the interpreter and the interpretation.

The systems of ancient wisdom, one could say, were given to human beings by God so that with them we could attain a better understanding of ourselves and recognize where the place of humankind is in the creative hierarchy. There is a basic need, inherent in us, after our need for food, shelter, and warmth are satisfied, to pose questions about the reason for living and being: "Where did I come from? Where am I? Where am I going? Why am I here? Why is all of this?"

God created us with a desire to have children and to know ourselves. He gave us the religions (in their pure form), as well as the ancient spiritual teachings, in order that we might realize the goal of self-realization.

By the way, it is possible to gain personal entrance to this objective truth with the help of shamanistic techniques and practices of systems such as Buddhism. But even having had such experiences, they are often colored and seen through the lens of what we've learned in our society. In the case of serious illnesses, accidents, emotional crises, near-death experiences, and so forth, a very sudden and direct access to objective truth can occur, even for people who have never sought it. Such experiences can change lives.

❦ ❦ ❦

---

[2] The Tarot is a card game that has been known of since the 14th century. It is said to have originated in ancient Egypt, or perhaps even earlier, and to contain all the secrets of life. It consists of 78 cards, 22 "Major Arcana," and 56 "Minor Arcana," divided into four suits: Wands, Cups, Swords, and Pentacles.

[3] The I Ching was originally a fortune-telling book. About 1000 B.C., it became a book of wisdom, a timeless treasure, with clear advice for right action.

If you look at the descriptions of the balance bottles in Chapter 8, you will find correspondences between the bottles numbered from 0 to 78 and the respective Tarot cards; and also between the bottles numbered 1 to 64 and the I Ching signs. If you are acquainted with Tarot or I Ching, wider dimensions of the bottles will unlock themselves by stating this information in it. If you are not acquainted with one or both systems, you may simply ignore it.

There is widespread data available about the Tarot and I Ching—for example, you may learn practical techniques in seminars and from books. Therefore, we shall not pursue this subject any further. But about the Kabbala and the Tree of Life, having for centuries been handed down by word of mouth, there is, up to the present, not much clear information available. That is not surprising. For, in spite of the fact that the "Tree" belongs to our cultural heritage, that manner of thinking needed to understand this complex symbol is still foreign to us. The fact that in many places an unusually strong patriarchal view shines through does not exactly simplify the situation: until rather recently, the "Tree of Life" was a subject for men only, and mostly for men over 40! For those who find it difficult to cope with Hebrew names, with highly complex thought processes, with an anti-feminist attitude, and a passionately God-fearing mindset, they will find it difficult to enter into the Tree of Life. But whoever makes the effort to jump over his or her own shadow and persevere, will be richly rewarded. For here, one can truly find the deepest knowledge and wisdom.

To many people, the Kabbala means numerology. But the Jewish secret teachings and its mystical aspects—for that is the Kabbala—embraces much more. Essentially, there are four subheads, and these are the categories:

- the practical Kabbala, which deals with ceremonial magic;
- the dogmatic Kabbala, which is the literature about the system;
- the interpretation of letters and numbers; and
- the "Tree of Life," which represents the basic symbol or system of symbols in the Kabbala.

At the time of Christ, the Kabbala was already ancient. Some believe that it dates back to prehistoric times. The old Kabbalists say that the people received this path to archetypal knowledge from the angels. (The word *Kabbala* originated from the Hebrew, a language that in its written form is set together with consonants only. QBL, or Kabbala, means *to receive.*) According to legend, it was the archangel Raphael who himself gave Adam the Kabbala after his expulsion from Paradise. This legend also says that this book contains the secrets and the keys by which Adam could find his salvation and his way back to the Paradise of God.

The Tree of Life is a diagram representing all factors affecting the universe, humankind, and the individual person. It depicts a living system as real and helpful today and in the future as it was in the time of Christ. It is applicable to all, including the most modern phenomena. For some, it signifies the only truly satisfying philosophy.

Hans-Dieter Leuenberger, in his second volume of *Schule des Tarot,* which deals with the "Minor Arcana" of the Tarot and its connection with the Tree of Life, writes this about the Kabbala:

> It is a strange mixture of theology and natural science, which in this combination and in a logical way is getting into a close relationship with magic. That may have been the main reason that throughout thousands of years, everything connected with the Kabbala has been cloaked in a mantle of secrecy, and is still being covered. This is wise and right. For whoever has understood the basic structure of the universe is also capable of destroying this universe in its basic structure.

Dion Fortune, the British esoteric author, writes in her book, *The Mystical Qabalah*, that in the 15th century, when the power of the church began to dwindle, a few had dared to write down the traditional wisdom of Israel. Sometimes, scholars considered the Kabbala to be medieval hocus-pocus because they could not find any earlier manuscripts. But all of cosmology and psychology could be expressed in this one glyph, which the uninitiated could not understand. She wrote that:

> The peculiar graphic descriptions together with this oral interpretation could be handed down from generation to generation without loss of the true meaning of its contents. If something about the meaning of a point difficult to understand evoked doubt, one focused on the holy symbol and meditated on it. As a result, information came to light, which for centuries had been placed there by meditation. Mystics know that a person who meditates over a symbol connected to earlier meditations, with specific preconceptions, will have access to those preconceptions.

Whoever is involved with the Tree of Life can gain a deeper understanding of how in the macrocosm of the universe and the microcosm of human beings—the body, the life situation—everything is interwoven. By the way, the ten different stations on the Tree have specific correspondences to the physical body, and there are color correspondences, as well.

There is a growing number of members in helping professions in the USA that use methods from the Kabbala so that others can be helped more effectively. Techniques that are used by teachers of the Kabbala are, among others, dream analysis, storytelling, and visualization.

The Kabbala teaches that each person needs to fulfill a certain life task that only he or she and no one else can take care of. To recognize this assignment, and to do it, and thus to attain a joyful and fulfilled life—is definitely a central theme.

❦ ❦ ❦

Now we come to the first important aspect that Aura-Soma has, so to speak, taken from the Kabbala: certainly the essential goal, a goal that is to be attained by using the substances is to find and fulfill your own mission in life, your own life task. For, all illnesses, all problems and hindrances are more or less related to your bypassing the real meaning of your life. An effort to change the direction toward your life purpose and to work on yourself in that regard will also free you, in time, from illnesses, problems, and hindrances on various levels.

A second important connection between the Kabbala and Aura-Soma was already described in Chapter 3: certain Kabbalistic invocations are used to energize the substances. An essential step in their preparation and production consists of using these invocations in a specific manner. Every bottle containing Aura-Soma substances carries a part of the Tree of Life within it, and hence, contains a key to certain aspects of consciousness within ourselves.

And here is the third aspect that the Kabbala and Aura-Soma have in common. As we mentioned, there are ten different stations on the Tree of Life corresponding to ten different colors. Via the colors, contact can be made with the different aspects of the stations. Even if the user of the substances has no inkling at all about the Kabbala, by using the substances in the bottles, a contact with these stations can be created; for the colors and color combinations in the balance bottles correspond directly to the various stations on the Tree. The establishment of this contact can be felt in dreams, in certain experiences in meditation, and even just in the way that the user's life flows. For him or her, it is a very personal experience, stemming from within. But a Kabbalist would declare, "The powers of Netzach are at work here, or those of Tipharet or Malkuth."

Just as the cosmos has neither found a form that is directly accessible for the human mind for the Tree of Life, this complex symbol; nor for the I Ching, which is nothing but a code; nor for Aura-Soma. The colors have to be translated. Just as the Tree of Life and the I Ching "work," whether one understands them or not, so do the colors of Aura-Soma. One can reach this conclusion since the substances have proven effective on sick plants and animals, on small children, and on mentally retarded people.

❧ ❧ ❧

In closing, let us add another thought or idea for a meditation theme in connection with the Kabbala.

Much has been said and written about the Jews over the course of centuries. One thing, however, is practically never mentioned: that they—or at least one certain group—have given humankind the Kabbalistic Tree of Life, one of the most precious instruments for understanding. "An initiate's way into the structure of the universe, God's blueprint of creation, the city map of the soul, a technique for using the mind, or also a manual for human intelligence." This is how the German author, Katja Wolff, describes the Kabbalistic Tree.

Wouldn't it be a good thing if more people were aware of this gift?

❧ ❧ ❧ ❧ ❧

THE COLORS

Everything around us has to do with light and color. All meaningful experiences are dependent upon their light and color. If we were to exist in darkness or grayness, it would not be possible for us to evolve. In fact, we could not survive.

We need light and color for so many reasons: to orient ourselves, to experience beauty and ugliness, to express ourselves creatively—in the arts, and with body language—and to be able to perceive the true expression of others. We also depend on light and color for determining whether we are safe or in danger, whether our environment is pleasant or repugnant, and for really getting to know ourselves and others.

American research has identified about 10 million color variations, and they can all be perceived and distinguished by the human eye. But, the ability to recognize, to differentiate, and to duplicate colors varies with each individual. In most people, color memory is not well developed. Ever since human beings have existed, they have been occupied with the phenomenon of color. Our ancestors during prehistoric times buried their dead in red ochre, or they painted their bones red, for they understood that red blood marked a significant border between life and death. Even then, red was considered to have a life-giving quality.

In the oldest Indo-European language, Sanskrit, *ruh-ira* means "blood." The first part of the word is to be found in many languages, as "red." In almost all documented cultures, red symbolizes life, and everything associated with life, such as vitality, strength, passion, and so on, or with death, which is also associated with red, as it has to do with the perception of blood.

People of earlier times had their experiences of life and death; they had the blue or the black sky; they had the whole color symphony of nature. From this, they developed names and symbols that at times corresponded with each other, but there are also variations. For the Celts, green was the color of Brigid, the earth goddess. For the ancient Chinese, green had a similar meaning to blue. Those colors signified wood and water. For Buddhists and Hindus, an intense green means life; pale green, the kingdom of the dead. Blue for the Celts was the color of bards and poets. For the ancient Greeks, it was that of Zeus and Hera as gods of heaven, as well as Aphrodite, the goddess of love. For those who study the Kabbala, blue symbolizes grace and mercy; for Native Americans, heaven and peace. In the Christian tradition, blue is the color of the mother of Christ—Mary, the queen of heaven. Note the parallels with Hera and Aphrodite. Besides that, for Christians, blue is the color of faithfulness, faith, and eternity.

❦ ❦ ❦

In his book, *Rainbow of Liberated Energy*, Ngakpa Chögyam, a Tibetan Lama born in Great Britain, clarifies the connection between nature and colors, as well as the connection between the patterns of human emotions and colors. He is clear in his view about the varying meanings of colors. His view and that of other color therapies may puzzle you while you are involved with Aura-Soma.

He compares the Tibetan system of colors and elements with the perspective of the Native Americans. He writes:

> Is it possible to learn something from the difference existing between the two systems? I fear the answer is no. We can actually learn very little and nothing of any worth for our lives except the joy that comes from gathering information. These systems are really separate ones. But when we try to mix them or to connect them, we simply distort them. They function in the context of their own sphere of action.

We could work with both or even more systems if our minds did not feel overburdened. But we should not deal with both or all at the same time. It would be impossible to answer the question of the "true" system. All would be true to the extent to which people at their level of growth support them. However, they would all be untrue if they were not truly experienced. They would only be reflections. Symbols are never absolute. They are bound to time and space and, therefore, to common cultural experiences.

Perhaps it would be helpful to clarify this for yourself from time to time in connection with Aura-Soma.

At the end of the 18th century, theories were being developed to systematize the phenomenon of color and to make it easier to understand. The two best-known ones are the mechanistic theory of the English physicist, Isaac Newton, and that of the German poet, Johann Wolfgang von Goethe, which today is considered esoteric. Aura-Soma is in sympathy with the view of Goethe for two reasons: he considered it more important to perceive the phenomenon of color rather than to theorize about it all too much. Another reason is that he—in contrast to Newton and his followers—did not accept three primary colors (blue, yellow, and red), but rather only two (blue and yellow). This premise has to do with duality, which plays a large role in life in general, in the spiritual domain (yin/yang, for example), and especially in Aura-Soma. The balance bottles are based on duality: two colors lie one over the other; above is a layer of oil, underneath is a layer of water. The "above" represents the personality ray, the "below" represents the soul ray of the person who chooses this particular bottle as his or her favorite. To Goethe, who followed the theory of the Greek philosopher and naturalist, Aristotle (384 B.C.–322 B.C.), the two colors blue and yellow were the most important ones. They were the primary colors. This interpretation fits that of Aura-Soma perfectly.

Goethe wrote in his color theory that he owed his knowledge to the ancient Greek philosophers. He believed that they have traced the phenomenon of color to its source, to the point beyond further explanation. Also, he hoped that natural scientists, chemists, dye-makers, artists, and physicians would take an interest in his color theory and would advance it.

Up until now, that has not happened, at least not until the time that Aura-Soma appeared on this earth....Goethe said that red is a combination of blue and yellow, the same as green. That is astonishing, for every child in kindergarten knows that blue and yellow never in the world make red, but always green. Goethe was also aware of the fact that the mixture of blue and yellow to make red does not function with color pigments, with crayons or oil paints. The combination works only with light! In this way, the combination is actually visible for everyone. This is demonstrated most impressively in the seminars at Dev-Aura, the Aura-Soma center in Great Britain, with the help of a glass container and an intensely bright flashlight. The glass contains a green oil intended later for the balance bottles. The flashlight then beams its light through the bright green oil. At that place where its light penetrates, one sees a red of the same intensity—an "Aha" experience for the participants in the seminar.

Goethe said that blue, yellow, and red are located opposite a complementary color, which represents a combination of both of the other colors. Opposite the blue is orange, a combination of yellow and red. Opposite yellow is violet, which consists of red and blue. Opposite red is green, a combination of blue and yellow. You can see the truth of this by looking at the Color Rose (the illustration in the center of the book that follows the bottles), which Aura-Soma has developed and which is a valuable aid for anyone using the bottles. You can also see, for instance, how blue gives off its influence in both directions. The same is true of yellow. A further step, then, is to picture how the meaning of blue and yellow transforms itself in both directions.

The inner rosette of the Color Rose includes the tertiary colors that are created by the primary and secondary colors, sharing borders: between blue and green is turquoise; between green and yellow, olive green (this is the specific name given by Aura-Soma). Between yellow and orange is gold; between orange and red is coral (also a specific color-name of Aura-Soma for this combination); between red and violet is magenta (the name originated from Goethe's color theory); and between violet and blue is royal blue. (In other systems, this color is called "indigo," where it contains a small part of black, which in Aura-Soma is not used at all.)

Every tertiary color lies directly opposite the tertiary color that represents the exact contrast. That means: turquoise lies opposite coral, olive green lies opposite magenta, and gold lies opposite royal blue.

You do not necessarily need to remember this information upon the first reading. However, you will see that it is important for understanding the language of color. Furthermore, you will also notice that you can absorb the contents and interpret them more easily than at first might have seemed possible. The knowledge is archetypal, having existed within human beings since ancient times. It has simply been buried in forgetfulness. It has remained in our genes and needs only to be stimulated. This is shown, for example, by the fact that many people, after just limited contact with Aura-Soma, already dream about specific bottles. Should you belong to this group, be sure to notice what your dreams tell you. They are a direct path to your subconscious, to the collective unconscious, and to other dimensions. If a bottle appears to you as a "medicine" for a particular problem, try it out. In this manner, some amazing processes have been introduced. And if using the contents does not produce any result, look at the Color Rose and pick out the color(s) directly opposite the one(s) in your dreams. The contents of dreams sometimes points out the exact opposite of what is really meant.

One user of Aura-Soma, for instance, dreamed of Bottle #43 (Turquoise/Turquoise) in connection with an emotional problem carried with him since childhood. The use of the contents produced no effect. But then, when he used #87 (Coral/Coral), lying exactly opposite the turquoise, he had a real breakthrough and could leave this "old pattern of behavior" behind in a short time.

❦ ❦ ❦

In the following pages, we have summarized the most important information about color. To give you an overview, we have kept it simple. We are limiting ourselves here to the interpretations exclusive to Aura-Soma. These interpretations were received by Vicky Wall and Mike Booth during meditation and have since been proven to be correct by thousands of people.

We shall follow the Color Rose and begin the sequence with red. Then we shall continue on with coral, orange, gold, yellow, olive-green, green, turquoise, blue, royal blue, violet, magenta, pink, and then end with clear.

Pink, for Aura-Soma, is red through which light shines. It is therefore the color in which the "red issues" have been transformed—for instance, the "red" passion turned into unconditional love. However, the opposite can also be the case. The pastel colors—in other words, the colors "through which the light shines"—can also indicate that the problems related to the corresponding color are even more intense. Pink can mean, for instance, that extreme problems related to sexuality or material issues are present.

"Clear" is related to the balance bottles, which contain a layer, transparent as water or a colorless oil. There is only one Aura-Soma bottle (#54), in which both layers are clear. It is the one containing pure light. It impresses some people as neutral and harmless. But the use of this oil often grows into extraordinarily deep, cleansing, and enlightening effects.

❦ ❦ ❦

If you use Aura-Soma and wish to become well acquainted with the "spirits in the bottles," we recommend that you read the following pages now and then to integrate the main points. However, we believe, as did Johann Wolfgang von Goethe, that colors must be experienced. Be open for this experience! Open your eyes to the colors in nature, in your environment, in yourself—the color of your hair, your eyes....Visualize colors with closed eyes—that is a very good exercise. (The way to protect yourself with a visualization on blue can be found in the meditation text beginning on page 214.) Look for and find rainbows in shiny objects, in water, in steamed-up window panes, and in soap bubbles. Allow yourself to feel whatever you find loosening up within you. Do not allow your brain to filter the experience. Color is energy that goes beyond words, beyond descriptions, beyond labeling.

But exercises and games in which the brain is used can also be meaningful, helping you to become better acquainted with the colors. For instance, you could think of ideas for symbols and associations with different colors. You could enjoy doing this activity by yourself, with a partner, or with children. What association comes up when you think of a particular color? Where in nature can you find it? What feelings are generated by this color? Which part of the body is associated with it? (Use the chakra chart.)

You can make a game of it. Such exercises can be fun. You and the people you are with will become ever more sensitive to the language of color and to the corresponding experiences.

❦ ❦ ❦

THE COLORS

Red

Most Important Associations: Energy. Grounding. "Survival issues." The material side of life.

Symbolic Meaning: Blood. Life. The "blood of life." Energy. Will power. Passion for life. Abundance. Maturity. Energy that is expressed quickly in communication. Inner warmth. Rebirth (on the various levels). (Blood) sacrifice. Red Cross (and the association with fast medical aid). The red rose and what it expresses—namely, love and passion. The red traffic light (warning of direct danger or punishment). Red as a symbol of brotherly love. Unity. Bondedness, but at the same time, suppression. Extremism. Grounding. Protection (but different from the protection of blue. Blue allows helpful and supportive energies from the outside in while it protects. Red offers isolating protection, shuts off the outer world, which can, in certain cases, be helpful and appropriate).

Spiritual Meaning: Flame—the cleansing flame and the flame of the Holy Spirit. Objectivity. Regeneration. Sacrifice. Urge for spiritual rebirth. Spiritual energy and strength. Phoenix, that rises out of the ashes. Transsubstantiation (for instance, turning water into wine). The potential for spiritual awakening.

Mental Meaning: Extraversion. Dominance. Authority. "Survival issues." Material side of life. Sacrifice. Energy for change (of oneself, of others, of things, situations, etc.). Stress. Chaos. Separateness (from oneself and others, from life).

Emotional Meaning: Passion. Temperament. Aggression. Heat. Fire. Anger. Resentment. Frustration. Violence. Embarrassment. Courage. Daring. Inconsistency.

Physical Associations: Sexuality (that has to do with conception and birth. The more playful form of sexuality is associated with orange). Womb. Menstruation cycle. Fertility, as compared to infertility. Potency, as compared to impotence. Blood and iron. Blood circulation. Cellular structure of the body. Fever. Swellings. Stimulation of the energy flow.

Crystals (used by Aura-Soma): Agate. Bloodstone or hematite. Garnet. Jasper. Karneol. Obsidian. Pyrite. Ruby.

Coral

Most Important Associations: Unrequited love. **Coral is a color that hardly has a role at all in Western society.** For Native Americans, however, it has a deep meaning. Among other colors, coral is used by them for jewelry, so rich in symbolism. The Persians weave this color into their carpets, for coral has the ability to bring happiness and good fortune into the home.

  With Aura-Soma, it is a "new" color. It can be seen only in Bottles #87, #92, and #93. However, it will appear in future bottles.

Symbolic Meaning: Coral grows in the sea. Therefore, it is associated with the unconscious and the subconscious. The little animals of which coral consists sacrifice their individuality for the good of the community. Coral reefs need light in order to grow. As a result, they strive for light.

  Coral is also a symbol for the skeletal structure of human beings. Coral represents a more intense version of the color orange, at least with respect to its symbolic content.

Spiritual Meaning: Higher intuition. Some see coral as the color of the new Christ ray.

Mental Meaning: Projection (of positive or negative characteristics to other persons, instead of recognizing them in yourself). Self-analysis. Possibility of getting beyond your own frustrations. Dependency. Co-dependency, and in the resolved form—independence and interdependence.

Emotional Meaning: Unresolved versus resolved relationships. Spontaneity. Protection from dishonesty. Ability to accept love. Joy in love. Feelings of aloneness and isolation versus *all-one-ness.*

Physical Associations: Glands. Elimination organs and sexual organs. Psychosomatic illnesses. Birth trauma and other shocks.

Crystals (used by Aura-Soma): Coral is not actually a stone (see above), but it is considered to be a stone for our purposes. Onyx. Rose quartz.

Orange

Most Important Associations: Dependency/Co-dependency/Independence. Shock. Trauma. Deep insight and ecstasy.

Symbolic Meaning: Harmony. Beauty. Art. Divinity and renunciation. (The robes of Buddhist monks are orange.) Sexuality. Trust.

Spiritual Meaning: Insight. Individuation. Devotion. The need to belong.

Mental Meaning: Wisdom. Indecision. Patience and perseverance. Deep insight. Lack of self-worth. Dependency/co-dependency/independence. Interdependence.

Emotional Meaning: Wisdom. "Gut feelings." Spontaneous wisdom. Camaraderie. Sexuality for pleasure and joy, not with the intent to conceive. Hysteria. Depression. Excitement. Extraversion. Shock. Trauma. Joy. Deep delight.

Physical Associations: Ovaries. Intestines, small and large (also constipation). Spleen (only the color orange can bring the spleen and its function into balance—see Chapter 4). Gall bladder (one who has difficulties with the gall bladder cannot stand oranges). The color orange has to do with food intake and assimilation.

Crystals (used by Aura-Soma): Agate. Amber. Coral. Topaz.

Gold

Most Important Associations: Wisdom and deep fear.

Symbolic Meaning: Transmutation (in the alchemical process, base metal is changed to gold through transmutation). Wealth on all levels. "The golden egg" as a symbol for wealth. The (golden) Holy Grail (as a symbol for something attained with great difficulty). The gold wedding ring (as a symbol for unity).

Spiritual Meaning: The wisdom of Solomon. The wisdom of discernment is golden. The ancient sun-worshiping religions are related to gold (ancient Egyptians, the Aztecs, and the Mayans). Holiness. Justice. Eternity. Wisdom. Purity. Beauty. Status. Splendor. Meditation. Enlightenment.

Mental Meaning: Wisdom. Support. Self-righteousness. False modesty. Cheating. Deception. Delusion.

Emotional Meaning: Desire. Ecstasy. Peace. Comfort. Delight. Constancy and trustworthiness. Problem with safety issues. Fear. Nervousness. Greed. Confusion.

Physical Associations: Nerves. Spine. Intestines. Skin (problems). Jaundice. Disgust. All kinds of addictions.

Crystals (used by Aura-Soma): Amber. Tiger eye. Topaz. Citrine.

Yellow

Most Important Associations: Acquired knowledge.

Symbolic Meaning: Sun. Light. In Chinese medicine, yellow stands for earth. "Yellow" on the traffic light means: caution! A yellow flag signifies quarantine.

Spiritual Meaning: Acquired knowledge. Light. Will power.

Mental Meaning: Stimulation. Cynicism. Mental confusion. Intellect. Indecisiveness.

Emotional Meaning: Warmth. Laughter. Joy and delight. Jealousy. Fear. Lack of trust. Cowardice. Nervousness. Confusion. Depression.

Physical Associations: The area of the solar plexus. Liver. Nerves. Skin. Central nervous system. Jaundice. Rheumatism. Arthritis.

Crystals (used by Aura-Soma): Amber. Topaz. Citrine.

Olive Green

Most Important Associations: Space and wisdom. Feminine leadership qualities.

Symbolic Meaning: Hope. New life on earth. Peace (after the Flood, a dove with an olive branch in its beak flew back to Noah). Light being manifested (in early times, olive oil was used for lamps). Transmutation (olives cannot be picked from the tree and eaten; they must be marinated and have to undergo a chemical process in order to be edible).

The Mount of Olives was a kind of power place for Jesus and His disciples. The last anointing (with oil) is a symbol for death and rebirth.

Spiritual Meaning: Clarity on the path. Ability to transform the spiritual into daily life. Joy and the ability to laugh at oneself as a spiritual quality. (Yellow, the color of joy combined with green, the color of space and truth). Groundedness.

Mental Meaning: Harmony. Completion.

Emotional Meaning: Self-love. Detachment from one's own emotions. Leadership qualities, combined with qualities of the heart.

Physical Associations: Gall bladder. Large intestine. Lungs. Calms diarrhea and cramps.

*Crystals (*used by Aura-Soma): Olivine. Peridot. Aventurine.

Green

Most Important Associations: Space. Search for truth. Panoramic view (intention of seeing 360 degrees, to turn around on one's own axis, to see all aspects of a situation).

Symbolic Meaning: Nature. Growth. Spring. Creativity. Overabundance. Devas. Fertility. Green is the symbolic color for money. The green light on the traffic light means free access, forward. Green harmonizes body, soul, and spirit.

Spiritual Meaning: Healing. Regeneration. Compassion. Love of the earth.

Harmony with nature and her laws.

Mental Meaning: Discernment. Compromise. Ability to make decisions. Generosity. Capability of making sound judgments. Balance.

Emotional Meaning: Openness. Calmness. Freedom. Generosity. Issues relating to the heart. Having a panoramic view (see above). Envy. Jealousy. Contentment.

Physical Associations: Heart. Lungs. Thymus gland. Ulcers. Space in connection with physical issues. The laws of nature in physical issues.

Crystals (used by Aura-Soma): Jade. Malachite. Opal. Olivine. Pyrite. Emerald. Tourmaline.

Turquoise

Most Important Associations: Mass communication. Communication through art and all kinds of creative expression.

Symbolic Meaning: Turquoise is the color of the often quoted "Age of Aquarius." It also stands for the legendary sunken continent of Atlantis, and the wisdom, technology, and art of that time. It stands for *transdimensionality,* meaning existence and presence beyond time and space. The fourth-and-a-half chakra, the ananda-khanda center, relates to the color turquoise. Turquoise stands for the sea. For dolphins. Freedom and intelligence linked with feeling.

Spiritual Meaning: (identical to the symbolic meaning)

Mental Meaning: Ability to trust intuition and to adjust to change easily. Idealism. Utopian outlook. Tendency to idealize. Teaching. Communication through mass media, through art and all kinds of creative expression. Awareness. Communication through foreign languages. Talent for technical things.

Emotional Meaning: Intuition having to do with feeling. The whole domain of emotions. Sympathy and empathy. Emotional expression. Optimism. Childlike in the positive sense of the word. Technophobia (fear of handling electronic apparatus) versus the talent for technical things.

Physical Associations: Heart. Throat. Thymus gland. Lungs. Upper neck. Shoulders, especially the right one. Circulation. Bronchitis. Asthma. Revitalization. Regeneration. Hay fever. Swellings. All sorts of strains in the body.

Crystals (used by Aura-Soma): Aquamarine. Malachite. Opal. Turquoise.

Blue

Most Important Associations: Peace and communication.

Symbolic Meaning: Maria, the nurturing and protective Mother of Jesus and the Queen of Heaven, and Kwan Yin, the far-Eastern goddess of mercy. Sympathy and healing. The "blue flower of romance." Rest. Peace. Safety.
    The autobahn in Germany has blue signs. Blue stands for speed and directness, straightforwardness. Officers of the military and of non-military institutions such as airlines and cruise lines wear blue uniforms. In so doing, they wish to show that they provide protection, and they let you know that they work for peace.

Spiritual Meaning: Blue is the color of the archangel Michael and of Krishna and Vishnu, two Hindu gods. They are described in the *Bhagavad-Gita,* one of the holy books of India, as living in blue bodies. This means that blue stands for Divinity. Water (baptism, blessing, spiritual cleansing). Trance mediumism. Protection (but different from that of the color red, which is isolating. Blue offers protection that lets helpful and supportive influences through).

Mental Meaning: Intuition. Diplomacy. Will power. Leadership. Uniformity. Authority. (Blue jeans, the most widespread uniform, demonstrated in Europe at first revolt against authority. Today they symbolize freedom and leisure time.)

Emotional Meaning: Serenity. Calmness. Softness. Emptiness. Frigidity. Feeling blue. Going within. The nurturing mother. The problematic father. (In Aura-Soma, blue relates to the positive experiences related to the mother and to the negative experiences with the father.)

Physical Associations: Thyroid. Throat. Everything having to do with communication. Cramps. Sprains. Infections. Neck problems. Calms. Effective for itching or sunburn.

Crystals (used by Aura-Soma): Lapis lazuli. Opal. Sapphire. Turquoise.

Royal Blue

Most Important Associations: To know why one is here.

Symbolic Meaning: Royal blue is the color of King David, the leader of the Jewish people. Royal blue is also the color of the Egyptian goddess of the night, Nuit, who symbolizes deep wisdom. Also represents femininity and the new moon. Mysticism. The third eye—psychic abilities such as clairvoyance, clairaudience, clairsentience. The meaning of royal blue is not referring to spontaneous phenomena, but rather that which is consciously accessible. Ability to make decisions, ability to "see through" situations. Paranoia. Extreme tendency to idealize. Resistance to seeing things as they are. Depression. Isolation. Separateness.

Spiritual Meaning: (Identical to the symbolic meaning)

Emotional Meaning: Neutrality. Objectivity. Ability to keep a distance. Reverence. Loneliness. To be alone, in the sense of all-one. Depression.

Physical Associations: Eyes. Ears. Nose. Forehead. Pineal gland.

Crystals (used by Aura-Soma): Lapis lazuli. Sapphire.

Violet

Most Important Associations: Spirituality. Healing. Service. (Too much) contemplation.

Symbolic Meaning: In Theosophy, the color violet represents the "flame of transmutation" that burns negativity and makes new growth possible. Individualism. To "bring to earth." To serve. Healing. Closure. To recognize and realize the reason for living.

Mental Meaning: To contemplate (too much).

Emotional Meaning: Suffering. Grief. Not wanting to be here. Difficulty with the material side of life. Addiction. Tendency to withdraw. Inner calmness.

Physical Associations: Production of mucus. Skull. Effective for overactivity. Calming.

Crystal (used by Aura-Soma): Amethyst.

Magenta

Most Important Associations: Love for the small, everyday things.

Magenta is important in Goethe's color theory and in the printing trade. Otherwise, it is hardly known. Even Aura-Soma has only limited information about it.

Magenta is the color of the "eighth chakra." It is located outside and above the body. The color is related to sacrificial love. Stimulates the ability to focus. Cooperation. Finding one's own reason for living and then living it.

Physical Associations: Hormonal system. Reproductive organs. Morning sickness. Stimulates the flow of energy. Magenta affects all chakras and all parts of the body.

Crystal (used by Aura-Soma): Amethyst.

With Aura-Soma, there are two types of magenta. One is Deep Magenta and can be seen, for example, in the lower layer of Bottle #0. It looks black, but when a bright light shines through it, one really sees a very dark magenta. The second type of magenta looks like an intense pink. It is found, for instance, in both layers of Bottle #67, as well as in the Color Rose between violet and red. (See the illustration in the center of the book.)

Pink

Most Important Associations: Unconditional love and caring.

With Aura-Soma, pink is considered red through which light is shining. That means that all "red issues" are either enhanced or negatively strengthened. This is especially applicable to passionate, sexually charged love, which can change to unconditional love or to sexual addiction and possessiveness. It relates not only to individual lessons, but also to the collective. In that way, for instance, the (red) so-called sexual revolution has led us away from prudishness and inhibition through times of promiscuity and other sexual excesses to new possibilities, such as Tantra. It could possibly lead us to a (pink-colored) true spiritual sexuality.

Pink represents unconditional love and caring. Feminine intuitive energy. Awakening. Also signifies the need for warmth and extreme problems with material issues. It stands for the feminine role model.

Physical Associations: Hormonal system. Reproductive organs. Eyes. Head. Deafness. Antidote for fear.

Crystals (used by Aura-Soma): Diamond. Rose quartz. Tourmaline.

Clear

Most Important Associations: Suffering and understanding of suffering. "Clear" is, of course, no color, but in Aura-Soma it is considered a color.

Symbolic Meaning: Clear is "frozen" light (therefore contains all colors). It has to do with the mirror and with the distorting mirror, in which we can recognize ourselves. Transparency. The source of light.

Spiritual Meaning: Karmic forgiveness. Deep reflection. Emptiness. Expansion. Transparency. Clarity. Purity. The energy of the moon. The "silver cord" that connects us to infinity. The white rose, as a sign of integrity. Honesty. Simplicity. Truth.

Mental Meaning: Clarity. Emptiness. Expansion.

Emotional Meaning: The "well of unshed tears." Suffering. The understanding of suffering. Clarity. Determination.

Physical Associations: Clear can be applied anywhere. It brings light into all chakras and all parts of the body. It cleanses and withdraws poisons with most of the combinations.

Crystals (used by Aura-Soma): Agate. Diamond. Moonstone. Quartz. Rose quartz. Zircon.

From the 14 described colors, a total of 28 different variations are considered valid by Aura-Soma.

Color	*"Opposite" Color*
Red	Green, Emerald Green
Pink/Rose Pink	Pale Green
Pale Pink	Pale Green
Coral	Turquoise
Pale Coral	Pale Turquoise
Orange	Blue
Pale Orange	Pale Blue
Gold, Pale Gold	Royal Blue
Yellow, Lemon	Violet, Purple
Pale Yellow	Pale Violet (Lilac)
Olive Green	Magenta, Deep Magenta

Clear

❦ ❦ ❦ ❦ ❦

WORKING WITH THE BALANCE BOTTLES

Now we are getting to practical matters. How do you know which Aura-Soma oils are right for you? Which oils can give you support for your very personal problems? Basically, there are three ways to choose.

The first and simplest way involves the Aura-Soma chakra chart. With this depiction of the human "rainbow," you can localize the problem for which you desire help. Let's say that you have difficulty reaching a meditative state because too many thoughts are active in your head. The cause of the problem lies in the violet area of your "rainbow." In view of the chart, then, you can look for the bottles containing violet in a store or at the establishment of an Aura-Soma practitioner. After that, you can study the descriptions yourself, or you can choose to have a counseling session. This is how you can find out which substances would most likely be the most beneficial. In this case, it would probably be Bottle #37 (Violet/Blue).

The effects of the oils chosen through this method are often not ideal, though. (However, when choosing Pomanders, one may have better results with this method, and it is usually reliable.) The reason why choosing the bottles in this manner is not the best way, is that the oils, in most cases, have their strongest effect if they are chosen with the heart and not with the head. If you find that you like Bottle #37 very much, you can probably expect to be helped by its contents. However, if you do not like it very much or feel neutral about it, the chances to benefit are not good.

Surprisingly enough, it often happens that your four favorite bottles, which we shall discuss later on in this chapter, contain a combination that can have an effect on virulent problems in your body. We find that women, for instance, who have difficulties in the lower part of their body, often choose a combination with pink, which is helpful in alleviating problems in that area.

The second, and more effective way of choosing bottles demands more intuition. It is best if you place the bottles directly in front of you, preferably during daylight hours. That means that doing it from the colored pictures in this book is not recommended.

Before choosing, it is best if you get yourself into a relaxed state. Then, you need to think about the problem you wish to resolve, and ask your inner voice which oil would be most beneficial. Of course, you may vacillate in your decisions. Or, you can close your eyes and move your left hand over and near the bottles to determine which one attracts you by its energy.

You can also hold your problem in mind while you pull a Tarot card. The numbered bottle that corresponds to the card would be the fitting "medicine." But if you choose this method, you should have really had some experience with the Tarot. The "Major Arcana" correspond to numbers 0 to 22. They relate to the first 22 bottles. With the "Minor Arcana," it matches the King of Wands (#23) and the Queen of Wands (#24), and so on. (Further notes appear in the section on the descriptions of the bottles.)

You could also throw an I Ching to know which bottle to pick out for yourself. The same applies here as with the Tarot cards. You should be well versed in using the I Ching. That same section containing descriptions of the bottles will be informative here, also.

If numerology interests you, you probably already have various ideas in mind to help you pick "your" bottles. Here are two possible methods: obtain the sum of your birth date in such a way that the result is a two-digit number. (That has proven more successful for Aura-Soma throughout the years than a single-digit number.)

Here is an example: If you were born on 2/2/1953, you would figure as follows: 2 plus 2 plus 1 plus 9 plus 5 plus 3 = 22. You would not, however, continue adding 2 plus 2 = 4, but rather, just hold on to the two-digit number, 22. Numerologically speaking, that would indicate the number of a bottle that has a lot to do with you, in this whole lifetime.

If you wish to find the bottle that coincides with the present phase in your life, you would use the numbers in the birth date, combined with those in the present year. For 1996, that would mean: $2 + 2 + 1 + 9 + 9 + 6 = 29$. Therefore Bottle #29 would be your "bottle of the year" for 1996.

And now we shall explain the "orthodox" way to choose your bottles and what information is contained in them that results from the sequence of the choice. With the help of the descriptions in Chapter 8, you can get an idea of what result a reading with an Aura-Soma practitioner might have for you. But it would certainly take much experience to keep an overview of all the various relevant approaches in mind and to draw meaningful conclusions. Because this book is meant to deliver only an entrance into Aura-Soma, and that in the most understandable way, we cannot say too much about this approach.

If you do decide to utilize the third method, and really want to gain some practical benefit, we would advise you to seek out an Aura-Soma practitioner, who can read the language of the colors and translate them for you.

Choosing Your Bottles

Imagine that you are being sent to a remote island where you will have to spend some time, and you are only allowed to take one single balance bottle with you for companionship. Which one would you choose? Consider your choice carefully, and choose when you are truly sure. Put the bottle aside, and start the process once again as you choose your second bottle. Now keep the same mission on that lonesome island in mind as before. Again, you may take only one bottle with you. Which is it this time?

Set your second-favorite bottle aside, also. Now, repeat this process two more times, for a total of four bottles. Now you have chosen your four most-favored bottles, in which a code is contained, a code that is personally right for you.

Now, what do these four bottles signify?

1. The first bottle shows your mission in life, the goal with which you incarnated this time.

2. The second bottle discloses your greatest difficulties and if you

have worked on them—your most valuable gift, the gift you received from the Creative Force, and at the same time, the gift that you can offer to the Creative Force.

3. The third bottle contains information about how you have progressed on your path.

4. The fourth bottle informs you about possible future perspectives.

The First Bottle

The lower fraction: shows what you have brought with you from the past (that is, from your former lives), and it shows your life task, which will possibly be held over to a future life. It also shows on which "soul ray" you incarnated. This ray (relevant to your life task) has to do with the attributes described in the chapter about colors. The lower half of your first bottle represents the color of your "true aura."

The upper fraction: shows the circumstances into which you were born in this life. It relates to the moment of your conception, but also to the circumstances of your childhood. It includes your adult years, through which you have allowed yourself to become what you are today. It embodies the personality ray on which you came into this life. (You can read more about what this may have to do with you in the color chapter, also.)

Both fractions together: make up your "soul bottle." You can be fairly certain that this bottle is, in fact, your soul bottle when you continually, and with great care, choose this bottle as your first choice.

Your soul bottle: points to what you want to learn and what you want to accomplish in this life. In Chapter 8, under the subhead for each bottle description called "Positive Personality Aspects," you can discover what your life task, talents, and goals are. Don't hesitate to also look at those aspects that need to be worked on. Even if they refer mostly to the second bottle, you will see that the descriptions also may hold true for the first. It is possible that you may need to work on them. Under the headings of Spiritual, Mental, Emotional, and Physical levels, you will find which effects the application of the shaken-up substances can have in these domains. Please realize that the process of taking Aura-Soma substances is more subtle than that of traditional medicines. The results do not always manifest themselves at once, often not until after many regular applications, and often in very subtle, delicate ways. It is not recommended that you try to solve serious health problems with Aura-Soma substances. Instead, you could place your trust in a physician or health practitioner—perhaps one who is open to alternative gentle healing methods. And you need to follow that person's advice, of course.

There is no conflict between Aura-Soma usage and that of therapies such as Bach flower essences, homeopathy, or with traditional medicine or psychotherapy. On the contrary, Aura-Soma supports all of these therapies. Even if for certain reasons you are obliged to take chemically based medicines, you may still use Aura-Soma substances, for they assist in the process of regaining your health.

The Second Bottle

When it comes to the second, third, and fourth bottles, it is not as important to look at the single layers of colors. Here, it is of greater value to look at the *combination.*

Both fractions together: tell you where your greatest difficulties and blockages relative to your problems are. At the same time, you will also find out about your greatest possibilities for growth. If you are working on that challenge, or already have worked on it, you will more extensively open the "gift-package" meant for you. At the same time and in the same form, this present also contains the gift that you can return to the cosmos—a wonderful paradox.

You can gain information about your difficulties, your blockages, and your problems under the subhead, "Personality Aspects That Could Be Worked On." You can find your gift under "Positive Personality Aspects" in your second bottle. Under the categories of Spiritual, Mental, Emotional, and Physical Levels, you will find the results of the application of the well-shaken substances.

The Third Bottle

Both fractions together: show how far you have come on your path up to this moment in your life. You might wish to take note of the positive personality aspects that are listed and judge as honestly as possible whether you have reached the goal, whether you are well on the way, or whether you will need to work on the problematic personality aspects represented by the second bottle. Most likely, some points from both aspects will apply to you. You might also look at the problematic personality aspects of your third bottle and allow yourself to be shown what additional hindrances may still block your way.

The interpretation of the third bottle poses some inherent difficulties, especially so if you want to do this interpretation alone. It requires a great deal of objectivity and an ability for self-critique to judge the situation somewhat realistically and objectively. It is difficult, as well, to develop strategies for yourself as to how to work on your problems, aside from the use of the substances. Because, however supportive Aura-Soma might be, when it comes to negative behavior patterns and life strategies, you simply need to vow sincerely to adopt a new way of behaving and to train yourself in it. To accomplish this task alone is very difficult. The support of a psychotherapist or a counselor can be a big help.

The Fourth Bottle

Both fractions together: reveal what the future may have in store for you. Please pay special attention to the "Positive Personality Aspects" in the description of this bottle, for we are co-creators of our future. It is very likely that the object of our concentration today will be our reality tomorrow. Therefore, be sure not to keep your focus on the problematic personality aspects or on your difficulties on the spiritual, mental, emotional or physical levels. Rather, direct your attention to whatever is most beneficial for you, for your fellow human beings, and for the planet—namely, to the positive personality aspects that the "spirits in the bottle" can help you attain.

It would be beneficial for you to place this fourth bottle near your bed to attract the positive energies concerning the future. Of course, you can also work with the shaken-up substances by applying them to the appropriate areas of the body. But this "work" of yours will not be experienced until after the second or third bottle. It is suggested that you let some time elapse between the use of the different bottles, generally.

❦ ❦ ❦

The second bottle in Aura-Soma counts as the "therapeutic" one, meaning that you should apply the contents of the second one first. In this way, you can attain positive, noticeable results. The benefit could also reach into areas not even included in the descriptions of the bottles. As such, Aura-Soma's completely "orthodox" method of solving a problem—a physical, emotional, mental, or spiritual one—consists of allowing the individual to choose his or her four favorite bottles and to give that person the "therapeutic bottle" for his or her use. Through this method, some really miraculous healings have come about—as we've said, even in areas not usually belonging to the well-known domains affected by these oils.

The content of your "soul bottle," which contains your innermost being (in terms of color theory), has a very strong effect. It is best if you come in physical contact with the substance in it only after you have experimented with the other bottles and know your reactions to them. You should allow yourself two to three weeks so that you can really become familiar with your soul colors. For instance, you could take the bottle along on a vacation when you are assured of some quiet time. Instead of applying the substance directly, you could, before going to sleep, place the bottle on your stomach for a while. This is how you can determine its effect and the dosage.

When you have used up the contents of the second bottle of your choice, the "therapeutic bottle," take a break for at least a week. Notice what has changed about you. Do you dream more often? What is the content of your dreams? What happens in your meditations or your stress-relieving practices? Do you recall things you had long forgotten? How is your sleep and your appetite? How are your emotions? Are you experiencing an unusual amount of joy, rage, frustration, tenderness, sexual arousal, or exhaustion? How well are you doing at work? Look up the corresponding descriptions of the bottles. Do you notice changes in the areas relating to your concerns? After a week, do you still have the feeling that there is a lot stirring within you? Then, lengthen the break! There is no hurry; take the time that you need. Make the most of every substance. Take the whole potential of the "spirit in the bottle" into yourself. Allow it to integrate.

Only after you really feel closure about the process will you make friends with a new bottle.

Next, we recommend that you use the contents of the third bottle of your choice. Your preference for this one can, in contrast to the first and second bottles (which should remain stable throughout), vary with the passage of time. Your preference for the fourth bottle can also change over the course of time. That is totally normal, for human beings are always evolving, especially if they regularly use the substances of Aura-Soma. You can accelerate the process and can enrich your personality with new facets, if you persevere. You will know that you have accomplished something when you notice the changes in your choice of the third and fourth bottles. However, we would like to impress upon you to be totally honest with yourself and to listen only to your inner voice.

We notice again and again that those users of the substances who are gaining increasing knowledge about the meaning of the single bottles are apt to allow themselves to be led by the intellect rather than by their feelings. One could say that they then tend to want to impress themselves or their Aura-Soma practitioner, or perhaps someone else. They are only wasting time and money by doing so, though, for it is highly unlikely that they will experience unfolding benefits from choices made through the intellect.

But luckily, something quite different often happens. Sometimes when you are looking over the bottles, a color combination that you had not noticed before will catch your eye. It may not have particularly appealed to you at first, but even so, you sense a strong attraction.

You would do well to follow that call and to accept and use the contents of that bottle. Often an actual problem reveals itself to you, one that begs to be solved. (What the problem might be you can usually determine by reading the accompanying description.) After being involved with Aura-Soma for only a short time, you will find that your instinct for color develops in a surprising way, and the reaction to a specific color can point up a difficulty even before you have consciously given it any thought.

The following occurrence happened at an Aura-Soma workshop: One day a participant felt strangely and intensely drawn to Bottle #78 (Violet/Deep Magenta). She seemed actually starved for the Violet. "I could drink it," she said. And the Deep Magenta had its message, too. This exact combination had crucial information hidden within it.

The woman began to use the substance, as prescribed. In a few days she began to dream about her mother, long deceased. It became clear to her that her inclination toward minor illnesses must have something to do with her mother. Because she could not solve the mystery through dreams, meditation, or contemplation, she consulted a trusted therapist engaged in breath work. In an intense rebirthing session in which she also applied the oil of Bottle #78, the secret was divulged. Having entered an altered state of consciousness through the breathing method, she became aware that her mother had been raped during the war. Her mother had never told anyone about this trauma. She had suppressed the shock all of her life. She had suffered until her death from a great variety of illnesses, especially dramatically severe throat inflammations.

Unaware she was doing so, and on a totally physical level, she had passed her own "shock program" on to her daughter, who was born after the war. The daughter had wondered all of her life why she was never really in good health. Obviously, she could not suspect what her mother had hidden within and what she had passed on as inheritance. Only with the help of Aura-Soma was it possible to uncover the secret that had caused her so many problems.

The woman needed a few weeks to work with Bottle #78 to allow the information that had been brought to light, to remain in the light. That meant that she had to retain it in consciousness and accept it. It meant that she had to tell herself over and over that the trauma and its effects were past, and that a new beginning had happened for her mother "on the other side" and also for herself.

She also told her body that shame, guilt, and atonement were no longer relevant. Whenever possible, she would lie in the sun—in other words, actually place herself in the light. She let all the cells in her body know that they were now well and free from the old "spells." She also told them that from now on they could work in harmony with all of the other parts of her personality. (You can find more specific information about this kind of inner work in Dr. Carl Simonton's book, *Getting Well Again*. This work relates to cancer patients, but it can also apply to people with other illnesses.)

After applying the substance in Bottle #78, the woman stopped for a while. Then she used #64 (Green/Clear), a balance oil meant especially for integration of difficult-to-accept truths. In addition, this oil supports new beginnings. Over the course of a number of months, her condition improved considerably.

❦ ❦ ❦

Allow us to summarize the sequence in which you might want to work with your bottles.

The second bottle of your choice is the "therapeutic" one. It is generally recommended that you use it first. (We remind you once more that if you notice no effect after several days, you might take Bottle #11 in the interim and as preparation. Or you might take them both at the same time.)

Then you need to pause for a week or more. The next one should be the third bottle of your choice. Please follow the directions and then pause again. After the third bottle, your fourth favorite bottle is the one to use. After another time lapse, you may very carefully begin to use your "Soul Bottle," but only after the necessary rest, and if you are sure you are at a place in your life when you can deal with the strong energies of this substance. It might be advisable to wait until your next vacation.

After using the contents of the first three or four bottles, some experiences with the "spirits in the bottle" will already be familiar to you. You will then be able to decide for yourself how you will proceed. It could be that you feel that you need to wait a longer interval, or you might welcome the effects of the contents of your bottles the second time. You might confront yourself with the whole process of choosing bottles again. You might look for a new "medicine" altogether. Tips on how to proceed from this point are found in the last chapter.

Body Contact with the "Spirits in the Bottle"

Now we shall present you with some important information regarding the handling of the bottles.

Please, always grasp the bottle with your left hand and always hold it by the lid only, whether it is yours or not. This is to make sure that the energies in the bottles are not disturbed.

If you want to apply a bottle's contents, you can be more relaxed. Handle it normally as you would any bottle. If at some time a drop or two spills, simply wipe it with a cloth or sponge. It is proper to treat the "spirits in the bottle" with respect, but don't overdo it. After all, they do want to have physical contact with you!

Take the bottle you are using in your left hand in such a way that the ring finger holds one "shoulder," the middle finger is over the metal top, and the index finger holds the other shoulder. Carry the bottle with the thumb clasping it. Now, open the lid, and shake the bottle, so that the two layers are well mixed. Put some of the quickly formed emulsion in your right hand, and spread it over the prescribed places (see Chapter 8). When you sense that the substance is difficult to shake out, you can then put the plastic stopper aside. (You need to save it, though, as you might want to re-insert it later.)

At first, the two layers will not mix that easily; they will separate again quickly. But the more you use the substance, and the more space is left in the bottle (as it is emptied), the easier it is to shake and mix. When applying the substance, it is very important that a wide band around the body is drawn with the emulsion, and that the spine is always included when the prescribed places relate to the trunk.

In the process of shaking the bottle, the energy of the user's electro-magnetic field goes into the content of the bottle. Thereby, the healing potential is heightened. This principle is also used in homeopathy when the doctor places a pill on the hand of the patient in order to allow the patient's energy to penetrate that pill. Furthermore, by shaking the bottle with the left hand, some of the potential of the right side of the applier's brain penetrates the substance. That is the side of the brain connected with creativity, the unconscious, and other dimensions.

We recommend that you apply the bottle's contents first thing in the morning, and in the evening immediately before going to sleep. With red combinations, you must be careful, though, as they can be too stimulating for some people, and their sleep may be disturbed when the substances are applied too late in the afternoon or evening.

Otherwise, we recommend, as we said before, to begin simply and not use more than one bottle until the contents are depleted. Do stay with it no matter what the reactions indicate. In rare cases, someone may react to a substance by getting bronchitis. If that should happen, stay with the bottle. This will only be a temporary crisis in the healing process, and it will be quickly overcome when you continue using the substance.

Only if you experience a skin reaction, you need to take a few days' break. The skin must first recuperate. What other possible problems could occur we have already mentioned in Chapter 3. For instance, unpleasant feelings or memories could surface. Be glad when these experiences occur, for it only means that old stories are there ready to bid you adieu.

The positive effects of the bottles we have already commented on: you will become more and more *yourself.* You will feel closer to understanding and attaining your life goal. This is a purely individual journey. Be optimistic, and look forward to it.

❦ ❦ ❦

Be sure that only you yourself shake the bottles that you use. Do not allow another person to touch them, except very carefully and in the prescribed manner, namely by holding them with the left hand by the metal top.

However, for exceptional situations, there are alternatives. Let us use the following case as an example: You are just now in the process of using the Shock Bottle #26 in order to finally deal with an old case of shock in your life. All of a sudden, someone within your circle of friends experiences a trauma, and you would like to give him or her support with your bottle. In this case, it is possible to completely cleanse the bottle of your own energies. The other person can energize it for him- or herself and can then use it until empty.

You can proceed with the cleansing process as follows: place the bottle upright on a bed of amethysts or in an amethyst geode (this is a natural cave consisting of amethyst, and it can be purchased in a crystal shop). The cleansing process takes about 12 hours. It is ready for use even if changes in color are noticeable and remain so.

The second-fastest method is to: place the bottle upright to the "shoulders" in sea salt. This method is as effective as the one with amethyst, but takes 24 hours.

And there is yet a third possibility, which takes about 36 hours: place the bottle up to the shoulders in a strong solution of sea salt and water. It is just as effective as the other two methods.

Should you wish to have some help, as in the case of massaging the oil onto your back, then shake the bottle yourself and put the emulsion in the hand of your friend, your partner, or your therapist. This person can then massage it into the skin as he or she normally would.

Sometimes a color disappears from a bottle that you want to use. Do not let it irritate you—that means that you have a need for this color. Look up what it means, and think about it. Then use the substance as usual. Or, if you are not using the oil, you might keep the bottle standing near your bedside, on your desk, and so on.

Often, the colors in the balance oils become dull and spotted. That means that the user has undertaken a very deep process. Then you need to be sure that the disturbing factors relate to yourself and not to another person. You must cleanse the bottle as described and not allow anyone else to come in contact with it. If the spots and dullness occur again, you can be sure that you yourself are responsible. The little energetic particles will support your healing process, in the same way as with a vaccination, where a number of pathogenic agents are brought into the body in order to stimulate the production of antibodies.

The Aura-Soma oils themselves do not spoil. They are produced with high-quality standards. There are still bottles in existence that hail from the time of Vicky Wall. Their contents have never been shaken, meaning that no one has made them his or her own. They are standing in Dev-Aura in the training center. For years they have experienced the rhythms of day and night, sunlight and moonlight, and total darkness. Their colors have remained as brilliant as ever. So, you can rest assured that when the appearance of the contents of a bottle changes, it is caused either by yourself or by a person in your vicinity.

In the beginning years of Aura-Soma, Vicky Wall noted very carefully what kind of bubbles and patterns were created in the fluid by shaking a bottle. These patterns were interpreted and incorporated into the contents of the readings. Shortly before her death in 1991, Vicky Wall tapered off with this part. She had reached the conclusion that Aura-Soma practitioners and users were losing themselves in noticing phenomena and interpreting them. She considered it essentially more important to use the oils so that the blessings through the workings of the oils could unfold. We are of the same opinion as Vicky Wall and shall delve no further into this subject.

❦ ❦ ❦

Aura-Soma is a system that cannot be approached in the same manner that you choose recipes from your kitchen file. If the products are to develop optimum effectiveness, then you cannot circumvent being involved in the system as a whole (at least, if you wish to work with Aura-Soma on your own). So that this fully involved participation is guaranteed, we as authors have decided against placing an index at the end of this book, thus ensuring that the entire text will be read. Concerning this decision, we ask for your understanding.

In closing, let us remark on one more thing: although all essential parts of the products are of natural origin and are totally harmless, that does not mean that the colors could not cause spots. The best place for shaking and applying the substances is in the bathroom, where you can immediately wipe away any spots or splatters. Please massage the oils into your body thoroughly, so that no streaks and spots on your clothing can form.

❦ ❦ ❦ ❦ ❦

THE DESCRIPTIONS OF THE BALANCE BOTTLES

This chapter provides explanations of the meanings of the color combinations in each balance bottle. In addition, we talk about the effects that each substance can have when it has been shaken together and applied in a proper way. We also explain where to apply them. But, before we begin, let us offer some clarifying comments in preparation for the descriptions.

Up to the present day, there are 94 different balance bottles (Bottle #0 to Bottle #93; #0 is counted, of course). There will be more added until one day the total number will be more than 100.

We have tried to present information about the bottles in an understandable and systematic manner. This has not been easy because of the abundance and the complexity of information. Each bottle represents a sort of universe within itself—a universe with "positive" and "negative" sides, with cycles that meet each other at opposite ends, and with paradoxes. The effects of one bottle, a bottle that you have made your own, are far-reaching. Sometimes they are so vast and so intimate that they can never be reported.

On the one hand, we have tried, as much as possible, to integrate personal experiences into the descriptions. But on the other hand, it has also been important to give you a clear orientation about the bottles and helpful recommendations. For that reason, we have left some thoughts and comments unsaid. We believe that in our selection we will accomplish both aspects.

For those of you who would like to become more deeply involved with Aura-Soma, you might decide to attend a seminar or let the bottles themselves speak to you. In time, you will find the best way to proceed. Here is just a little idea to start: take a bottle that seems meaningful to you and from which you would like to get some information into your meditation. Ask for help and support. Look at it carefully; take the colors and the energies in without the filter of the intellect. You could also lay it on your third eye, on your heart chakra, or any other part of your body that seems appropriate to you. Simply notice what the bottle sends out to you. Do not be impatient if at first "nothing" comes. Colors contain a language that can only be unlocked over the course of time, for this language has sunk into the realm of forgetfulness. Just think how long it took you to learn your mother tongue.

When Vicky Wall received instructions for the creation of the Aura-Soma substances, she did not know how they would serve people. In addition, it was not at all clear to her that the sequence in which they "were born" was in harmony with the Kabbala, the Tarot, and the I Ching. These correlations were discovered later. When this happened, she "asked" for information from above, and she readily received it. And thus, the specifications that you find in this chapter came into being.

Here, we will introduce the essential coordination with the Tarot and I Ching. For those of you who are already familiar with these systems, you will accept this additional attempt to bring an understanding of the bottles and their respective characteristics as helpful. For those of you who do not know much about the Tarot and the I Ching, you can simply ignore this information.

It is important to note that the numbers of the bottles do not correspond to the Kabbalistic numerology. For instance, numerologically, Bottle #0 is the number 1, and Bottle #1 is the number 2. Later, there are other differences to be noted. If we would integrate these statements, you would definitely be led into confusion.

The names for the bottles up to #44 originated with Vicky Wall and relate directly to her experience and background. Beginning with Bottle #45, the names originated with Mike Booth, drawn from his background. In one sense, the names express the characteristics of the respective bottles—that is, their content. The category, or basic theme, aims to further clarify the characteristics, goals, and functions. However, the basic theme can vary considerably for the individual and can deviate from our definitions.

The category of "Positive Personality Aspects" relates to the choice and to the sequence of choice of the four preferred bottles described in the previous chapter. These aspects apply to the first choice and, in decreasing effect, to the third and fourth. Those "Personality Aspects that Could Be Worked On" relate to the second bottle. That bottle represents the difficulties to be overcome. It should really be used first.

It is not intended that all the listed attributes in the two categories apply—not any more than everything in the following four sections. Aura-Soma is a subtle energy therapy, and its beneficial effects and the process leading to it cannot be determined in the same way as the instructions on a prescription pill bottle.

The four sections: Spiritual, Mental, Emotional, and Physical, show what effects the substance can have on the corresponding aspects if used according to instructions. Actually, all four domains are more or less treated as one. A human being is a complete unit. The crossing from one level to another is very tenuous. We have decided on these subdivisions only for the sake of clarity.

As already mentioned, every bottle represents a universe in itself. And so it is that parts of the problematic personality aspects also fit the person who has this bottle as his or her first choice. If someone works with this as his or her "therapeutic bottle" (his or her second choice), then this person will be able to discover more and more what a treasure he or she has been carrying alongside of what is mentioned in the "Positive Personality Aspects." Perhaps on the first reading this may seem confusing. According to linear thinking that we have been taught in school, it is baffling. But as soon as you have really been in contact with the Aura-Soma bottles and have experienced some effects, you will understand exactly what is meant.

Under the subhead, "Where to Apply the Substance," precise directions are given for the application. (How the bottle is to be shaken and how you should handle the short-term emulsion, we have already described in the previous chapter.) You always need to spread the substance in a wide band around your body so that the spine is included. That is important for its efficacy.

We do not mention in the following sections that the substances can also be applied to the hands and feet. The energies in the contents can be transported to anywhere in the body where they are needed, by way of the reflex zones. It could be very meaningful to know this, especially in the case of an emergency when certain areas on the body cannot be reached for the application of the suitable substance.

Under the heading, "Distinctive Qualities," you will find, among other things, information about whether certain bottles are components of the "Chakra Set." The meaning of that will be explained in Chapter 12.

As far as the wording is concerned, you will often find certain phrases used in the extreme, both positive and negative. When we have decided on such forms, it is to be clear, and not to offend. When we speak of egocentricity or self-deception or emotional immaturity, we are merely referring to tendencies. When, on the other hand, we speak of capabilities to heal, or of other wonderful talents, we do not mean that you should give up your job and become a healer. In everyday affairs—while working in an office, in a flower shop or a clothing store, or in normal occurrences within the family, such talents can be applied effectively.

The characteristics of the Tarot cards are consistent with those of the deck of the British author, A.E. Waite, of the "Rider Waite Deck," which is the deck mostly used. Some of the affirmations have been inspired by statements in Hans Dieter Leuenberger's Schule des Tarot (see Appendix). We thank him for these ideas.

The affirmations can help to incorporate the level of consciousness and thereby possibly strengthen the effect of the oils—but only if that appeals to you. If not, then you can ignore the affirmations, just as you can ignore the remarks on the Tarot cards and the I Ching.

We suggest that you write the affirmation meant for the bottle that you are using presently on a slip of paper. You might lay it next to the lamp on your nightstand. Read the affirmation evenings before going to sleep and mornings after awakening. Include the content of the statement in your meditation. Or, you might fasten the paper to your bathroom mirror, on the refrigerator, or to the dashboard of your car. You will surely think of many other ways of focusing your attention on the concepts presented. And, of course, you can create your own affirmations.

❦ ❦ ❦

The Aura-Soma substances can open you up to new possibilities—they may soothe and relieve, or they may stimulate awareness and give you courage. But what they cannot do is this: change the situation in which you find yourself, teach you completely new ways of conducting yourself, or provide you with social and professional success. That you need to strive for yourself, supported by the "spirits in the bottle." Should you, for example, discover in the course of your work with Aura-Soma that now is the time to make an effort to go forth and speak in public, you could attend a seminar in public speaking. When you come to the realization that it's best to call a halt to old, negative childhood experiences, find a therapist or a group where you can find professional help. Should you come to realize that addiction, dependency, or co-dependency are influencing your life, you might turn to Alcoholics Anonymous or similar self-help groups, where you will find support and encouragement from others in similar circumstances. If you notice that you are no longer happy in your profession and that you would like to do something else, begin gathering information about another career, or make inquiries at an employment agency.

Make sure that your growth becomes something concrete. Spirituality is not genuine if it is not implemented in totally normal affairs of the day and if it is not evident there. It needs to be applied through humanness, truthfulness, friendliness, reliability, fairness, authenticity, understanding, and compassion. If it is not, then it is "put on" and not genuine. The substances will provide you with the best possible support so that the changes on all levels will really take hold and come to be realized.

❦ ❦ ❦

THE 94 BALANCE BOTTLES (#0 – #93)

#0

Name of Bottle: Spiritual Rescue
Color: Royal Blue/Deep Magenta
Shakes Together As: Deep Magenta
Chakra: Crown
Tarot Card: The Fool
I Ching Sign: Starts with Bottle #1
Main Theme: Helps to transfer deep intuitive insights into practical every-day life

Positive Personality Aspects: Emotionally balanced. Searching for truth, especially with regard to spiritual matters. Possesses psychic and healing qualities, as well as the ability to leave the body during sleep (out-of-body experiences) and to do healing work in areas of crisis. With some people, this happens consciously, but with most, it happens unconsciously. These people often feel more tired when getting up in the morning than they felt the evening before. In this case, it is very useful to apply "Spiritual Rescue" to the temples of the forehead each morning.

Personality Aspects That Could Be Worked On: Can tend to be occupied excessively with spiritual matters. There can also be a tendency toward foolishness, self-deception, and a lack of restraint. There is often a lack of self-love and a need to be healed—"the wounded healer."

Spiritual Level: Stimulates inspiration. Heals deep spiritual problems. Clears the path for spiritual or religious experiences.

Mental Level: Helps to uncover self-deception. Facilitates a new start, a new step forward. Aids in establishing contact with your own power.

Emotional Level: Brings deep peace and deep joy, as well as trust in a higher order.

Physical Level: Alleviates chronic headaches, insomnia, mental restlessness, serious injuries, heavy contractions during childbirth, and birth defects.

Where to Apply the Substance: Along the entire hairline, around the ears. In acute cases, it can be applied everywhere on the body.

Affirmation: I love life. Life loves me.

Distinctive Qualities: None.

1

Name of Bottle: Physical Rescue
Color: Blue/Deep Magenta
Shakes Together As: Deep Magenta
Chakra: Third Eye and Crown
Tarot Card: The Magician
I Ching Sign: Heaven above, heaven below, No. 1, "The Creative"
Main Theme: Helps one understand and accept that everyday life is spiritual; the healer's bottle.

Positive Personality Aspects: Knows his or her ideals and is able to realize them. Has strong analytical, charismatic, and leadership qualities. Strong male ("animus") qualities, regardless of whether the person occupies a male or female body.

Personality Aspects That Could Be Worked On: Difficulty with the female side of being. Tendency toward mental overexcitement and negative manipulation of others. Hard time expressing him/herself.

Spiritual Level: The substance helps the person connect with his/her life purpose, which has to do with service. Facilitates the process of letting go of old belief systems.

Mental Level: Helpful with poor memory and mental overexcitement. Stimulates the process of bringing up old memories to be resolved in positive ways.

Emotional Level: Calms emotions, especially during crises. Aids in overcoming feelings of separation and in contacting inner strength through self-love.

Physical Level: Relieves the discomfort associated with burns, bruises, and abrasions; with all pain, especially back pain; with bronchitis; high blood pressure; cystitis; diarrhea, and sciatica. With all these conditions, it is especially helpful during the acute stages.

Where to Apply the Substance: Along the entire hairline, around the throat, neck, and ears (see "Distinctive Qualities" below).

Affirmation: I am whole. I integrate every aspect.

Distinctive Qualities: Belongs to the Chakra Set. Relates to the crown chakra and the third eye. Physical Rescue is one of the few balance oils that can be applied locally, on the affected areas, along with the prescribed areas. It can be applied to a painful area, in a similar way to the Bach Flower Remedy "Rescue Cream." It is not only available in 50-ml and 25-ml glass bottles, but also in 25-ml plastic bottles that are easily carried. Therefore, it can also be used by someone other than just the "owner."

 # 2
Name of Bottle: Peace
Color: Blue/Blue
Shakes Together As: Blue
Chakra: Throat
Tarot Card: The High Priestess
I Ching Sign: Earth above, earth below, No. 2, "The Receptive"
Main Theme: Establishes contact with true inner peace

Positive Personality Aspects: Is peaceloving and in harmony with him/herself. Is committed to peace. Utilizes creativity, which is linked to the throat chakra (for example, in relation to public speaking). Supports other people. Possesses strong female ("anima") qualities and a close link with the archetypes Eve and Isis, regardless of whether the person occupies a male or female body. Is able to become a channel for information from other dimensions.

Personality Aspects That Could Be Worked On: Difficulty in finding inner and outer peace. On the one hand, there is difficulty with the male aspect; on the other hand, there is a great deficit of nurturing energy. (Has neither received it nor can one give it.) Fear of the unknown.

Spiritual Level: Helps to establish contact with the deeper aspects in one-self; also, the ability to become a channel, which means to allow information from other dimensions to pass through. Cleanses the aura. Enables the dying to make an easier transition. Deals with the personification of the moon. (Aids people who experience mood swings at various stages of the moon cycle). Establishes access to deep intuition.

Mental Level: Comforts those who fear the unknown; also useful with problems related to concentration and speech. Establishes contact with creativity and intuition.

Emotional Level: Makes transitions easier—for example, with the dying, for women giving birth, or for people in a crisis. Establishes access to the "strength of silence," to balance in or after emotionally charged situations and to the feeling of being protected. Helps to decipher dreams.

Physical Level: Useful when applied to an over- or underactive thyroid. Helps with problems of the endocrine system and the neck, speech impediments, infections and bruises; and with labor, and teething in babies.

Where to Apply the Substance: The upper line of the band to be applied is around the hairline, on the neck, and the line between the lower jaws; the lower line of this band is at the level of the collarbone: apply around the whole throat/neck.

Affirmation: I breathe in peace. I breathe out peace.

Distinctive Qualities: Part of the Chakra Set, relates here to the throat chakra. This may seem strange, but it is a proven fact—it helps to prevent stretch marks. In this case, apply to the area concerned. With teething babies, apply the substance around the jaw area. For external use only!

 # 3
Name of Bottle: Atlantean/The Heart Bottle
Color: Blue/Green
Shakes Together As: Turquoise

Chakra: Heart
Tarot Card: The Empress

I Ching Sign: Water above, thunder below, No. 3, "Difficulty at the Beginning"

Main Theme: Problems of the heart; the whole emotional side of life

Positive Personality Aspects: Has intuitive knowledge. Helps other people to find their direction. Possesses the ability to be an artist, teacher, therapist. Can attain spiritual awakening through artistic, physical, and especially eco-logical work. Truth is very important to this person. Has the talent to achieve success. Brings in the harvest of many previous incarnations.

Personality Aspects That Could Be Worked On: Goes to the extreme to ful-fill others' expectations. Gives off ambiguous messages. Does not know what he/she feels. Difficulty in finding or creating a space where he/she can evolve.

Spiritual Level: Helps to advance spiritually and to discover what creates advancement. Creates a space where the essence of the soul can express itself.

Mental Level: Provides access to imagination and creativity. Useful when dealing with depression, especially exogenous (those which are not of genetic origin but caused by external circumstances or experiences).

Emotional Level: Removes difficulties in the entire emotional area, espe-cially when it comes to expressing feelings.

Physical Level: Eases abdominal pain, asthma, chronic bronchitis, angina pectoris, all heart conditions and rashes on the chest, and the growth or swelling of connective tissues.

Where to Apply the Substance: Across the entire chest area, in a wide band starting at the collarbone, down to the lowest rib.

Affirmation: I express love and truth.

Distinctive Qualities: Part of the Chakra Set. Corresponds here to the heart chakra. In past-life therapy, it helps establish contact with Atlantean incarnations. This bottle is an effective animal healer, whatever the ailment. Of particular use to people who deal with animals professionally or privately. Enables them to use their healing potential to the fullest for the animals. People with this bottle in the first, third, or fourth position will find Karma Yoga very suitable as a spiritual discipline.

4

Name of Bottle: The Sun Bottle/Sunlight
Color: Yellow/Gold
Shakes Together As: Golden Yellow
Chakra: Solar Plexus
Tarot Card: The Emperor
I Ching Sign: Mountain above, water below, No. 4, "Youthful Folly"
Main Theme: Opens the door to inner knowledge and inner wisdom

Positive Personality Aspects: Possesses authority and a great talent for management and organization; combines these talents with wisdom. Has access to knowledge from past times and can utilize this knowledge. Possesses the ability to realize a vision. Sees the funny side of life. This person knows that it is more valuable to know something than to possess something.

Personality Aspects That Could Be Worked On: Is marked by deep fear, lack of joy, and emotional immaturity. Leans toward utopianism. Behaves in a very authoritarian and, therefore, immature manner.

Spiritual Level: Transforms spiritual ideas into concrete form. Establishes contact with intuition and inner guidance. Brings about "solar" awareness. Raises perceptive faculties.

Mental Level: Is helpful with phobias that have their cause on the mental plane.

Emotional Level: Provides trust, safety, and joy.

Physical Level: Helps with problems of the nervous system and spine, with hiatal hernias, fractures, chronic rheumatism, arthritis and anorexia, with nausea, flatulence, constipation, diabetes, and menopausal problems.

Where to Apply the Substance: At solar plexus level, in a wide band around the body.

Affirmation: I am safe. I know that I know nothing.

Distinctive Qualities: Part of the Chakra Set. Relates here to the solar plexus chakra. In past-life therapy, can establish contact with incarnations in Ancient Egypt.

5
Name of Bottle: Sunrise/Sunset
Color: Yellow/Red
Shakes Together As: Scarlet
Chakra: Base
Tarot Card: The Hierophant
I Ching Sign: Water above, heaven below, No. 5, "Waiting" or "Nourishment"
Main Theme: Helps to utilize the available energy wisely

Positive Personality Aspects: Possesses a lot of energy, and is able to express this energy. Is dynamic and charismatic. Manages the material side of life very well. Radiates an atmosphere of joy in which people feel good. Possesses teacher qualities.

Personality Aspects That Could Be Worked On: A very insecure person of little trust. Has messianic tendencies and a tendency to not want to develop. Ruled by fear in sexual relationships; on the other hand, wishes that life was a big party. Survival fears, suppressed anger. In private life, finds great difficulties establishing relationships with other people.

Spiritual Level: Helps to distinguish "good and bad" and to develop a spiritual generosity. Enables the user to recognize that spiritual awakening is also possible through joy (one's own and that which is transmitted to others).

Mental Level: Supports the process of learning. Helps give structure to concepts.

Emotional Level: Brings suppressed anger to the surface, together with the reason for its origin. Helpful with stage fright. Clears the way to find joy, security, and profound relationships (including those of the sexual kind).

Physical Level: Useful with sexual problems (frigidity and impotence), infertility, problems of the uterus, bladder, and colon, painful menstruation, diabetes, kidney problems, and pain of the lower back. Provides energy.

Where to Apply the Substance: The contents of this bottle relate specifically to the base chakra and should, therefore, be applied as low around the trunk as possible—that is, around the entire lower abdomen.

Affirmation: I open myself to the joy in my life.

Distinctive Qualities: Part of the Chakra Set, relating here to the base chakra. On top of everything else, it also contains similar effects to the "Shock Bottle" (# 26). In past-life therapy, it helps to establish contact with Tibetan and Chinese incarnations. Possibly indicates abuse, not only when this bottle is in the second, but also when it is in the first, position. However, the user needs to be very careful before making an assessment of this type. If abuse actually has taken place, the aim of the working process should never be vengeful or guilt-apportioning. An experienced therapist is recommended for any work in connection with this subject.

6
Name of Bottle: The Energy Bottle
Color: Red/Red
Shakes Together As: Red
Chakra: Base
Tarot Card: The Lovers
I Ching Sign: Heaven above, water below, No. 6, "Conflict"
Main Theme: Sacrificial love

Positive Personality Aspects: A very brave person, ready to love under the most adverse circumstances. Possesses a lot of vitality, has a magnetic attraction, and feels an incredible joy towards life. Is fulfilled. Has no difficulty with material matters.

Personality Aspects That Could Be Worked On: Can be addicted to material things and may misuse his/her charisma. Will not take on responsibility, especially when it comes to the material side of life. Is frustrated, leans toward a laissez-faire attitude, laziness, and a lack of interest in life.

Spiritual Level: Aids in expanding awareness through love, especially love under difficult circumstances. Allows a person to recognize that loving another person enables him/her to love God. Establishes access to sacrificial love.

Mental Level: Supports the process of getting to know oneself with the aim to love more truthfully. Gets one's feet (back) on the ground.

Emotional Level: Helps give the best in relationships, to overcome resentments stemming from unrequited love, to recognize heart's desires and to fulfill them, but also to release these desires. Aids in overcoming survival problems originating from a difficult birth.

Physical Level: Eases muscle cramps, frostbite, sexual problems (frigidity, impotence). Recommended for iron deficiency, useful for the mobilization of limbs after a stroke or paralysis.

Where to Apply the Substance: Everywhere below the hip area. Especially suitable for application to the soles of the feet.

Affirmation: Whatever I do makes the love in my life grow.

Distinctive Qualities: Especially recommended after serious operations or at times of fatigue. Should not be used too late in the afternoon or evening because it is very energizing and may result in sleep difficulties.

 # 7
Name of Bottle: Garden of Gethsemene
Color: Yellow/Green
Shakes Together As: Olive Green

Chakra: Heart and Solar Plexus
Tarot Card: The Chariot
I Ching Sign: Earth above, water below, No. 7, "The Army"
Main Theme: Test of faith

Positive Personality Aspects: For this person, belief and faith are a life theme (also see "Distinctive Qualities"). A pioneer of the New Aeon. An idealist, a philosopher, who understands the needs and sufferings of humanity. Possesses inner wisdom and strength. Has learned lessons about ethics in previous incarnations, and is able in the here and now to express and utilize that. Likes to travel, loves nature, especially trees—in fact, is often very knowledgeable about trees.

Personality Aspects That Could Be Worked On: A disillusioned seeker. An egocentric who acts against his/her own principles. Is not honest with him/herself and knows it deep within, but continues this self-deception.

Spiritual Level: Helps put mind over matter, to attain inner wisdom, and to establish a connection with deep inner knowledge. Enables the user to recognize what is blocking his/her own path and aids in the removal of these blockages.

Mental Level: Stimulates the brain. Helps with decision making and reduces exaggerated speculation and introspection. Eases agoraphobia (fear of wide, open spaces) and claustrophobia (fear of enclosed spaces).

Emotional Level: Releases fear, brings joy. Helps overcome jealousy and envy, as well as fear of emotions. Aids in development of emotional maturity.

Physical Level: Alleviates hyperglycemia, problems with the nervous system and thymus gland, all heart conditions, the pain following fractures, and constipation.

Where to Apply the Substance: Everywhere in heart and solar plexus area, around the width of the body.

Affirmation: I have no limits apart from those I set for myself.

Distinctive Qualities: The energy in this balance bottle is analogous to the situation in the Garden of Gethsemene, where Jesus underwent his last test of faith.

8

Name of Bottle: Anubis
Color: Yellow/Blue
Shakes Together As: Green
Chakra: Solar Plexus, Heart and Throat
Tarot Card: Justice
I Ching Sign: Water above, earth below, No. 8, "Holding Together" (Union)
Main Theme: Too much thinking disturbs the inner peace

Positive Personality Aspects: Has an excellent sense for time, balance, justice, and linear order, as well as a distinctive feeling for equality (of all people, all spiritual traditions, etc.). Knows the laws of life and the consequences if they are (not) followed. Ability to teach, but not in the spiritual domain. Outstanding abilities in management, control, and organization. A person who knows him/herself.

Personality Aspects That Could Be Worked On: Too busy with superficial chatter. This leads to not receiving the information needed. Exaggerated desire for harmony, unable to make decisions because of an acute awareness of both sides of a situation. At the same time, has a tendency toward dictatorial behavior. Possesses strong prejudices.

Spiritual Level: Helps to unveil the law of love, to come to the here and now, as well as get in contact with eternity. (An 8 on its side, the "lemniscate" is the symbol for infinity.)

Mental Level: Facilitates the process of getting to know oneself and becoming clear about plans for the future. Eases nervousness and stuttering, in both adults and children.

Emotional Level: Releases old guilt feelings; creates a balance when conflicts exist on different personality levels. Brings into the light of day suppressed rage and is helpful in bringing a new perspective to difficult situations.

Physical Level: Calms the liver, balances the adrenal level. Alleviates digestive disorders, stomach weakness, and menopausal problems.

Where to Apply the Substance: Around the entire trunk.

Affirmation: I am in the here and now. Here and now is the only moment for changing.

Distinctive Qualities: In past-life therapy, it can help to resolve guilt feelings from previous lives.

9

Name of Bottle: Crystal Cave/Heart Within the Heart
Color: Turquoise/Green
Shakes Together As: Deep Turquoise
Chakra: Heart
Tarot Card: The Hermit
I Ching Sign: Wind above, heaven below, No. 9, "The Taming Power of the Small"
Main Theme: The individual search for truth

Positive Personality Aspects: A selfless person. Is in contact with his/her own subconscious and inner voice. Discovers the hidden secrets of life and can interpret them. Creative talents for painting and writing poetry. Understanding of philosophy. Is occupied with questions concerning humanity. A developed human being who possesses the ability to speak from a universal perspective and, therefore, a person who can reach many.

Personality Aspects That Could Be Worked On: Possesses a strong tendency for self-deception and for lying and deceit when it comes to others. Is jealous and tends to gossip. Is unaware of all these weaknesses.

Spiritual Level: Helps the user find the way out of limbo, to overcome loneliness, and to reach aloneness (in the sense of all-one-ness). Gives spiritual protection. Promotes the process of going within and learning self-trust.

Mental Level: Brings awareness of own self-deception. Helps find a new direction, especially concerning communication (for example, when it comes to the fear of public speaking).

Emotional Level: Enables the person to cope with feelings such as strong jealousy, idealized love, old emotional entanglements, and loneliness.

Physical Level: Eases all problems in the chest area, including the back, especially serious heart conditions, asthma, and bronchitis. Balances the thymus gland.

Where to Apply the Substance: Around the entire chest area.

Affirmation: In the search for truth, I listen to my inner voice.

Distinctive Qualities: In past-life therapy, helps establish a connection with Atlantean incarnations.

10
Name of Bottle: Go Hug a Tree
Color: Green/Green
Shakes Together As: Green
Chakra: Heart
Tarot Card: The Wheel of Fortune
I Ching Sign: Heaven above, lake below, No. 10, "Treading" (Conduct)
Main Theme: Helps to make decisions

Positive Personality Aspects: A person who leads without dominating, who gives space for growth to others. Is concerned about the problems of humankind from the heart level. Recognizes what needs to be done and does it. Discovers gain even in loss. A person who is a good listener, who works on him/herself, who is honest and truly independent and in harmony with fate. Can realize creative ideas. Possesses a deep connection to nature.

Personality Aspects That Could Be Worked On: Occupied excessively with the past and the future; withdraws intellectually. Does not have both feet on the ground. Does not create the necessary space and resources or perspectives for him/herself. Is outside the rhythms of nature and life. Does not understand why spiritual development is necessary.

Spiritual Level: Aids in being honest and in clearing karma. Allows the person to see that an inner change causes external change. Stabilizes and centers the astral body (the deepest dimension) and expands it.

Mental Level: Makes the user aware that there is work to be done on him/herself. Brings clarity to mental disturbances. Provides inner peace. Protects from external attacks.

Emotional Level: Is useful in the search for a new space, a new perspective; lets the person find the ability to stand on his/her feet, especially when things have gone wrong.

Physical Level: Builds up muscles and tissue, helps generally with cellular problems. Eases tension and fatigue. Helps the individual regain independence after an operation. Recommended in all heart conditions, circulatory problems, and all problems in the chest area.

Where to Apply the Substance: Around the entire chest area.

Affirmation: I have the space to do what needs to be done.

Distinctive Qualities: This bottle contains a lot of information on all levels. In it are "hidden," for example, #2 (Blue/Blue) and #42 (Yellow/Yellow). Much of the information given for these bottles also applies to #10.

#11
Name of Bottle: A Chain of Flowers/Essene Bottle I
Color: Clear/Pink
Shakes Together As: Pale Pink
Chakra: Mainly Base, Heart, and Throat, but also all other chakras
Tarot Card: Strength
I Ching Sign: Earth above, heaven below, No. 11, "Peace"
Main Theme: To get a feeling for what unconditional (self) love is about

Positive Personality Aspects: A very strong, powerful personality who radiates great warmth and tenderness, as well as strong empathy; someone who can truly love. A healer and teacher of the New Aeon. Even looks at troublesome situations as growth promoting and is still friendly, even in difficult circumstances.

Personality Aspects That Could Be Worked On: Is extremely vain and arrogant, especially in spiritual matters. Has lost hope. Feels like a failure. Is convinced that he/she has acted correctly, even though it is obvious to everyone else that he/she has made a mistake.

Spiritual Level: Reduces spiritual arrogance. Stimulates intuitive female energy and encourages the ability to express this energy clearly. Opens to messages from other dimensions. Promotes self-love.

Mental Level: Helps overcome self-doubt, to build up trust in oneself and to find clarity. Allows people, especially those who have this bottle in the first position, to become independent of the recognition and approval of others.

Emotional Level: Opens up the user to self-love, love for others, and to self-forgiveness. Helps to overcome psychosomatic illnesses and fears from childhood. Useful in coping with the disappointment one feels after having given a lot and received practically nothing in return.

Physical Level: Cleanses, detoxifies, and balances the hormonal system. Helpful with ear problems, especially in children, as well as with problems during menstruation and in the lower back area.

Where to Apply the Substance: Around the hips, the lower abdomen, the lower back. Can also be applied around the entire trunk and the throat.

Affirmation: I love myself as I am.

Distinctive Qualities: Part of the New Aeon Child's Set. Functions as a mediator, which means it clears the way where other Aura-Soma substances are not yet working. In past-life therapy, it can establish contact with Essene incarnations. Can help a woman to conceive if she desires a child.

12

Name of Bottle: Peace in the New Aeon
Color: Clear/Blue
Shakes Together As: Blue
Chakra: Throat
Tarot Card: The Hanged Man
I Ching Sign: Heaven above, earth below, No. 12, "Standstill" (Stagnation)
Main Theme: Peaceful, friendly communication

Positive Personality Aspects: A person who acts from a peaceful, yet emotionally heartfelt base. Is very much in contact with his/her feelings and instinctive intelligence. Nurtures and carries others, and feels deeply connected to them. Possesses a clear vision of his/her initiatives. Feels guided, and can speak about this feeling, as well as his/her intuitive insights. Possesses writing talents.

Personality Aspects That Could Be Worked On: An egocentric who is shut off from spiritual matters. It is also possible that this person knows his/her spiritual truth but does not live it because it is easier this way. Feels "above" others, is arrogant, has no inner peace, has difficulty with communication, and has an exaggerated need to be carried and nurtured by others.

Spiritual Level: Allows the person to find the courage to live spiritual truth. Establishes contact with Divine guidance and an orientation of the soul. Brings about a meditative, calm, peaceful access to clarity.

Mental Level: Reduces egocentricity and leads to a feeling of wholeness and orientation. Supports children when they find it difficult to learn to speak and to express themselves.

Emotional Level: Encourages the release of deep emotional problems (for example, through the shedding of tears), and aids in regaining peace. Establishes contact with the inner voice. Is helpful with problems of dependency and co-dependency.

Physical Level: Possesses antiseptic and astringent (skin contracting) properties. Balances the thyroid gland. Eases pain, particularly sore throats (especially in children).

Where to Apply the Substance: Around the entire neck.

Affirmation: The more at peace I am, the more light I am given.

Distinctive Qualities: Part of the New Aeon Child's Set. When we mention under "Positive Personality Aspects" that this person feels guided and can speak about it as well as about his/her intuitive insights, we do not mean public speaking. Rather, that it is possible for this person to express deep matters when he/she is in an atmosphere of trust.

13
Name of Bottle: Change in the New Aeon
Color: Clear/Green
Shakes Together As: Green
Chakra: Heart
Tarot Card: Death
I Ching Sign: Heaven above, flame below, No. 13, "Fellowship with Men"
Main Theme: Space in connection with transition and change

Positive Personality Aspects: A leader who imparts knowledge clearly and kindly and can demonstrate new perspectives to people. Likes to discover new things in all areas of life. Is knowledgeable in astrology, does not approach it in an intellectual way, but rather from the heart and from the feelings. Loves nature. Often supports the dying.

Personality Aspects That Could Be Worked On: Is stuck in negative patterns and emotional dilemmas. Is afraid of nature. Is obsessed by the thought that he/she will never be able to forgive him/herself. Has great difficulty making decisions.

Spiritual Level: Helps establish contact with the present moment and to let go of the past. Supports the release of the fear of death, and aids in the integration of information from states of higher awareness.

Mental Level: Promotes self-forgiveness. Memories become less important, therefore, a better contact with the here and now comes about.

Emotional Level: Enables the user to release feelings. Provides access to peace and joy by overcoming stuck emotions. Helps bring order in emotional matters and to decide which of these matters may live and which should die.

Physical Level: Relieves bronchitis, pain of the middle back, eczema (especially in children), and asthma (again, especially in children).

Where to Apply the Substance: Around the entire heart area.

Affirmation: In each ending there is a new beginning.

Distinctive Qualities: Part of the New Aeon Child's Set. Is supportive in rebirthing sessions. On all levels, this bottle deals with metamorphosis, the transformation of the caterpillar to the butterfly. The substance helps overcome "spiritual materialism" (the expression originates from Chögyam Trungpa). It means that some people tend to think they can earn their spiritual development, something like: "If I meditate so-and-so many hours, then the universe will return to me so-and-so much. After so-and-so many years, I will be enlightened." The oil supports the process of understanding that things do not work like this, but that progress in these dimensions always depends on the grace of "the other side."

14

Name of Bottle: Wisdom in the New Aeon
Color: Clear/Gold
Shakes Together As: Gold
Chakra: Solar Plexus
Tarot Card: Temperance
I Ching Sign: Flame above, heaven below, No. 14, "Possession in Great Measure"
Main Theme: Becoming a clear channel for wisdom

Positive Personality Aspects: An inspired, purposeful herald of the New Aeon who is in contact with deep inner wisdom. Disseminates harmony and balance. Is able to feel deep joy. Possesses a profound understanding of natural forces. A clear-thinking person who has learned from past mistakes and draws wisdom from that knowledge.

Personality Aspects That Could Be Worked On: A person who is not in balance, neither with him/herself nor with his/her life. Someone who acts in extraordinarily negative ways, thereby spreading chaos. Is possessed by deep fear but does not really know what there is to be afraid of.

Spiritual Level: Allows for contact with his/her own guardian angel. Reduces fear of expectations. Brings supportive, positive energies. Aids in the realization that goals should not be set too high, but rather, that one progresses safest and fastest by taking one step at a time.

Mental Level: Builds bridges between the conscious and subconscious, and is very helpful with dream work. Gives the courage to look more closely at difficult facts in one's own life. Also helps in releasing unpleasant memories.

Emotional Level: Provides and maintains centeredness, even during tumultuous times. Builds up the heart, the emotional level, particularly in regard to general fears and anticipation.

Physical Level: balances the solar plexus, adrenal secretions, and function of the liver. Helpful with diabetes (especially with children), as well as all difficulties having to do with the thighs.

Where to Apply the Substance: Around the entire solar plexus area.

Affirmation: The more I let go of my fear, the more I open myself to my own inner truth.

Distinctive Qualities: Part of the New Aeon Child's Set. In past-life therapy, this substance helps to heal wounds and scars from previous lives. In children, it alleviates the fear of starting school.

15
Name of Bottle: Healing in the New Aeon
Color: Clear/Violet
Shakes Together As: Violet
Chakra: Crown
Tarot Card: The Devil
I Ching Sign: Earth above, mountain below, No. 15, "Modesty"

Main Theme: To gain one's own healing power

Positive Personality Aspects: A strong person with authority in the best sense of the word; a person who has spiritual strength. Someone who stands for what he/she believes in, even under the most unfavorable circumstances. Leads a truly spiritual yet "grounded" life. Assists other people, especially with respect to helping them become aware of their illusions. Has overcome negativity and unknown fears. Has learned to withstand temptations.

Personality Aspects That Could Be Worked On: Great difficulty in perceiving his/her "shadow," as well as in finding out the truth—this applies to all areas of life. A person who is obsessed by material things, sex, and other addictions; who is easily distracted and directs power against him/herself. Possesses little self-love and needs to be praised at all times. Believes that all evil comes from "outside" and that he/she is the only one to whom unfortunate things happen.

Spiritual Level: Helps to attain healing powers (for him/herself and others). Promotes understanding of spiritual matters.

Mental Level: Useful in overcoming sexual egocentricity. Allows the person to release the idea that he/she is the only unfortunate one.

Emotional Level: Brings distance to emotional entanglements, raises identification with feelings. Allows the person to get acquainted with the shadow and to give up negative emotions. Lessens fear of other people (this applies especially to children).

Physical Level: Reduces exaggerated anxiety, headaches, and sore throats. Useful with certain types of epilepsy and with speech impediments—for example, stammering. All of the above applies particularly to children.

Where to Apply the Substance: Along the hairline and around the entire head.

Affirmation: The more light I let into myself, the more I heal.

Distinctive Qualities: Part of the New Aeon Child's Set. When working with the "inner child," this substance brings balance to the male and female personality aspects. For women in labor, it eases the intensity of contractions and helps to bring about a conscious birth experience.

16
Name of Bottle: The Violet Robe
Color: Violet/Violet
Shakes Together As: Violet
Chakra: Crown
Tarot Card: The Tower
I Ching Sign: Thunder above, earth below, No. 16, "Enthusiasm"
Main Theme: Spiritual surrender

Positive Personality Aspects: Is in accord with the Divine plan and lives life based on this concept. Often gets spontaneous "enlightenments." Is in touch with the transformative process and helps others with their transformation. Often attends to the dying. Gifted with respect to healing others on the psychological and/or mental level (for example, as a psychiatrist or psychotherapist). Knows that his/her own behavior influences the behavior of others.

Personality Aspects That Could Be Worked On: An oppressor, marked by lack of joy and by self-destruction; can have suicidal tendencies. Does not want to be here (that is, does not want to be incarnated). Cannot forgive him/herself. Clings to old patterns and behavior patterns. Cannot distinguish between the real and unreal.

Spiritual Level: Opens up the user to the idea that one has to give everything in order to receive that which is truly needed and desired, that everything not in harmony with the true calling is really senseless and useless. Establishes contact with the true self and the recognition of the user's own life purpose.

Mental Level: Aids in releasing old patterns and behaviors, as well as self-destructive tendencies.

Emotional Level: Protects children before going to school (alleviates the fear of attending school). Helps the person overcome grief and the desire to not be here. Allows for the realization of the positive aspects of a separation.

Physical Level: Alleviates acute pain, insomnia, migraine, infections, nerve pain, and shocks that result from a near-death experience.

Where to Apply the Substance: Along the entire hairline.

Affirmation: The more I realize my purpose, the brighter my life will be.

Distinctive Qualities: None.

17

Name of Bottle: Troubadour I/Hope
Color: Green/Violet
Shakes Together As: Dark Green
Chakra: Heart and Throat
Tarot Card: The Star
I Ching Sign: Lake above, thunder below, No. 17, "Following"
Main Theme: A healing heart

Positive Personality Aspects: Great interest in spirituality and the hidden secrets of life. Experiences joy through loving others and bringing them in contact with their own spirituality. Someone who gives very much. A good listener who truly understands others. As a result, people can easily accept this person's advice. Strives for unity and freedom. A brave person who searches for truth and examines it time and again. Possesses a clear perspective. Has the ability to see into the future.

Personality Aspects That Could Be Worked On: Leans toward self-pity. Feels misunderstood. Has no trust and no hope, even to the extent that life doesn't seem worth living. Harbors self-doubts, no matter how much competence there is.

Spiritual Level: Establishes contact with the Higher Self and with his/her own psychic abilities. Broadens horizons. Brings about the ability to talk about spiritual experiences.

Mental Level: Improves the ability to handle time. Helps get in touch with the truth when emotions obscure the mind. Expands mental horizons.

Emotional Level: Is useful in overcoming the feeling of being misunderstood. Resolves the impression of being on his/her own. Revives strength when too much has been exerted. Heals the grief after a disappointing relationship.

Physical Level: Recommended for problems with the shoulders, the thyroid gland, and with circulation. Also relieves structural problems in the chest.

Where to Apply the Substance: Around the entire chest. If problems are of a spiritual or mental variety, also apply along the hairline.

Affirmation: I seek and find the truth.

Distinctive Qualities: In this bottle, there are many others "hidden"—for example, #20 (Blue/Pink). In past-life therapy, it aids in contacting the era between the 12th and 16th centuries, when secret mystical traditions existed (for example, with the Cathars and Knights Templar). The Troubadours spread these teachings through theater performances, dance, and songs. Often, Troubadours were persecuted.

The phrase, "helps to talk about spiritual experiences," does not imply that this person should necessarily go on about these issues in public or in groups; rather, that it can be clarifying and healing to talk to an understanding friend or partner about these matters in order to gain more confidence and the ability to integrate. This substance can be helpful in transforming the unspeakable into words and in handling these matters in an atmosphere of trust.

18
Name of Bottle: Egyptian Bottle I/Turning Tide
Color: Yellow/Violet
Shakes Together As: Deep Gold
Chakra: Solar Plexus and Crown
Tarot Card: The Moon

I Ching Sign: Mountain above, wind below, No. 18, "Work on What Has Been Spoiled" (Decay)
Main Theme: Overcoming self-deception

Positive Personality Aspects: Has arranged life in just the way he/she has always dreamed. Possesses the courage to change, and enjoys fulfilling his/her life purpose. This person's healing qualities come to show in everything he/she does. A charismatic personality, a spiritual teacher, a very intuitive person. Truly wants to help others.

Personality Aspects That Could Be Worked On: Cannot distinguish between reality and fantasy. A dreamer in the negative sense of the word. Does not dare to move forward or to try something else due to the perception that things can only get worse. Is obsessed with material things and fears of all kinds.

Spiritual Level: Assists the user in realizing how much he/she is programmed, and awakens the soul from "being asleep" (Gurdjieff). Brings joy to life. Through the use of this substance, healers learn to distinguish when to be active and when not to be.

Mental Level: Connects "head and belly"; aids in overcoming self-deception, and stimulates discernment.

Emotional Level: Helps overcome the role of being a victim. Gives courage to express one's fears. Releases the feeling of being betrayed and being spied on. After emotional difficulty, it establishes a clearer vision of the future.

Physical Level: Recommended in all degenerative conditions (for example, multiple sclerosis, Parkinson's disease, etc.), ulcers, and blockages of the solar plexus area.

Where to Apply the Substance: Around the solar plexus and the entire hairline.

Affirmation: The more I let go of my fear, the more I am healed.

Distinctive Qualities: In past-life therapy, can establish access to incarnations in Ancient Egypt.

 # 19
Name of Bottle: Living in the Material World
Color: Red/Purple
Shakes Together As: Deep Red
Chakra: Base and Crown
Tarot Card: The Sun
I Ching Sign: Earth above, lake below, No. 19, "Approach"
Main Theme: To build up new energy

Positive Personality Aspects: Is in harmony with him/herself, and conveys this feeling to others. Owns a lot of energy, including psychic energy. Others feel magnetically drawn to this person. Possesses talent for work in the social, nursing, and helping professions. When working in other areas, this person is also successful and puts money into charitable or spiritual causes. Is balanced in his/her conscious and unconscious intentions.

Personality Aspects That Could Be Worked On: A person whose spirituality is eclipsed by material interests, who always wants to be the center of attention, who misuses psychic abilities, and is obsessed by sexual fantasies. Clings to the past and is always tired. Lacks energy.

Spiritual Level: Awakens the kundalini energy. Brings deep peace and at the same time a fresh breeze into life. Allows deep insights into one's own inner world even in very concrete ways—for example, certain meditations and creative visualizations can be improved. Helps radiate and receive love.

Mental Level: Enables the person to examine the shadow sides of his/her personality and to release them. Stimulates new mental energy. Facilitates the process of releasing sexual obsessions.

Emotional Level: Assists in overcoming conscious anger, resentment, and frustration. Encourages involvement and initiative. Offers a new perspective and an acceptance of the body. Raises self-esteem.

Physical Level: Alleviates sexual problems (frigidity, impotence, etc.), and physical problems having to do with a lack of energy (for example, low blood pressure, constipation); and reduces foot problems, particularly those with accompanying pain.

Where to Apply the Substance: Around the entire lower abdomen; in mental or spiritual matters, also along the hairline. Not to be used too late in the afternoon or evening because it is very energizing and can lead to sleep problems.

Affirmation: I say "yes" to life and to myself.

Distinctive Qualities: "Hidden" in this bottle is #6 (Red/Red).
Helps with sexual abuse issues, poltergeist phenomena, and in handling or releasing other undesired past or present interferences or beings. The contents of this bottle are especially useful when too much energy has been spent—for example, after working too hard, and so on. Regarding the subject of "sexual abuse," also see the "Distinctive Qualities" of Bottle #5.

20
Name of Bottle: Child's Rescue/Star Child
Color: Blue/Pink
Shakes Together As: Blue
Chakra: All chakras, meaning that this substance can be applied to all parts of the body
Tarot Card: Judgment
I Ching Sign: Wind above, earth below, No. 20, "Contemplation" (View)
Main Theme: Aids children in all areas, even the children that we once were (psychotherapeutic work with the "inner child")

Positive Personality Aspects: An optimist who can utilize his/her optimism constructively. Possesses deep inner peace and has freed him/herself of fear. Is in touch with the feminine, intuitive aspect and can express it. Faces life with a childlike openness and has great compassion. Feels deeply for others, is concerned and cares for them, and is in contact with unconditional love.

Personality Aspects That Could Be Worked On: Feels disconnected from inspiration and love. Permanently questions, judges, and condemns him/herself. Is unstable and has a hard time being assertive. Has a "peace and love" mentality.

Spiritual Level: Establishes reconnection to the soul level. Joins with that level of love that transforms everything. Promotes a spiritual new beginning and resolves spiritual disillusionment. Helps with the integration of soul parts that have not yet been integrated.

Mental Level: Supports the healing of the "inner child" and establishes balance between the male and female energies. Is useful with all problems that have originated, and which occur, during childhood (making it applicable to children and adults alike). Enables the person to actually attain what he/she needs.

Emotional Level: Lifts the feeling of love deficit, which affects and changes all emotional patterns. Provides support during difficult situations. Helps reach one's intuition through love.

Physical Level: Recommended during pregnancy, with teething babies, burns, abrasions, bruises, and fever. Particularly useful with children up to 12 years of age. (With older children, Bottle #1 is more effective.)

Where to Apply the Substance: Can be applied to all parts of the body. With teething babies, apply to jaws and around the entire neck. For external use only!

Affirmation: Love is letting go of fear.

Distinctive Qualities: Part of the New Aeon Child's Set. One of the most important bottles. Especially useful in polarity work and work with the "inner child." Helps people whose conditions are affecting only one side of the body. With regard to the "Spirits in the Bottle," the following note: this bottle contains the love of a child, with a child's potential for forgiveness. This substance is a available in a 25- or 50- ml glass bottle, as well as in a 25-ml plastic bottle. Like this, it is easy to carry, and it enables it to be used by people other than the "owner."

21

Name of Bottle: New Beginning for Love
Color: Green/Pink
Shakes Together As: Green
Chakra: Base and Heart
Tarot Card: The World
I Ching Sign: Fire above, thunder below, No. 21, "Biting Through"
Main Theme: New beginning for love

Positive Personality Aspects: A truly mature personality of highest aware-ness, who loves God and humanity. Someone who gives and receives love and works with it in constructive ways (for example, writing, art, public speaking, but also within the family circle). Can realize and materialize dreams. Is aware of goals and works to attain them. A person who is need-ed by others and who knows that love is the basis of all life. Someone who is able to let the world run its course.

Personality Aspects That Could Be Worked On: Possesses little self-love, does not feel loved by others, and always keeps looking for love. Never receives love in the desired fashion. A dreamer in the negative sense, who is fragmented and feels disconnected from God. Feels he/she is more important than is actually the case. Refuses to accept life's lessons. Is dis-satisfied with his/her situation, yet is unable to change it.

Spiritual Level: Helps recognize that the love of God is expressed in the love of and for other people. Aids in overcoming resistance, giving up struggling, and finding new joy and dedication to love.

Mental Level: Connects with one's life purpose, makes space for new "pro-grams," new behavioral patterns, new self-love. Helps overcome present difficulties.

Emotional Level: Enables recognition of the love that is already in one's life. Balances giving and taking in the love area. Makes it easier to under-stand dreams. Helps the person cope with the consequences of (external) aggression.

Physical Level: Relieves certain skin complaints—for example, eczema, all heart conditions, especially those of psychosomatic origin, pain in the upper back, asthma, bronchitis (particularly in children), and inflammations.

Where to Apply the Substance: Around the entire heart area.

Affirmation: I hold the world in my hands.

Distinctive Qualities: This is a variation of Bottle #28.

 # 22
Name of Bottle: Rebirther's Bottle/Awakening
Color: Yellow/Pink
Shakes Together As: Pale Gold
Chakra: Solar Plexus
Tarot Card: The Fool (this is a different aspect of "The Fool" than that which has been the subject of #0)
I Ching Sign: Mountain above, fire below, No. 22, "Grace"
Main Theme: Love without dependency

Positive Personality Aspects: A teacher of the New Aeon who lives spirituality in a "grounded" manner. Is in contact with the Divine intelligence and therefore feels liberated. Is in touch with his/her own eternal aspect. Communicates knowledge in such a way that it is easily understood by everyone. Puts determination behind every action.

Personality Aspects That Could Be Worked On: A manipulative personality who seems generous, but who is really only interested in self-gain. Expects too much in return in view of what is given. Can be merciless. Needs constant recognition. Possesses a deep-seated fear of disappointment in the area of love.

Spiritual Level: Initiates spiritual rebirth. Brings about deep self-forgiveness. Supports recognition of the Divine spark within.

Mental Level: Releases the identification with one's shadow. Encourages a more optimistic perception and the formulation of new life goals. Helps the user realize what love is.

Emotional Level: Reduces the exaggerated need for love. Aids in coping with unrequited love and resultant problems. Helps the person deal with fear, shocks, dependency, and co-dependency.

Physical Level: balances glands, digestive system, and skin.

Where to Apply the Substance: Around the entire solar plexus area.

Affirmation: I breathe in love. I breathe out love.

Distinctive Qualities: In rebirthing therapy, it helps the client and the therapist to attune to the process. The substance has to do with the Bible passage in Mark 10, Verse 15: "I assure you that whoever does not accept the reign of God like a little child shall not take part in it."

23

Name of Bottle: Love and Light
Color: Rose Pink/Pink (this is the only bottle to contain Rose Pink)
Shakes Together As: Pink
Chakra: Base and Crown
Tarot Card: King of Wands
I Ching Sign: Mountain above, earth below, No. 23, "Splitting Apart"
Main Theme: Regaining self-love

Positive Personality Aspects: Has a strong need to get to know him/herself and also carries out this self-knowledge (for example, through therapy, meditation, etc.). Accepts fate in a positive and practical manner. Has a lot of strength, yet this strength is manifested in tenderness, warmth, empathy, and the ability to give and receive.

Personality Aspects That Could Be Worked On: Is very insecure. Feels unloved. Develops one symptom after another because as a child, he/she received care only when illness was present. Has kept this pattern up.

Spiritual Level: Encourages spiritual strength and energy, as well as harmony. Opens the door to unconditional love.

Mental Level: Promotes self-understanding. Allows the user to lose his/her false self-image and any illusions about him/herself.

Emotional Level: Aids in overcoming feelings of frustration and futility when love is unrequited. Helps to free any blockages impeding the flow of communication. Useful in releasing guilt feelings and insecurity. Renews the love for oneself if it has been lost through separation or divorce.

Physical Level: Brings relief from allergies. Balances the gland functions, particularly during puberty and menopause.

Where to Apply the Substance: Around the entire lower abdomen. During difficult emotional situations, apply around the whole heart area. When there are spiritual and mental problems, apply along the hairline, too.

Affirmation: I am in harmony with life, and life is in harmony with me.

Distinctive Qualities: None.

24

Name of Bottle: New Message
Color: Violet/Turquoise
Shakes Together As: Violet
Chakra: Heart and Crown
Tarot Card: Queen of Wands
I Ching Sign: Earth above, thunder below, No. 24, "Return" (The Turning Point)
Main Theme: New possibilities

Positive Personality Aspects: A visionary who has the talent to teach and meet people at their level. Awakens self-love in others. Possesses charisma, integrity, and maturity and concentrates on joy. Always finds a challenge and is willing to take it on. Is creative and at peace. Creates harmony in relationships (this can literally mean that somebody may work as a matchmaker or marriage counselor).

Personality Aspects That Could Be Worked On: Inclined to magnify worries. More than anything, focuses on what difficulties other people present to him/her and what problems they cause. Deceives him/herself and others, suspecting people of all kinds of things.

Spiritual Level: Aids the process of awakening, particularly with respect to relationships. Brings forth spiritual integrity. Enables the person to become aware of self-deception. Facilitates the development of extrasensory perception. Helps find the way back to one's own path.

Mental Level: Brings peace after emotional difficulty, as well as clarity regarding his/her own childhood problems. Assists in meeting challenges. The ability to deal with authority improves. Helps in deciphering dreams.

Emotional Level: Opens new levels in personal and business relationships. Facilitates the healing of emotional injuries due to patriarchal, male-oriented behavior.

Physical Level: Useful in dealing with heart conditions, as well as speech impediments (dyslexia, stutters), especially with children. Balances the thymus gland function.

Where to Apply the Substance: Around the heart area; when there is a problem with speech, apply around the throat.

Affirmation: I am open to new opportunities in my life.

Distinctive Qualities: The contents of this bottle have very much to do with the energies of the planet Venus.

25

Name of Bottle: Convalescence Bottle/Florence Nightingale
Color: Purple/Magenta (this is the only bottle containing purple)
Shakes Together As: Bright Purple
Chakra: Crown
Tarot Card: Knight of Wands
I Ching Sign: Heaven above, thunder below, No. 25, "Innocence" (The Unexpected)
Main Theme: To be liberated from disappointment

Positive Personality Aspects: A healer who has a lot of energy to give. Has the ability to look deep within. Completes tasks that have been planned. Loves other people, has warmth for them, and often works in a caring profession. May be a spiritual crusader/pioneer.

Personality Aspects That Could Be Worked On: Often feels extreme disappointment with life. Does not know how to get well or how to recover. May have been through a serious illness or operation but has not yet fully coped with it.

Spiritual Level: Opens up the person for information from "above." Brings forth spiritual awareness and the strength to achieve the unachievable. Frees the user from spiritual utopianism. Provides an idea of what the "Divine Plan" is.

Mental Level: Stimulates creativity. Assists the individual in dealing with serious disappointments from the past. Helps with extreme nervousness and wishful thinking.

Emotional Level: Provides perspective and courage. Aids in overcoming extreme sexual desires and exaggerated needs for love and care.

Physical Level: Eases the consequences of serious illnesses and difficult operations, as well as all nerve problems—for example, nerve pain. Reduces the necessity to absorb potassium through the intake of nutrients.

Where to Apply the Substance: Along the hairline.

Affirmation: I let go of my disappointments.

Distinctive Qualities: This substance is very effective in cases of myalgic encephalomyelitis (ME), an illness with symptoms of extreme lethargy and fatigue, as well as headaches and muscle pain. In extreme cases, temporary paralysis may result. The substance can bring relief even when the acute state has already occurred.

26
Name of Bottle: Shock Bottle/Etheric Rescue/Humpty Dumpty
Color: Orange/Orange
Shakes Together As: Orange
Chakra: "Second Chakra"

Tarot Card: Page of Wands
I Ching Sign: Mountain above, heaven below, No. 26, "The Taming Power of the Great"
Main Theme: Shock and its consequences (on all levels)

Positive Personality Aspects: A very independent person who is creative, possesses deep, instinctive wisdom, and who learns by teaching others. Is intelligent and cautious and not given to excess in any way. Acts rather than reacts. Is able to feel deep joy. Loves animals. Is sexually fulfilled in a loving and harmonious way.

Personality Aspects That Could Be Worked On: May have been abused sexually, but also on various other levels). Has been through an "emotional storm." Reacts in extreme ways to people and situations. Is restless and disorientated. Makes hasty and irrational decisions.

Spiritual Level: Helps the user recover from disappointment resulting from spiritual deceit (such deceit puts the soul into a state of shock). Brings about higher insights.

Mental Level: Useful with nervous depressions and unknown fears that have led to deep depressive states. Establishes mental/spiritual orientation. Brings the user into the here and now. Recommended in all cases of shock.

Emotional Level: Liberates the individual from resentful thoughts and the results of possible physical, emotional, and/or sexual abuse. Supports the psyche during dramatic changes in life.

Physical Level: Alleviates problems associated with the thyroid gland, tense muscles, gallstones, post-accident stresses, operations, and other traumas. Can also be used before operations to prevent shock.

Where to Apply the Substance: This is the only substance that needs to be applied in a very specific way—around the entire abdomen; also from the left earlobe to the left shoulder in a small band downward. Then, beginning under the left arm in a wide band down the whole left side of the trunk to the ankle. With thyroid gland problems, apply around the throat. When muscles are tense, massage on the affected areas.

Affirmation: The only constant in life is change.

Distinctive Qualities: Belongs to the Chakra Set. Here, it relates to the "second chakra." On the left side of the body is the "etheric gap" where the "true aura" moves in shock situations. The contents of this bottle, if applied as prescribed, bring the aura back to its original position. This has a radical effect, very quickly restoring the person's health. Due to these fantastic effects, Bottle #26 is the most popular bottle in the Aura-Soma system. It also helps to heal animals, particularly after unconsciousness due to shock or anesthetics. In animals, the substance needs only to be applied around the abdomen. Apart from being sold in a 50-ml and 25-ml glass bottle, it is also available in a 25-ml plastic bottle, which can be easily carried. It can be used by others as well as the "owner."

(With respect to "abuse," see also "Distinctive Qualities" of Bottle #5.) In many people, this bottle triggers great delight, or they dislike it very much. These feelings usually point to a shock situation that needs healing. In such a case, it is recommended that the Shock Bottle be used first, then after a break, select your favorite bottle(s) anew.

27
Name of Bottle: Robin Hood
Color: Red/Green
Shakes Together As: Red
Chakra: Base and Heart
Tarot Card: Ten of Wands
I Ching Sign: Mountain above, thunder below, No. 27, "The Corners of the Mouth" (Providing Nourishment)
Main Theme: Assertiveness

Positive Personality Aspects: A successful person who works hard, who can concentrate well, who has great stamina, and is decisive. Is assertive and self-reliant. Has an infectious enthusiasm for life. Someone with courage and heart, who dares to push forward into the unknown. Is very centered and has a good feeling for harmony.

Personality Aspects That Could Be Worked On: There are problems with one's own gender—with one's masculinity or femininity. In some way, this might be a dual personality. Life is considered very difficult. This person is not in harmony with him/herself. Feels "bogged down." Loves intrigue.

Spiritual Level: Causes transformation. Clears stuck situations on the spiritual level. Encourages the user to follow his/her path more effectively and gives space for the soul to unfold. Awakens the individual to spiritual discipline and inspires him/her to give this area more importance.

Mental Level: Helpful with dual personalities. Provides for more self-confidence and assertiveness, especially in relationships in which one has, up to this point, been too passive.

Emotional Level: Aids in overcoming hurt(s) and anger after a separation or divorce. Enables the individual to cope with the feeling of being spied upon and of being deceived.

Physical Level: Helps strengthen the immune system.

Where to Apply the Substance: Around the entire trunk.

Affirmation: I see the light through the trees.

Distinctive Qualities: This combination, if chosen by a woman, can indicate someone who has a problem relating to men. It often shows that the person is about to go through a separation or divorce or has just done so (this applies to men as well as women). This substance helps a person to handle their transsexuality (that is, feeling like a woman living in a male body, or vice versa).

28
Name of Bottle: Maid Marion (Robin Hood's consort)
Color: Green/Red
Shakes Together As: Red
Chakra: Base and Heart
Tarot Card: Nine of Wands
I Ching Sign: Lake above, wind/wood below, No. 28, "Preponderance of the Great"

Main Theme: New beginning

Positive Personality Aspects: A pioneer who is always ready to look at a situation from a new, fresh perspective. A reliable and happy person who is honest with him/herself. This person is knowledgeable and possesses clarity of thought. Can trust his/her own intuition, does so, and is able to stand up for him/herself.

Personality Aspects That Could Be Worked On: Permits others to be domineering and likes to play the martyr. Lets others walk all over him/her. Finds it difficult to trust, and usually makes wrong decisions when these somehow have to do with trust. Believes others are against him/her. Suffers in coming to terms with a separation or divorce.

Spiritual Level: Assists the individual in breaking free of old relationships and entanglements, as well as in finding a new source of power to change things. Gives clarity and helps overcome self-doubts.

Mental Level: Enables the person to see him/herself anew. Encourages assertiveness. Makes difficult decisions easier and helps the individual communicate more easily about difficult decisions that have to be made.

Emotional Level: Releases limiting patterns, especially those that permit others to dominate. Gives a person the strength to stand up for him/herself. Encourages a feeling of happiness. Helps open up to space and freedom after a period of restraint.

Physical Level: Strengthens the immune system.

Where to Apply the Substance: Around the entire trunk.

Affirmation: I find the strength to be who I am.

Distinctive Qualities: If a man chooses this bottle, it can indicate a problem with a woman or women. If chosen by a woman, it often indicates that she allows herself to be treated as a "doormat." This substance, like that in Bottle #27, helps to cope with the impression of being a female in a male body or a male in a female body.

 # 29
Name of Bottle: Get Up and Go
Color: Red/Blue
Shakes Together As: Violet
Chakra: Base and Throat
Tarot Card: Eight of Wands
I Ching Sign: Water above, water below, No. 29, "The Abysmal" (Water)
Main Theme: To bring order into life

Positive Personality Aspects: A reformer who wants to change conventions and does so. Commits him/herself to peace, protects others, and wants the best for humanity. This person's lifestyle shows that spiritual and material matters are in harmony. Has integrated various personality aspects. Possesses a strong constitution and is healthy. Feels fulfilled both physically (also sexually) and spiritually.

Personality Aspects That Could Be Worked On: Puts material aspects of life above inner peace. Carries around a lot of anger, frustration, and resentment; therefore, has difficulty relating to other people.

Spiritual Level: Inspires communication about spiritual matters. Brings about harmony and deep peace. Awakens the soul from its "sleep" (Gurdjieff). Helps the individual recognize spiritual dangers and to draw the appropriate conclusions.

Mental Level: Beneficial during trying times. Supports integration of higher aspects into everyday life.

Emotional Level: Draws out the "skeletons in the closet"—sheds light into dark, oppressed areas. Balances the male and female aspects of a personality.

Physical Level: Increases hormone secretion. Restores energy to those who have been fatigued for a long time. Provides energy for self-expression (speaking, for example, in group situations).

Where to Apply the Substance: Around the entire trunk.

Affirmation: I open up to inner peace.

Distinctive Qualities: Helpful when one feels an energy drain (applies to all levels).

30
Name of Bottle: Bringing Heaven to Earth
Color: Blue/Red
Shakes Together As: Violet
Chakra: Base and Throat
Tarot Card: Seven of Wands
I Ching Sign: Fire above, fire below, No. 30, "The Clinging, Fire"
Main Theme: To get energy through communication

Positive Personality Aspects: Transforms ideas into action. Sees things clearly, also in the sense of clairvoyance. Often a teacher for spiritual or physical disciplines (yoga, martial arts, etc.). Male and female energies are in harmony. Understands what the "quality of life" is about: not only is the result of an action important, but also the way in which it is carried out.

Personality Aspects That Could Be Worked On: Has very rigid, fixed ideas. Is extremely competitive, holds grudges, and holds on to old stories. Feels inferior, especially with respect to intellectual capacity. Glorifies own results. Cannot express passion. Finds it difficult to keep the peace.

Spiritual Level: Opens new dimensions for psychic abilities. Provides a grounding influence after meditations. Brings head and belly together. Helps the individual get in touch with his/her life purpose. Stimulates communication of spiritual experiences (in small groups, and also in larger public arenas).

Mental Level: Calms mental hyperactivity. Releases rigid ideas. Gives courage and helps the user express creativity and passionate feelings.

Emotional Level: Brings peace. Allows for the expression of suppressed rage, and also heals the "inner child." Helps overcome feelings of frustration.

Physical Level: Relieves thyroid gland problems, headaches that are related to congestion, as well as ailments associated with the genital organs.

Where to Apply the Substance: Around the entire trunk. When there are spiritual problems and headaches, apply along the hairline, too.

Affirmation: Head in heaven, feet on earth, center flowing free.

Distinctive Qualities: "Hidden" in this bottle is #20 (Blue/Pink).

31
Name of Bottle: The Fountain
Color: Green/Gold
Shakes Together As: Olive Green
Chakra: Heart and Solar Plexus
Tarot Card: Six of Wands
I Ching Sign: Lake above, mountain below, No. 31, "Influence" (Wooing)
Main Theme: Overcoming deep fear

Positive Personality Aspects: Is diplomatic, maintains relationships of the heart with other people and establishes good team spirit. Accepts responsibilities and does not look at responsibilities as a burden, but rather as a joy. Possesses teaching abilities, also loves the arts and sciences. Builds a bridge between the two. Knows how to create space within and without. Has overcome many fears. Possesses deep faith in the Divine and in him/herself. Loves nature very much and is connected with devas and earth spirits.

Personality Aspects That Could Be Worked On: Knows no trust and no happiness. Feels cut off from the world. Wants to be rewarded for everything. Driven by hidden fears and emotions. Is rarely on time and delivers things late.

Spiritual Level: Helps to connect with the "sunshine of the heart"—that is, finding inner happiness. Opens the door to the inner prison (of conditioning, of self-inflicted limitations, etc.). Aids the individual in becoming more observant and also to connect with devas and earth spirits.

Mental Level: Brings back mental stability after a trauma. Resolves confusion. Gives hope. Connects the user with his/her inner truth.

Emotional Level: Useful when it comes to decisions of the heart. Injects happiness into a joyless life. Supports the letting go of fears and traumatic experiences, including the general fear of speaking.

Physical Level: Relieves ailments associated with the heart, liver, pancreas, kidneys, and is useful after physical traumas. Also alleviates stammering problems and chronic skin conditions (for example, allergies and eczema).

Where to Apply the Substance: Between the heart and the area just below the navel.

Affirmation: I let go of my fear and find sunshine in my heart.

Distinctive Qualities: Can help the user find a personal power spot, a place in nature, where he/she feels content and especially "connected." Is supportive and calming in examination situations.

32
Name of Bottle: Sophia
Color: Royal Blue/Gold
Shakes Together As: Deep Magenta
Chakra: Solar Plexus and Third Eye
Tarot Card: Five of Wands
I Ching Sign: Thunder above, wind below, No. 32, "Duration"
Main Theme: Imparting of inner truth

Positive Personality Aspects: Possesses a lot of charisma and, at the same time, discipline. Gives warmth, support, and attention to others. Is at peace with him/herself. Has knowledge of the powers of nature. Lives in the moment. Able to communicate in a clear manner. Material things are not important to this person; he/she lives a simple life. On the other hand, this person can obtain anything that is needed at any time. And (on yet another hand!), he/she also can attain what is unattainable to many others (this applies to all areas of life).

Personality Aspects That Could Be Worked On: Does not know who he/she is. Does not feel at peace. Always feels stressed. Has difficulty being in the here and now. Danger of drug abuse. Is obsessed by all kinds of fears and anxieties, mainly anticipation, and has a general fear of life.

Spiritual Level: Helps overcome illusions and to separate from "lofty" ideas in order to turn to more realistic spiritual aims. Introduces the idea that we humans possess great creative powers (the possibility of "co-creation"). Helps the user to find his/her true identity.

Mental Level: Provides a clear mental direction. Reduces "stress in the mind." Strengthens the mind. Reduces anxieties, increases tranquility.

Emotional Level: Brings about breakthroughs after stagnation. Helps to clear mother-issues as well as finding general clarity in matters of the heart. Gets one to act rather than *re*act.

Physical Level: Helps with problems of the stomach, liver, kidneys, pancreas, colon (especially in nutritional assimilation), with nervousness in the stomach, and with skin complaints, especially "age spots."

Where to Apply the Substance: Anywhere between head and navel.

Affirmation: I let go of my fear and open to inner wisdom.

Distinctive Qualities: Helps the individual access ancient memories. In past-life therapy, this substance can connect with Aztec, Mayan, and Toltec incarnations. It is possible that somebody who chooses this as the first bottle was born with the umbilical cord around the neck.

 # 33
Name of Bottle: Dolphin/Peace with a Purpose
Color: Royal Blue/Turquoise
Shakes Together As: Royal Blue
Chakra: Heart and Third Eye
Tarot Card: Four of Wands
I Ching Sign: Heaven above, mountain below, No. 33, "Retreat"
Main Theme: Peaceful communication

Positive Personality Aspects: An artist who works for peace. One who is connected to intuition, to inner guidance. Is absolutely devoted to his/her purpose in life. A reformer who would never let authority or authority figures oppose this aim. At the same time, this individual is a lovable, gentle person who wants to bring heaven to earth. Has access to other dimensions. Loves nature. Can laugh about life's mysteries.

Personality Aspects That Could Be Worked On: A martyr in the negative sense of the word. Has difficulty understanding him/herself. Has no commitment or involvement. Wants others to take care of him/her. Is still suffering from a difficult relationship with his/her father. The love is deep, but this person cannot express love. Is uncomfortable among other people.

Spiritual Level: Assists the user in finding inner beauty through meditation. Establishes contact with other dimensions. Facilitates the process of self-discovery. Helps to open the Third Eye (enabling one to interpret symbols more clearly and become generally more clairvoyant).

Mental Level: Aids the individual in better understanding dreams and helps him/her draw strength from the awareness gained in this way. Gives access to original, creative ideas.

Emotional Level: Supports the letting go of feelings of isolation, as well as extreme insecurity and shyness. Allows the person to give the nurturing, motherly care that he/she needs.

Physical Level: Useful with eye conditions.

Where to Apply the Substance: In the neck and jaw area, along the hairline, just above the eyebrows along the forehead, and around the throat. Also, around the entire chest area. With eye conditions, apply near the eye sockets (only in the vicinity of the bone structure).

Affirmation: Peace is all I am striving for.

Distinctive Qualities: In past-life therapy, can establish contact with incarnations in Lemuria and Atlantis. Helpful in polarity work.

 # 34

Name of Bottle: Birth of Venus
Color: Pink/Turquoise
Shakes Together As: Light Violet Sprinkled with Pink
Chakra: Heart and Base
Tarot Card: Three of Wands
I Ching Sign: Thunder above, heaven below, No. 34, "The Power of the Great"
Main Theme: Integration of many different levels within the personality

Positive Personality Aspects: A self-sufficient person in all areas of life. Needs no external help, is self-reliant, has inner strength. Can give and receive deep love. Does not deviate from his/her life path, no matter what happens. Has already come a long way and is close to mystical completion. Loves the ocean and is possibly involved with seafaring.

Personality Aspects That Could Be Worked On: Experiences constant disappointment and does not learn from it. Does not trust his/her inner guidance. Sells him/herself too cheaply. Becomes lost in fantasies. Does not see things as they are. Has great difficulty with the reality of life and withdraws from this truth. Gets carried away by passion.

Spiritual Level: Establishes access to the hidden secrets of life and love. Brings up lost secrets from the depths of the soul. Useful as an escort for "inner journeys" (for example, in an isolation tank, in hypnosis, etc.).

Mental Level: Promotes balance between the male and female sides of a personality and leads to love between both aspects.

Emotional Level: Opens up the heart. Is especially recommended where new love blossoms. Releases the pain of the past and brings joy. Helps the user stand on his/her own feet.

Physical Level: Relieves all heart conditions, juvenile acne, growing pains of youngsters, and menstruation problems.

Where to Apply the Substance: Mainly around the heart area. With menstruation problems, around the abdomen/lower abdomen; in dream work, along the entire hairline.

Affirmation: I am who I am.

Distinctive Qualities: Helpful with dream work and for children who feel threatened. Choosing this bottle may indicate that the person concerned could be taken in by flattery.

35
Name of Bottle: Kindness
Color: Pink/Violet
Shakes Together As: Violet
Chakra: Base and Crown
Tarot Card: Two of Wands
I Ching Sign: Fire above, earth below, No. 35, "Progress"
Main Theme: Getting closer to the spiritual through love

Positive Personality Aspects: Experiences deep satisfaction through helping others, thereby helping oneself. Possesses the gift of healing, also of distant healing (that is, healing someone who is not in the immediate vicinity). This person's thoughts are ruled by love. He/she is a gentle, spiritual soul who is concerned about the welfare of humanity. Is in connection with love from "above." Possesses self-confidence and strength.

Personality Aspects That Could Be Worked On: Carries unresolved anger and frustration from childhood. This person's wish to help is egotistic. Is easily dominated. Has too much sensitivity and can easily fall into depressions.

Spiritual Level: Brings back energy to helpers (with burn-out syndrome). Protects from aggressive energy. Revives mind and soul. Establishes access to empathy for oneself and others. Helps the user get in touch with his/her life's purpose.

Mental Level: Encourages self-acceptance and the development of intuition. Opens up to love. Makes "old tapes" unnecessary—that is, things that the person has been telling him/herself or has been told for a long time. Helps the individual release oversensitivity and exaggerated self-love.

Emotional Level: Breaks up old patterns of despair. Enables the person to cope with disappointment in love and with extreme depression.

Physical Level: Useful with problems during menopause, pain in the chest, headaches and insomnia, especially when caused by emotional problems. Brings tenderness into sexuality.

Where to Apply the Substance: Everywhere around the body.

Affirmation: In healing others, I heal myself.

Distinctive Qualities: Helpful in situations in which someone suffers physically—for example, if one is in pain, but no specific reason can be found.

36
Name of Bottle: Charity
Color: Violet/Pink
Shakes Together As: Violet
Chakra: Base and Crown
Tarot Card: Ace of Wands
I Ching Sign: Earth above, fire below, No. 36, "Darkening of the Light"
Main Theme: Spiritual love

Positive Personality Aspects: Is aware of his/her life purpose. In everything this person does, he/she has inner goals in sight even when the path is not straight. Feels connected with the Creator and has a love for all things. Is a child of love (that is also meant literally: this person's parents truly loved each other). Has the gift of strong healing powers and serves selflessly. Often involved with alternative medicine.

Personality Aspects That Could Be Worked On: Harbors hidden frustrations. Is particularly frustrated because he/she felt unloved by the mother. Clings to the affection and caring of others. Possibly does not want to be here (that is, did not want to be born). Is uncomfortable in the physical body. Lives the part of a victim. Is not in the here and now. Holds on to false hopes.

Spiritual Level: Establishes access to inner goals, personal healing powers, and enables the user to be more in the present moment. Stimulates contact with the Creator, with all living things, and with the individual's life purpose. Protects against spiritual confusion resulting from too many workshops, or the like.

Mental Level: Aids in overcoming false hope. Enables the person to see life anew and to appreciate it again. Helpful in preventing the head from ruling the heart too much.

Emotional Level: Brings about more self-love. Dissolves frustrations, as well as deep depressions. Helps the individual say "yes" to being here. Makes it easier to access new identity patterns. Brings about general positive changes.

Physical Level: Useful for pain throughout the body, energy blockages, head injuries, knee and hip problems.

Where to Apply the Substance: Everywhere around the body (for example, when necessary, just around an injured or bothersome knee).

Affirmation: I love the challenges of life.

Distinctive Qualities: Helpful in working with the "inner child."

37

Name of Bottle: The Guardian Angel Comes to Earth
Color: Violet/Blue
Shakes Together As: Deep Violet
Chakra: Crown and Throat
Tarot Card: King of Cups
I Ching Sign: Wind above, fire below, No. 37, "The Family" (The Clan)
Main Theme: Effectiveness

Positive Personality Aspects: Follows his/her ideals. Is disciplined, inspired, and has great intuition. The way this person behaves shows how effective and successful in life he/she is. Is engaged in different spiritual activities. May have to shoulder a lot of responsibility which, however, does not present a problem or cause difficulties. Is able to see the overall perspective. Has noble intentions. Wants to create beauty and impart a sense of aesthetics to others.

Personality Aspects That Could Be Worked On: Responsibility rests heavily on this person's shoulders. Does not want to face life. Wants to go "home"—that is, this person is suicidal. On the other hand, is very enamored of him/herself. Has not yet found the primary life purpose. Manipulates others, but also tends to idealize them.

Spiritual Level: Stimulates meditative energy. Transforms. Nurtures and protects. Opens the higher chakras (outside the body). Helps the user get in contact with deep inner peace and the truly spiritual purpose and direction in life.

Mental Level: Brings clarity into thoughts and speech. Gets the user to come to terms with his/her male role model (and, therefore, authority issues). Establishes contact with hidden rhythms.

Emotional Level: Works in an encouraging and supportive way in cases of deep depression and when the user wishes to give up old emotional patterns. Enables the person to adjust more easily to external and internal circumstances, lessening the desire to commit suicide.

Physical Level: Can be useful with headaches that result from toxicity of the body; and with thyroid, jaw, neck, and throat problems.

Where to Apply the Substance: Along the entire hairline and around the throat/neck area.

Affirmation: I fill my cup so it can overflow into the world.

Distinctive Qualities: Can balance and stimulate the Third Eye, as well as help develop psychic abilities.

38
Name of Bottle: Troubadour II/Discernment
Color: Violet/Green
Shakes Together As: Deep Green

Chakra: Heart and Crown
Tarot Card: Queen of Cups
I Ching Sign: Flame above, lake below, No. 38, "Opposition"
Main Theme: To get from thinking to feeling

Positive Personality Aspects: This person possesses natural authority and individuality in the best sense of the words. Is in contact with the heart. At the same time, has a strong feeling for the community. This is also his/her life purpose. Has the ability to see both sides of a situation and then make the right decisions. Understands the laws of karma. A seeker with emotional and intuitive maturity who is friendly, sensitive, and comforting. One who likes to give freely, yet who is independent. Is connected with the power of the Goddess. A good person, yet he/she is unaware of this.

Personality Aspects That Could Be Worked On: This person does not trust his/her female side. Is envious, jealous, suspicious, and has a sharp tongue. Has a strong desire for peace, independence, and solitude; also needs a lot of acceptance and appreciation from others. Yearns for nature, but never makes the effort to go there. A disillusioned person who has no spiritual focus. Searches for balance between the conscious and subconscious.

Spiritual Level: Furthers the process of finding the truth and reaching a new spiritual direction. Allows the user to discover inner secrets and to stimulate intuitive abilities. Resolves spiritual illusions. Brings spiritual experiences from the head to the heart.

Mental Level: Gives an overactive mind some rest. Helps the individual cope with his/her own (and external) authority and to integrate the female side. Brings about more self-confidence and independence from being accepted by others.

Emotional Level: Heals heart problems on all levels, especially when the mind has ruled the heart. Helps the user gain understanding of his/her own suffering. Encourages the person to come to terms with feelings of mistrust, envy, and jealousy.

Physical Level: Beneficial for all kinds of heart problems, psychosomatic illnesses, frozen shoulder, arthritis, rheumatism, bladder and kidney conditions.

Where to Apply the Substance: Along the entire hairline, around the heart area; with bladder and kidney problems, around the abdomen; with rheumatism and arthritis—wherever the pain is.

Affirmation: I give a name to my feelings.

Distinctive Qualities: In this bottle, many others are "hidden," which means that it is very complex. Its contents bring psychic abilities and spirituality together (sometimes these two areas are poles apart). In past-life therapy, this substance can establish access to medieval incarnations (see "Distinctive Qualities" of Bottle #17).

39
Name of Bottle: Egyptian Bottle II/The Puppeteer
Color: Violet/Gold
Shakes Together As: Orange
Chakra: Solar Plexus and Crown
Tarot Card: Knight of Cups
I Ching Sign: Water above, mountain below, No. 39, "Obstruction"
Main Theme: Healing of deepest fears

Positive Personality Aspects: Possesses the strength to change the world and understands that this change has to begin within oneself. Finds freedom in action. Enjoys attaining knowledge and passing it on to others. A humble and dignified person who possesses excellent discernment. Has universal understanding—that is, perceives and comprehends many things in life. An idealistic "crusader" who has an important life mission and possesses great inner wisdom.

Personality Aspects That Could Be Worked On: Harbors deep unresolved fears and holds on to them. Is confused and very occupied with fears. Aims at things that are really unattainable ("paper moon" mentality). Has difficulty establishing friendships. Condemns him/herself and others. Indulges in fantasies and illusions in order to withdraw from reality.

Spiritual Level: Encourages the user to change his/her ideals. Helps to resolve fears. Supports the transformative process of learning to know oneself.

Mental Level: Reduces the desire to condemn others by becoming gentler with oneself. Allows the user to cope more easily with confusion, fantasies, and illusions and to view the world more realistically.

Emotional Level: Helpful in overcoming deep current and past fears. Brings joy into a joyless life. Stimulates sympathy and empathy.

Physical Level: Helps with psychosomatic skin conditions, psoriasis, digestive problems, and fractures.

Where to Apply the Substance: Along the entire hairline and around the abdomen.

Affirmation: I have a lot to learn and a lot to share.

Distinctive Qualities: In past-life therapy, can establish access to incarnations in Ancient Egypt.

40

Name of Bottle: "I am"
Color: Red/Gold
Shakes Together As: Red
Chakra: Base and Solar Plexus
Tarot Card: Page of Cups
I Ching Sign: Thunder above, water below, No. 40, "Deliverance"
Main Theme: Self-realization or self-knowledge

Positive Personality Aspects: Carries deep wisdom within, and can express this. Is very close to awakening—meaning he/she is in the process of self-discovery and has already come a long way. A person who, when planning, weighs the existing opportunities and then commits him/herself to the most probable. Is in harmony and is of healthy mind and body. Usually a very successful businessperson who enjoys his/her work. Can present a good appearance to others. Has ecological interests, also. Is creative and constantly reviews his/her own thinking.

Personality Aspects That Could Be Worked On: A very dominant person who frightens others. Carries a lot of guilt within. Has inner conflicts and perceives him/herself unrealistically. At the same time, judges and condemns others. Always feels misunderstood. A naive person, in the negative sense of the word. Has sexual problems. Finds it especially difficult to express sexuality.

Spiritual Level: Encourages the user to get in contact with earth energies (philosophically and concretely, as in dowsing, etc.). Furthers the utilization of sexual energies for spiritual work (for example, through Tantra). Allows the individual to perceive the wealth of the soul in him/herself and in others. Transforms meditation into action. Awakens the Christ energy.

Mental Level: Resolves mental conflicts, especially in connection with anticipation fears. Useful in freeing the user from dependency, co-dependency, and certain addictions, as well as in finding out what his/her real responsibility is.

Emotional Level: Resolves fears, frustration, shocks, and the feeling of being misunderstood, and helps the person connect with joy. Beneficial in overcoming emotional naivete, as well as fears—especially fears having to do with money and health issues. Allays guilt feelings and the tendency to blame others. Frees the person from old, limiting patterns.

Physical Level: Eases shoulder problems, skin inflammations, stress-related stomach ailments. Makes the energy flow.

Where to Apply the Substance: Everywhere between the base and solar plexus chakras.

Affirmation: I say "yes" to life.

Distinctive Qualities: None.

41
Name of Bottle: Wisdom Bottle/El d'Orado
Color: Gold/Gold

Shakes Together As: Gold
Chakra: Solar Plexus
Tarot Card: Ten of Cups
I Ching Sign: Mountain above, lake below, No. 41, "Decrease"
Main Theme: Assimilation

Positive Personality Aspects: A farmer in the best sense of the word and in all areas of life—that is, somebody who sows and reaps, who lives in harmony with the rhythms of nature, who sees things from a "natural" point of view, and so on. (All of this can be taken both literally and figuratively.) Loves adventure. Feels great happiness. Discovers possibilities for growth in all trials and difficulties. Finds joy in simplicity. Helps others to start a new life. Is connected with his/her own inner wisdom. Has high expectations of him/herself and others, but it does not matter much to this person if these expectations are fulfilled or not.

Personality Aspects That Could Be Worked On: Is obsessed with self-doubt and patterns of the past. Has difficulty with the material side of life, especially concerning the desire for luxury. Feels no joy and has great inner conflicts. Leans toward dependency in relationships. Concentrates only on that which he/she is supposedly entitled to, instead of giving something out. Harbors guilt feelings and blames others.

Spiritual Level: Beneficial for bringing more light into all personality aspects. Allows the individual to take in *prana* (life energy). Reveals his/her own truth. Leads to "right(eous) speech, right(eous) action, right(eous) life." Establishes access to wisdom from the past.

Mental Level: Balances logic and intuition. Improves the ability to care for self and others. Helps the user attain what he/she wants and needs and also to take responsibility for the consequences resulting from satisfied desires.

Emotional Level: Brings happiness, even to the happy. Enables the person to overcome bitterness and to cope constructively with confusion. Injects a fresh breeze into paralyzing situations. Opens the user to joy and fun by constructively dealing with fear.

Physical Level: Eases kidney problems (especially when the body retains water), as well as skin and spine problems. This substance is highly recommended when the body is slightly toxigenic.

Where to Apply the Substance: Around the entire solar plexus area.

Affirmation: I search for and find the pot of gold at the end of the rainbow.

Distinctive Qualities: Can dissolve blockages in the middle of the body.

42
Name of Bottle: Harvest
Color: Yellow/Yellow
Shakes Together As: Yellow
Chakra: Solar Plexus
Tarot Card: Nine of Cups
I Ching Sign: Wind above, thunder below, No. 42, "Increase"
Main Theme: Spontaneity combined with joy

Positive Personality Aspects: A kind, harmonious, "sunny" person. This is also reflected in the way this person moves (for example, he/she may possess dancing abilities). Is in a natural flow, goes with the flow of life. In the positive sense, knows no inhibitions. Finds his/her own way in the most varied life situations. Easily absorbs information, which this person often utilizes in his/her work.

Personality Aspects That Could Be Worked On: Keeps searching for a new identity, but never changes. Tries unsuccessfully to rely on the mind. Has little sweetness in life; therefore, indulges in overeating sweets. Is unhappy and permanently focused on future events instead of being in the present moment.

Spiritual Level: Helps experience more joy and self-realization. Facilitates awakening. Casts light into the shadow areas of the personality. Points out those things that are truly desired.

Mental Level: Resolves feelings of limitation and nervous depressions. Stimulates the intellect and the intake of information, but is also helpful for balancing over-intellectuality and intellectual dominance. Facilitates decision-making processes.

Emotional Level: Inspires "higher feelings" (love, warmth, compassion, etc.). Clears emotional confusion. Encourages freedom from fear; brings joy.

Physical Level: balances the solar plexus and the central nervous system. Helps to heal wounds. Relieves liver problems and diabetes; aids in the assimilation of nutrients, as well as skin and digestive disorders that originate from acidity.

Where to Apply the Substance: Around the entire solar plexus area. When experiencing seasonal depression (usually in the winter), apply along the entire hairline.

Affirmation: From my outer knowledge, I create inner knowledge.

Distinctive Qualities: Beneficial during seasonal depression and at exam preparation time (for children, teenagers, and adults). This substance affects the astral body (see Chapter 4). It helps to let go of illusions.

43
Name of Bottle: Creativity
Color: Turquoise/Turquoise
Shakes Together As: Turquoise
Chakra: Heart
Tarot Card: Eight of Cups
I Ching Sign: Lake above, heaven below, No. 43, "Breakthrough" (Resoluteness)
Main Theme: Communication through art and mass media

Positive Personality Aspects: A searcher of truth who constantly examines him/herself, but feels in harmony anyway. Exhibits "elasticity of the mind"—meaning that he/she is very flexible and open to new things. Has an affinity for the stars, directly and abstractly—for example, concerning astrology, astronomy, and the experience of the night sky. Possesses communication abilities beyond the verbal level (dance, painting, music, etc.). If not artistically talented, applies a creative note to everything that is done. Has a good spiritual connection. Is in contact with angels and devas.

Personality Aspects That Could Be Worked On: A sad person who is ruled by the patterns of the subconscious. Is not in touch with the feelings, does not know him/herself, but on the other hand, is narcissistic. Feels rebuffed due to rejection. Someone who is not awake.

Spiritual Level: Improves self-perception. Helps decipher the secrets of life. Gives courage to perform in front of larger groups, not so much as the "great guru," but in a way that includes the listeners in the auditorium.

Mental Level: Inspires one to formulate and verbalize ideas, as well as to "dig out" subconscious matters and to talk about them. Supports people who impart knowledge beyond language (for example, massage, dance, and music teachers).

Emotional Level: Helps to feel accepted and to feel well overall. Releases blockages. Assists in overcoming foolish infatuations.

Physical Level: Balances the thymus gland, especially in children. Useful with bronchitis and all problems in the chest, with cardiac rhythm disorders and speech impediments, especially when resulting from extreme nervousness. Awakens the body for sexuality.

Where to Apply the Substance: Around the entire heart area.

Affirmation: Everything is flowing. I go with the flow.

Distinctive Qualities: This bottle relates especially to the ananda-khanda center, the chakra on the right side of the body at the heart level (see Chapter 4).

44
Name of Bottle: The Guardian Angel
Color: Pale Violet (Lilac)/Pale Blue
Shakes Together As: Pale Violet (Lilac)
Chakra: Throat and Crown
Tarot Card: Seven of Cups
I Ching Sign: Heaven above, wind below, No. 44, "Coming to Meet"
Main Theme: Transformation of negativity to peace

Positive Personality Aspects: A transformer who liberates him/herself and others. A person with a peace mission, who is in contact with God and transforms that in very practical ways (co-creation). Is aware of his/her own Divine spark. A healer who is very inspired and in contact with the Higher Self. Communicates in a kind, easy, yet profound way. Is very focused and is a good co-worker/team worker. Has to work hard to fulfill his/her life purpose, but is happy to do so. Is connected with the realm of angels, with the etheric spheres, and can talk about these subjects.

Personality Aspects That Could Be Worked On: Lacks inner peace. Is not grounded. Is desperate about his/her life circumstances, about existence in general, and doubts God. Had a difficult childhood, which is still unresolved. Deceives him/herself and spends time in wishful thinking. Fosters expectations that everything will turn out all right, even in situations that make such an outcome impossible.

Spiritual Level: Encourages Divine inspiration and support from "above." Connects the user with the inner flow and enables him/her to trust this flow. Brings the ability to find his/her own philosophy of life outside fixed structures (for example, religions). Unites the person to the "oasis of the soul"—that is, to the knowledge that "deep within me there is a place where I can recharge."

Mental Level: Encourages integration of the different aspects of life. Opens the mind for "higher intelligence"; for example, for extrasensory perception. Has a grounding effect. Helps to erase old patterns.

Emotional Level: Brings joy and a clear motivation that is independent from the desires of the ego. Releases suffering that results from egocentricity. Frees from childhood trauma and from the results of possible physical, mental, or sexual abuse.

Physical Level: Helps balance the thyroid gland and the hypothalamus. Beneficial for psychosomatic illnesses, jaw and neck problems, especially on the right side of the body.

Where to Apply the Substance: Around the throat and along the hairline.

Affirmation: I let go and do not expect anything.

Distinctive Qualities: Gives strength to people who have had encounters with UFOs, extraterrestrials, and angels, and who, as a result, feel threatened and insecure. The color lilac, as it is used in the upper part of this bottle, appears in only two other bottles. "Lilac" in Aura-Soma means "pale violet."

Regarding the subject of "abuse," also see the "Distinctive Qualities" of Bottle #5.

45

Name of Bottle: Breath of Love
Color: Turquoise/Magenta
Shakes Together As: Violet
Chakra: Base, Heart, and Crown
Tarot Card: Six of Cups
I Ching Sign: Lake above, earth below, No. 45, "Gathering Together," (Massing)
Main Theme: Give and take in love

Positive Personality Aspects: Has access to ancient knowledge and understands this knowledge very well. A sensitive person with strong intuition. Loves beauty in all areas of life. Creative but determined, is in contact with his/her feminine aspect. Endeavors to achieve inner balance and always establishes it anew. This person's love is linked to his/her life purpose, which means that he/she may be in a caring profession and really love that work. Has the ability to plan things carefully and in such a way that they are beautiful and pleasant. Is concerned that the people being planned for feel good.

Personality Aspects That Could Be Worked On: Holds on to a past love, which has a negative influence on the current situation. This person's emotional blocks hamper his/her sexuality. Has difficulty expressing him/herself. Because there is a problem verbalizing feelings, tends to experience them vicariously. Takes on other people's problems and tries to fix them. Is very ambitious, overestimates own abilities and withdraws.

Spiritual Level: Helps the user develop compassion and to feel unconditional love. Gives a feeling of growth and expansion. Fosters recognition
of clairvoyant abilities and a renewal of inner strength.

Mental Level: Useful in coping with the consequences of suppressed sexual feelings. Inspires creativity. Enables the person to distance him/herself
from all kinds of problems and entanglements.

Emotional Level: Helps to give more authenticity to the soul and to the
expression of feelings; gives emotions a new focus. Connects the user with
his/her own emotions so that he/she no longer needs to feed off those of
others. Encourages the person to care for him/herself.

Physical Level: Supports during dietary changes. Assists in recognizing the
needs of the body. Recommended for anorexia and overeating; helpful with
heart conditions, stress, and overwork.

Where to Apply the Substance: Everywhere on the body. When there is
stress, apply around the heart area, especially.

Affirmation: Everything is beautiful in its own way.

Distinctive Qualities: Helps overcome disappointments in love.

46

Name of Bottle: The Wanderer
Color: Green/Magenta
Shakes Together As: Deep Jade Green
Chakra: Heart and Crown
Tarot Card: Five of Cups
I Ching Sign: Earth above, wind/wood below, No. 46, "Pushing Upward"
Main Theme: New beginning for love

Positive Personality Aspects: A loyal person whose life is very centered
and who trusts the process of the "great whole," even when life has its ups
and downs. "Works hard and plays hard," which means that whatever the
task, it is performed well and thoroughly. Loves the garden (the garden outside, but also the garden within, the place where things grow and blossom

and are reaped and where relaxation can be found). Carries the love inside that opens the hearts of others. Is in contact with the "inner child." May be working with birth processes, again, in both the literal and the abstract sense.

Personality Aspects That Could Be Worked On: Is extremely possessive in love. Can be addicted to love and sex. Wants to fall in love time and time again, but never comes to truly love. This person's life is ruled by patterns that he/she does not want to look at. Is paralyzed by jealousy and envy. Does not know the feeling of trust. Always needs the permission of others when thinking about doing anything for him/herself.

Spiritual Level: Helps develop spiritual discipline (for example, for regular meditation) and spiritual strength. Facilitates the process of attaining a higher aim. Enables the user to develop compassion, encourages the user to allow him/herself to do whatever has to be done for him/herself.

Mental Level: Enhances creativity and an optimistic view of life. Helps to get rid of addictions and dependency. Heals limiting patterns from childhood, especially those of childlike jealousy.

Emotional Level: Releases envy, jealousy, and possessive behavior. Brings a new, positive direction to the emotional world. Helps to forgive oneself and others. Eases the pain after a shattered love.

Physical Level: Beneficial for candida, abdominal growths, and all menstrual problems (too strong, too weak, or irregular menstruation, etc.), as well as bronchial infections.

Where to Apply the Substance: Around the heart; with menstrual problems, also around the abdomen.

Affirmation: I see the fountain in the garden of my heart.

Distinctive Qualities: None

 # 47

Name of Bottle: Old Soul
Color: Royal Blue/Lemon (this is the only bottle containing lemon)
Shakes Together As: Green
Chakra: Solar Plexus and Heart, as well as the Third Eye
Tarot Card: Four of Cups
I Ching Sign: Lake above, water below, No. 47, "Oppression" (Exhaustion)
Main Theme: Connecting head and belly

Positive Personality Aspects: Gifted with extrasensory perception. Is in contact with the Higher Self. Possesses mystical knowledge. Has a clear direction in life and teaches by example. Is in contact with the heart and can express this. Acts instead of reacting.

Personality Aspects That Could Be Worked On: Pretends to be centered and balanced, but in actuality, there is nothing but inner tension. An amateur in the worst sense. Manipulates others. Life gives this person a lot, yet he/she does not know what to do with these blessings. May be inspired, but this inspiration is controlled emotionally.

Spiritual Level: Helps develop extrasensory perception and the ability to be inspired through meditation. Connects the individual with the Higher Self. Encourages discrimination in the spiritual field. Resolves self-deception.

Mental Level: Brings balance to the right and left hemispheres of the brain, which means it balances the analytical and creative mind. Makes logical thinking and the ability to remember easier; inspires the formulation of goals, and helps gain new access to readily available knowledge.

Emotional Level: Enables the user to perceive and define emotions more clearly. Aids in coping with fears, especially mentally based ones. Eases neuroses.

Physical Level: Useful with degenerative illnesses (Alzheimer's disease, etc.), with fatigue and lack of stamina or the development of stamina. Calms pain of the middle back and heart conditions, especially when of mental origin.

Where to Apply the Substance: Around the solar plexus and heart area, as well as along the hairline.

Affirmation: I make the best of my opportunities.

Distinctive Qualities: In some circles, an "old soul" is regarded as one that has already had many incarnations. Others are of the opinion that all humans are "old souls." Today, Aura-Soma is in conflict about the name of this bottle because it inspires spiritual vanity in some people.

48
Name of Bottle: Wings of Healing
Color: Violet/Clear
Shakes Together As: Pale Violet (Lilac)
Chakra: Crown
Tarot Card: Three of Cups
I Ching Sign: Water above, wind/wood below, No. 48, "The Well"
Main Theme: To clarify one's life purpose

Positive Personality Aspects: This person is often professionally involved in healing, psychology, or psychotherapy. Has great enthusiasm for life and a lot of energy for communicating with others. Holds a deep belief in him/herself, and is probably religious. Feels "at one" with God and existence. Is aware of his/her personal life purpose.

Personality Aspects That Could Be Worked On: Is often misunderstood, feels internally driven, and rarely finds peace. Harbors a lot of frustration and resentment. Says: "If only I had..." and makes other people and circumstances responsible for his/her own unhappy state. May have suicidal tendencies. Is unable to use one's own talents, hides his/her light under a bushel (in the negative sense of the expression).

Spiritual Level: Encourages one to undergo a cleansing process, especially when "spiritually congested" (too much information, too many workshops, too many teachers, etc.). Supports transformational work on oneself. Establishes contact with Divine inspiration. Helps overcome suicidal tendencies.

Mental Level: Releases poverty consciousness. Inspires the sense that each moment gives cause for celebration, that everyday living is full of miracles. Enables the user to concentrate on important issues and to pursue them.

Emotional Level: Releases the feeling of inner emptiness. Brings accumulated tears to the surface, especially after the loss of a loved one.

Physical Level: Detoxifying. Helps to get rid of fungus (both externally and internally). Eases pain of the lower back, as well as hormonal problems.

Where to Apply the Substance: Along the hairline; with hormonal and back problems, also apply around the abdomen.

Affirmation: I find joy because the light nourishes me.

Distinctive Qualities: This substance is especially recommended after cranio-sacral work to stabilize the body. (Cranio-sacral work is a body therapy that harmonizes the cerebral-spinal fluid and the bones of the brain.)

49

Name of Bottle: New Messenger
Color: Turquoise/Violet
Shakes Together As: Deep Violet flecked with Turquoise
Chakra: Heart and Crown
Tarot Card: Two of Cups
I Ching Sign: Lake above, fire below, No. 49, "Revolution" (Molting)
Main Theme: Expression of feelings

Positive Personality Aspects: A flexible, creative person with many new ideas and great interest in development. Has a good feeling for rhythms, sequences, and time planning, as well as a talent for speaking. Often works in mass media. Brings his/her spirituality together with a down-to-earth attitude, especially with respect to love. Is able to share feelings with others. Sees that positive and negative sides in others actually mirror a part of oneself.

Personality Aspects That Could Be Worked On: Is in search of the perfect relationship, therefore often misses existing opportunities. A discouraged person, held back by guilt feelings. Has difficulty sharing (money, feelings,

#0: Royal Blue/
Deep Magenta
Spiritual Rescue

#1: Blue/
Deep Magenta
Physical Rescue

#2: Blue/Blue
Peace

#3: Blue/Green
Atlantean
The Heart Bottle

#4: Yellow/Gold
The Sun Bottle/Sunlight

#5: Yellow/Red
Sunrise/Sunset

#6: Red/Red
The Energy Bottle

#7: Yellow/Green
Garden of Gethsemene

#8: Yellow/Blue
Anubis

#9: Turquoise/Green
Crystal Cave
Heart Within the Heart

#10: Green/Green
Go Hug a Tree

#11: Clear/Pink
A Chain of Flowers
Essene Bottle I

#12: Clear/Blue
Peace in the New Aeon

#13: Clear/Green
Change in the New Aeon

#14: Clear/Gold
Wisdom in the New Aeon

#15: Clear/Violet
Healing in the New Aeon

#16: Violet/Violet
The Violet Robe

#17: Green/Violet
Troubadour I
Hope

#18: Yellow/Violet
Egyptian Bottle I
Turning Tide

#19: Red/Purple
Living in the Material World

#20: Blue/Pink
Child's Rescue
Star Child

#21: Green/Pink
New Beginning for Love

#22: Yellow/Pink
Rebirther's Bottle
Awakening

#23: Rose Pink/Pink
Love and Light

#24: Violet/Turquoise
New Message

#25: Purple/Magenta
Convalescence Bottle
Florence Nightingale

#26: Orange/Orange
Etheric Rescue
Humpty Dumpty

#27: Red/Green
Robin Hood

#28: Green/Red
Maid Marion

#29: Red/Blue
Get Up and Go

#30: Blue/Red
Bringing Heaven to Earth

#31: Green/Gold
The Fountain

#32: Royal Blue/Gold
Sophia

#33: Royal Blue/Turquoise
Dolphin
Peace with a Purpose

#34: Pink/Turquoise
Birth of Venus

#35: Pink/Violet
Kindness

#36: Violet/Pink
Charity

#37: Violet/Blue
The Guardian Angel Comes
to Earth

#38: Violet/Green
Troubadour II
Discernment

#39: Violet/Gold
Egyptian Bottle II
The Puppeteer

#40: Red/Gold
"I Am"

#41: Gold/Gold
Wisdom Bottle
El d'Orado

#42: Yellow/Yellow
Harvest

#43: Turquoise/Turquoise
Creativity

#44: Pale Violet (Lilac)/ Pale Blue
The Guardian Angel

#45: Turquoise/Magenta
Breath of Love

#46: Green/Magenta
The Wanderer

#47: Royal Blue/Lemon
Old Soul

#48: Violet/Clear
Wings of Healing

#49: Turquoise/Violet
New Messenger

#50: Pale Blue/Pale Blue
El Morya

#51: Pale Yellow/Pale Yellow
Kuthumi

#52: Pale Pink/Pale Pink
Lady Nada

#53: Pale Green/Pale Green
Hilarion

#54: Clear/Clear
Serapis Bey

#55: Clear/Red
The Christ

#56: Pale Violet/Pale Violet
Saint Germain

#57: Pale Pink/Pale Blue
Pallas Athena & Aeolus

#58: Pale Blue/Pale Pink
Orion & Angelica

#59: Pale Yellow/Pale Pink
Lady Portia

#60: Blue/Clear
Lao Tsu & Kwan Yin

#61: Pale Pink/Pale Yellow
Sanat Kumara &
Lady Venus Kumara

#62: Pale Turquoise/
Pale Turquoise
Maha Chohan

#63: Emerald Green/
Pale Green
Djwal Khul & Hilarion

#64: Emerald Green/Clear
Djwal Khul

#65: Violet/Red
Head in Heaven and
Feet on Earth

#66: Pale Violet/Pale Pink
The Actress

#67: Magenta/Magenta
Divine Love
Love in the Little Things

#68: Blue/Violet
Gabriel

#69: Magenta/Clear
Sounding Bell

#70: Yellow/Clear
Vision of Splendor

#71: Pink/Clear
Essene Bottle II
The Jewel in the Lotus

#72: Blue/Orange
The Clown (Pagliacci)

#73: Gold/Clear
Chang Tsu

#74: Pale Yellow/Pale Green
Triumph

#75: Magenta/Turquoise
Go with the Flow

#76: Pink/Gold
Trust

#77: Clear/Magenta
The Cup

#78: Violet/Deep Magenta
Crown Rescue

#79: Orange/Violet
The Ostrich Bottle

#80: Red/Pink
Artemis

#81: Pink/Pink
Unconditional Love

#82: Green/Orange
Calypso

#83: Turquoise/Gold
Open Sesame

#84: Pink/Red
Candle in the Wind

#85: Turquoise/Clear
Titania

#86: Clear/Turquoise
Oberon

#87: Coral/Coral
The Wisdom of Love

#88: Green/Blue
Jade Emperor

#89: Red/Deep Magenta
Energy Rescue

#90: Gold/Deep Magenta
Wisdom Rescue

#91: Olive Green/Olive Green
Feminine Leadership

#92: Coral/Olive Green
Gretel

#93: Coral/Turquoise
Hansel

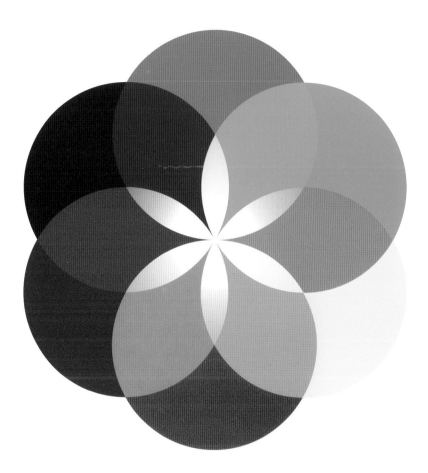

The Color Rose

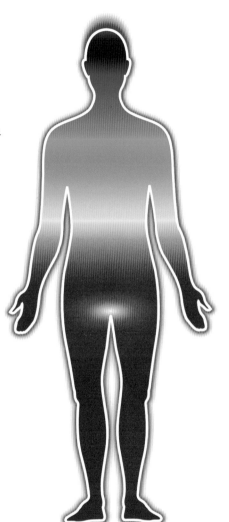

Eighth Chakra   Magenta

Crown Chakra   Violet

Third Eye   Royal Blue

Throat Chakra   Blue

Fourth-and-a-half Chakra
(ananda-khanda center)   Turquoise

Heart Chakra   Green

Solar Plexus Chakra   Yellow

Second Chakra   Orange

Base Chakra   Red and
Pink

Dev-Aura, the Aura-Soma
Training Center in
Tetford, England

Vicky Wall

all types of things). Finds it difficult to change his/her situation. Allows others to walk all over him/her.

Spiritual Level: Brings about the ability to more clearly recognize one's own path and to talk about spiritual matters with others. Helps overcome utopianism and exaggerated idealism. Inspires a deep understanding of the need for change, therefore resolving the despair that some changes bring with them.

Mental Level: Effective for those who have problems with authority. Effects a new sense of balance when the analytical mind is too strong. Establishes contact with seriousness, trust, discernment, and a feeling of time—that is, with respect to sequence and planning.

Emotional Level: Resolves old guilt feelings and discouragement, as well as past, emotionally loaded memories from childhood. Helpful at the beginning of a new relationship (also applies to professional relationships).

Physical Level: Helpful with shoulder problems, tennis elbow, adenoids, sinusitis. Balances the thymus gland and the thyroid.

Where to Apply the Substance: Around the chest area and along the hairline; with speech impediments, also around the throat/neck.

Affirmation: I open myself to love.

Distinctive Qualities: Beneficial for speech impediments, which have their origin in some type of trauma.

50
Name of Bottle: El Morya (see "Distinctive Qualities")
Color: Pale Blue/Pale Blue
Shakes Together As: Pale Blue
Chakra: Throat
Tarot Card: Ace of Cups
I Ching Sign: Fire above, wind/wood below, No. 50, "The Cauldron"
Main Theme: Readiness to live life from now on in harmony with the greater whole

Positive Personality Aspects: A pioneer who is selflessly committed. Is in harmony with his/her life purpose, fate, and soul. Trusts God and life. Is highly evolved spiritually; this person's love overflows into the world. Great talent for communication of different kinds. Knowledgeable in numerology and astrology. Possesses a clear mind. Forgives easily (others and him/herself) and is able to feel great joy. Can be detached enough to gain direct access to the subconscious.

Personality Aspects That Could Be Worked On: Has not yet overcome the extreme difficulties that arose in the past with his/her father. Probably has been mentally abused (brainwashed to a greater or lesser extent, but not necessarily by the father). Always wants somebody to care for him/her. Sees all things in life in a negative way. Is not at peace with him/herself and feels disconnected from (cultural) roots. A person blocked on all levels.

Spiritual Level: Makes faith more real, which means it shows in what one really believes. Brings spiritual inspiration and connection with the life purpose. Initiates a correspondence between God's will and one's own will. Helps open up to the light and for new realities that fit into our times.

Mental Level: Supports the integration of the male aspects of the personality and helps to balance a too-analytical view. Instills a clarity and balance if there are authority problems.

Emotional Level: Inspires profound peace and self-forgiveness. Balances emotional extremes. Releases blockages, especially those related to speech and communication.

Physical Level: Balances the thyroid gland; especially helps children with sore throats. Cools and calms in the most diverse circumstances.

Where to Apply the Substance: Around the entire throat.

Affirmation: Thy will be done through me.

Distinctive Qualities: Part of the Master Set (see Chapter 10).

51

Name of Bottle: Kuthumi
Color: Pale Yellow/Pale Yellow
Shakes Together As: Pale Yellow
Chakra: Solar Plexus
Tarot Card: King of Swords
I Ching Sign: Thunder above, thunder below, No. 51, "The Arousing" (Shock, Thunder)
Main Theme: The intellect in search of wisdom

Positive Personality Aspects: A spiritual warrior, a person who is willing to take the initiative to defend something. Is of high mental flexibility, thinks and acts independently. Teaches and leads in a supportive way without interfering too much. Inspires others to live up to their potential. Is a master of his/her own fate. The intellect is clear and strong, in a positive sense. Has a very good understanding of numbers (in all connections, from mathematics to numerology).

Personality Aspects That Could Be Worked On: A joyless person who can be very dogmatic and therefore goes through life with blinders on. Expects and fears all kinds of things instead of being in the present moment. Is inflexible. Has invested too much in the intellect and realizes that this is a hindrance to progress.

Spiritual Level: Inspires spiritual discrimination, empathy, and compassion. Helps to show others where they are destined to go. Brings more clarity to wisdom from the past.

Mental Level: Facilitates the process of solving intellectual problems and, as a result, aids in the integration of knowledge and wisdom that has been gained from this process. Stimulates mental flexibility. Brings forth an understanding of how the microcosm works.

Emotional Level: Aids in overcoming fears, especially fears of anticipation. Brings joy into a joyless life.

Physical Level: Helps with anorexia and bulimia, with chronic skin complaints, nausea, digestive ailments, and problems with assimilation.

Where to Apply the Substance: Around the solar plexus area.

Affirmation: I am standing at the gate and know that joy is just behind it.

Distinctive Qualities: Part of the Master Set. Opens up for perception of devas and angels, as well as for communication with them; also for the awareness of the entire mineral and plant realms and for communication, globally or in parts, with both.

52

Name of Bottle: Lady Nada
Color: Pale Pink/Pale Pink
Shakes Together As: Pale Pink
Chakra: Base and Crown
Tarot Card: Queen of Swords
I Ching Sign: Mountain above, mountain below, No. 52, "Keeping Still, Mountain"
Main Theme: To experience unconditional love

Positive Personality Aspects: A reformer who allows him/herself and others to be idealistic. Is concerned with questions of ecology and humanity. Has a lot of empathy; is not attached to material things. Possesses a very high level of concentration, which is very emphatic. That is apparent to everybody who is with this person. Cares in very practical ways for others, which often shows in his/her profession. Recognizes when other people need love and, so, gives it to them.

Personality Aspects That Could Be Worked On: Is still giving even when abused and exploited. Harms him/herself by this. Has a restless mind, can hardly relax. Feels fragmented and empty. Feels unloved. Everything is too much for this person. Indulges in spiritual illusions (for example, identifies with a very beautiful aspect of the self that he/she might have encountered during meditation, and does not recognize that he/she, like everyone else, still needs to work a lot on the self in order to realize this aspect).

Spiritual Level: Supports and speeds up the process of awakening. Helps to be concentrated during meditation. Brings spiritual illusions back to earth. Facilitates the understanding of the Christ energy, the Christ consciousness. (This energy has nothing to do with the historical Jesus and is accessible to each person, no matter whether he/she is Christian, Moslem...nonreligious, or even an atheist (see Chapter 10).

Mental Level: Calms a restless mind. Stimulates intuition as well as concentration; particularly helpful before and during examinations.

Emotional Level: Aids in the integration of positive aspects of the mother or, more abstractly, of the female role model. Facilitates the processing of possible abuse (not only with sexual, but also physical [beatings], mental and spiritual). In most cases, the victims are convinced they are unworthy and do not deserve love. This substance also assists in the process of resolving these difficulties and in the development of self-love.

Physical Level: Balances the whole hormone system. Useful for problems associated with the uterus, menstruation, and menopause.

Where to Apply the Substance: Around the abdomen. With mental problems, apply one drop to top vertebra at the head, one drop to the temples, and one drop to the neck, and rub in.

Affirmation: I love myself as I am.

Distinctive Qualities: Part of the Master Set. In past-life therapy, it can establish contact with Essene incarnations. This substance relates to the Third Eye with respect to music, meaning that it can intensify the experience and understanding of music.

Regarding the subject of "abuse," also see the "Distinctive Qualities" of Bottle #5.

53
Name of Bottle: Hilarion
Color: Pale Green/Pale Green
Shakes Together As: Pale Green
Chakra: Heart
Tarot Card: Knight of Swords
I Ching Sign: Wind/wood above, mountain below, No. 53, "Development"

(Gradual Progress)

Main Theme: The Way, the Truth, and Life (this is meant literally, not as a Christian reference)

Positive Personality Aspects: A practical scientist who understands the cosmic laws. Knows his/her way. Has a very good memory and discernment, knows exactly when he/she is on the wrong track or when a process is heading towards deceit. Because this person has become free of deep tension, he/she can easily attain altered states of consciousness.

Personality Aspects That Could Be Worked On: Harbors all kinds of guilt feelings within. Can be extremely envious and jealous. Feels disconnected from others. Believes that others deceive him/her. Finds that in the spiritual realm, materialism prevails. This person's dogmatic views do not change. Does not recognize the system of which he/she is a part, which leads to rigidity.

Spiritual Level: Helps to connect with nature in a spiritual way and to build more stamina. Inspires faith. Aids in perception of the different aspects of a situation and in finding a true direction. Deepens the spiritual connection through awareness of correct body posture, proper breathing, etc.

Mental Level: Refreshes the mind when there is the feeling of being stuck. Resolves phobias and hidden fears. Instills clarity into a situation when deception has occurred and when there are tendencies toward *self-deception*.

Emotional Level: Eases guilt feelings. Helps to cope with jealousy and envy, as well as with fears that are related to space (claustrophobia and agoraphobia). Makes it easier to live one's own truth. Helps the individual feel comfortable with him/herself.

Physical Level: Eases all chest problems, especially asthma and bronchitis. Gives a new body-consciousness (to those who are simply uncoordinated, but also to those who have suffered an accident, shock, rape).

Where to Apply the Substance: Around the entire heart area. When working with the body therapies mentioned below, apply on the whole body.

Affirmation: I find my own truth.

Distinctive Qualities: Part of the Master Set. In past-life therapy, it can establish contact with Lemurian incarnations. This bottle is often chosen by people who work with body therapies such as Rolfing, Trager, Alexander Technique, or Feldenkrais.

54
Name of Bottle: Serapis Bey
Color: Clear/Clear
Shakes Together As: Clear
Chakra: All chakras
Tarot Card: Page of Swords
I Ching Sign: Thunder above, lake below, No. 54, "The Marrying Maiden"
Main Theme: Cleansing and detoxification on all levels

Positive Personality Aspects: A philosopher with strong personal ideals. Has recognized a lot and has realized quite a bit, also. Understands conflict, pain, and suffering. Has a clear view of the most varied things and for the most different levels of problems. Has access to universal knowledge. A "rainbow warrior" (an expression by Vicky Wall), meaning that this person has the potential and strength to awaken the rainbow within. And to "awaken the rainbow" means to balance the chakras and to have them at one's fullest disposal.

Personality Aspects That Could Be Worked On: Holds on to institutions of the past. Always feels unprepared, is completely thrown by unexpected events. Is obsessed and tormented, places too much attention on details. Suffers enormously. This person's tears have washed the color out of his/her life.

Spiritual Level: Allows for a change in energy. Removes the cobwebs of the past. Brings old sexual matters into consciousness so that they can be solved. Aids in becoming aware of the light body (this is dealt with in Chapter 4). Cleanses, and is especially recommended during and after fasting.

Mental Level: Gives freedom of decision making as well as understanding in conflict and pain situations. Helps release exaggerated expectations and to accept what is there.

Emotional Level: Frees accumulated tears, which leads to refreshment. Aids in clearing deep levels of suffering and inner conflict. Gives courage to cope with difficult emotions.

Physical Level: Facilitates the cleansing process during a fast; is very detoxifying. Helps the body to eliminate water and mucus.

Where to Apply the Substance: Everywhere on the body.

Affirmation: Whether I laugh or cry, I see the rainbow in my tears.

Distinctive Qualities: Part of the Master Set.

Everyone incarnates on a color ray. This bottle in the first position shows that the subconscious of the person is not yet ready to give out information about his/her soul ray and personality ray. Serapis Bey can open the user to find the colors that relate closest to him/her. However, people should not force themselves to use this substance, nor should they persuade anybody to use it, because it can release deep inner processes—for example, related to problematic sexual experiences of the past—with which the user can only cope constructively when truly ready to look at these matters.

55

Name of Bottle: The Christ (not the historical Jesus is meant here, but the Christ consciousness—more about this in Chapter 10)
Color: Clear/Red
Shakes Together As: Intensive Light Red
Chakra: Base
Tarot Card: Ten of Swords
I Ching Sign: Thunder above, flame below, No. 55, "Abundance" (Fullness)
Main Theme: To develop sacrificial love

Positive Personality Aspects: A spiritual pioneer and also a pioneer in the concrete, material world. Is very aligned to the truth. Possesses a lot of wisdom but does not show off with it. Is willing to sacrifice him/herself for a higher cause. Often works without asking for money. (This is meant in the best sense—gives without expecting anything in return.) Is objective and can, once having embarked on a task, see exactly how it will end up. An idealist who manifests ideas in a practical way. Equality for women is a matter of concern for this person. Has no problems at all with sexuality. Understands the material side of life very well.

Personality Aspects That Could Be Worked On: Harbors a lot of frustration, resentment, and anger from the past. Has possibly been very affected by a material loss. On the one hand, suffers as far as worldly matters are concerned; on the other hand, is very focused on the material world and sensuality. Has had a lot of conflicting experiences in life and cannot cope with them. Demands a personal revelation (from the universe, from existence...) but that may not happen because this person is too tense.

Spiritual Level: Facilitates the process of initiation and transformation of the self. Creates a clear channel for energy. Leaders experience humility when using this substance. The feeling of being disconnected from existence is reduced.

Mental Level: Brings about clarity of thought. Helps to stop identifying with everything, as well as to let go of resentment.

Emotional Level: Frees the individual from the feeling that he/she is not being heard. Resolves anger and frustration and helps to transform these emotions in a positive way. Useful in overcoming childhood traumas, as well as the sense of being a martyr.

Physical Level: Helps with sexual problems of all kinds and with lack of energy. Acts as a detoxicant.

Where to Apply the Substance: Around the entire lower abdomen. (Should not be used too late in the afternoon or evening, because this substance is very energizing, which can lead to sleep problems.)

Affirmation: I have the energy to follow my ideals.

Distinctive Qualities: Part of the Master Set. Helps to awaken the kundalini power. Supports the process of coping with possible sexual abuse. The

Tarot card, "Ten of Swords," as well as this substance, relate to the test that shows whether or not someone is able to take on spiritual responsibility.

56

Name of Bottle: Saint Germain
Color: Pale Violet/Pale Violet (Lilac/Lilac)
Shakes Together As: Pale Violet (Lilac)
Chakra: Crown
Tarot Card: Nine of Swords
I Ching Sign: Fire above, mountain below, No. 56, "The Wanderer"
Main Theme: Releasing negativity on all levels

Positive Personality Aspects: A reformer and inspired teacher who is humorous, masters thought processes, and possesses a creative intellect. Can subordinate him/herself and knows when this is appropriate. Situations can be influenced positively through this person's presence; acts as a catalyst. Keeps fit; knows exercise is important for overall well-being. Possesses a strong intuition and strong psychic abilities. Likes to be on his/her own, feels at home in his/her own personal world, but also likes to travel and seek out new adventures.

Personality Aspects That Could Be Worked On: A martyr in the negative sense of the word. Is caught up in personal thought and behavior patterns, which is why this person's life circumstances do not change. Feels internally stressed and finds the material world threatening. A loner who feels homeless, in the literal and figurative sense. Longs to be anywhere else but here. Is trapped in his/her own world and in the past. Carries out physical castigation and physical training to the extreme.

Spiritual Level: Supports the search for higher truth. Frees the user from the difficulties that can arise if he/she is too occupied with the suffering of the world. Establishes a link with self-love and inner peace. Helps one live with less self-torment and to find sense in meditation practices. Awakens psychic abilities.

Mental Level: Interrupts thoughts that move in circles. Stimulates intuition. Helps release self-denial tendencies and patterns from the past.

Emotional Level: Clears negative emotional patterns, especially in relation to criticism. Gives clarity with respect to conflicts.

Physical Level: Can be calming—for example, with fever, overexcitement, insomnia. Helpful with migraine and nervous headaches. Is especially useful with children.

Where to Apply the Substance: Along the hairline.

Affirmation: I trust that my intuition is based on reason.

Distinctive Qualities: Part of the Master Set. Brings male and female aspects together. Helps people who believe they have had a religious experience to integrate it into a larger perspective—not to see it so much in a religious, but rather in a general, spiritual context. This substance relates very much to the energy of Jupiter.

57
Name of Bottle: Pallas Athena & Aeolus
Color: Pale Pink/Pale Blue
Shakes Together As: Pale Violet (Lilac)
Chakra: Base, Throat, and Crown
Tarot Card: Eight of Swords
I Ching Sign: Wind/wood above, wind/wood below, No. 57, "The Gentle" (The Penetrating, Wind)
Main Theme: To release the patterns of the past

Positive Personality Aspects: An artist who can express him/herself through writing, painting, music, dance, etc. Is dynamic and in the flow; does the right things at the right time. Finds it easy to go on "inner journeys" (visualization, meditation, dreams, etc.). Has access to great strength because male and female aspects are balanced. Has overcome many difficulties and is aware of his/her own limitations. Works for the advancement of humanity in different areas (art, society, ecology, and so on). Has access to knowledge, sometimes even to material things from the past (for example, through inheritance).

Personality Aspects That Could Be Worked On: Reason and emotions often conflict. Sets goals too high. It is difficult for this person to let go of the past. Male and female personality aspects are not balanced, which results in difficulties in integrating further personality aspects.

Spiritual Level: Establishes access to ancient knowledge, to creative inspiration from a deep (soul) level and to a balance of the male and female personality aspects. Shows where on the spiritual path the user is at the moment. Enables the individual to reduce dogmatic behavior and to communicate spiritual information in a human, understandable way.

Mental Level: Stimulates love of life, thereby instilling inner peace. Enables the person to get in "the flow." Encourages a positive view of the material side of life and of life in general.

Emotional Level: Harmonizes the emotional and mental level. Brings freshness into relationships.

Physical Level: Beneficial for all menstrual problems, especially with heavy bleeding. Also helps with speech impediments and dyslexia.

Where to Apply the Substance: Around the lower abdomen, around the throat, and along the hairline.

Affirmation: I let go and trust.

Distinctive Qualities: Part of the Master Set. In past-life therapy, it can establish contact with Ancient Egypt and Ancient Greece. Enables the user to better recall dreams.

58

Name of Bottle: Orion & Angelica
Color: Pale Blue/Pale Pink
Shakes Together As: Pale Violet (Lilac)
Chakra: Base, Throat, and Crown
Tarot Card: Seven of Swords
I Ching Sign: Lake above, lake below, No. 58, "The Joyous Lake"
Main Theme: Inner and outer journeys

Positive Personality Aspects: A sensitive person who can build bridges between matter and mind. Experiences the miracles of life like a child and uses this ability very constructively. This is meant in a very positive way. Can express him/herself skillfully and precisely; is well balanced and patient and in the present moment. Concerned with transformation. At the same time, is aware of his/her own Divine spark and also perceives the Divine spark in other people. Loves the earth, often works in ecological areas. Likes to travel.

Personality Aspects That Could Be Worked On: Manipulates him/herself and others with emotions. Is convinced that this is done in the name of truth. His/her "inner child" needs healing, which means that this person is emotionally immature. Finds it difficult to express feelings and has difficulty with physical contact.

Spiritual Level: Opens up to information from other dimensions and enables a recognition of the Divine spark in oneself and in others. Supports changes in this person's spiritual life. Cleanses—for example, after a stay in surroundings with a negative atmosphere.

Mental Level: Helps teenagers with problems during puberty. Eases emotional crises, especially those related to male or female role models (father or mother). This applies to teenagers as well as adults.

Emotional Level: Aids in overcoming irrational fears and frustrations of the "inner child." Helps to develop stronger resistance, to change negative feelings, and to reduce oversensitivity.

Physical Level: Increases the joy in touching and being touched. Helpful after operations of the spine and with all serious illnesses in children. Balances both sides of the body.

Where to Apply the Substance: Around the abdomen, the throat, and along the hairline.

Affirmation: I reach the here and now, and change is taking place.

Distinctive Qualities: Is part of the Master Set. This bottle is an intensive version of Bottle #20 (Blue/Pink). Everything that applies to that bottle does to this one, as well.

59
Name of Bottle: Lady Portia
Color: Pale Yellow/Pale Pink
Shakes Together As: Pale Yellow
Chakra: Base, "Second Chakra"
Tarot Card: Six of Swords
I Ching Sign: Wind above, water below, No. 59, "Dispersion" (Dissolution)
Main Theme: Justice and discernment

Positive Personality Aspects: An excellent speaker with great discernment and a sense of justice, who has a feeling for balance. Knows about the structures of the past, especially in view of religion; at the same time, possesses an orientation to the future. Acts selflessly. Is kind and at the same time possesses leadership qualities. This person's sense of humor and joy is transmitted to the people around him/her. Is in the process of awakening and enjoys this search. Is thankful for what life has to offer. Tells others what they need to hear.

Personality Aspects That Could Be Worked On: Cannot see what has been already achieved, but is always concentrating on what still needs to be done. Judges and condemns him/herself constantly. Talks too much. Even if very able and talented, has difficulty seeing what can be achieved. Has no joy in life. Harbors guilt feelings. Often a person with excess weight.

Spiritual Level: Establishes contact with the user's own truth. Brings spiritual discrimination, generosity, and gratitude. Encourages the individual to stop judging and condemning him/herself and others constantly.

Mental Level: Breaks up old patterns and leads to new understanding, also to new self-understanding. Helps to give up exaggerated analytical thinking.

Emotional Level: Assists in understanding that some things in life cannot be attained. Cleanses the emotional area very gently. Brings joy and helps overcome fears; especially the fear of not being good enough.

Physical Level: Facilitates elimination via colon and bladder. Eases skin complaints, especially during puberty.

Where to Apply the Substance: Around the entire abdomen.

Affirmation: I understand the laws of life, and I grow.

Distinctive Qualities: Part of the Master Set. Helps therapists and clients with rebirthing, especially when the client is already experienced with it.

60
Name of Bottle: Lao Tsu and Kwan Yin
Color: Blue/Clear
Shakes Together As: Pale Blue
Chakra: Throat
Tarot Card: 5 of Swords
I Ching Sign: Water above, lake below, No. 60, "Limitation"
Main Theme: To find such deep peace that one calmly accepts everything that life places in one's path

Positive Personality Aspects: Has attained wisdom because this person always questions him/herself and life anew (this is meant in the most positive sense). Is connected with the deepest depths. Recognizes the lessons that are inherent in difficult situations. On the one hand, he/she has a charismatic quietness and a charismatic silence, which means that through these qualities, can influence a situation very positively; on the other hand, though, it is a pleasure to talk to this person. Has a realistic evaluation of one's own abilities. Can receive very well, therefore is able to give (for example, by listening and thereby giving support to other people). Has developed a strong presence.

Personality Aspects That Could Be Worked On: Gives too much without being aware that overexertion is the result. Pays too much attention to other people's opinions and therefore, feels fragmented and disconnected. Hides one's own qualities. Finds it difficult to share what weighs heavily on the mind, which is, above of all, uncried tears. Has no feeling for proportions, which means that this person places too much importance on details.

Spiritual Level: Inspires feelings of peace. Frees from limitations. Helps keep the inner light burning—that is, maintains the awareness that something is living inside that can never be destroyed.

Mental Level: Brings the roots of unconscious suffering to awareness, thereby helping this person become free from that suffering. Makes it easier to question oneself and gives support to achieve positive, growth-facilitating results.

Emotional Level: Calms exaggerated impulsiveness. Helps to express emotional problems.

Physical Level: Soothing and cooling for infections in certain body parts. Relieves speech impediments that are of a physical origin (for example, cleft palate) by acting on the psychological level. That means that the cleft palate isn't cured, but the underlying problems are. Shame and bashfulness are reduced.

Where to Apply the Substance: Around the throat and neck.

Affirmation: I free myself from all limitations.

Distinctive Qualities: Part of the Master Set. Can act as an "in-between" substance and precursor for other Aura-Soma oils (see explanation of Bottle #11).

61
Name of Bottle: Sanat Kumara & Lady Venus Kumara
Color: Pale Pink/Pale Yellow
Shakes Together As: Pale Coral
Chakra: Base, "Second Chakra"
Tarot Card: Four of Swords
I Ching Sign: Wind above, lake below, No. 61, "Inner Truth"
Main Theme: Personal loss, transpersonal gain

Positive Personality Aspects: Is kind in everything he/she does, is positive and considerate. Knows what is good for him/herself. Sees own strengths, and expresses them in a natural manner. Has overcome sexual fears and problems and is balanced and happy in his/her sexuality. Possesses the talent for writing, teaching, and doing administrative work. Knows the secrets of success. An honest person with a lot of love and feeling, for him/herself and others. Uses meditation and reflection in very constructive ways.

Personality Aspects That Could Be Worked On: Needs an excessive amount of love and is concerned about it. These worries and fears are in the way and prevent this person from opening up to possible love. Tendency to enter into relationships that create dependency, which applies to people, but also to alcohol, drugs, etc. Is sexually immature, and suffers as a result. Has had a personal loss. Battles on, but has no real success. Believes that the masks people wear represent their real personalities, and is not able to look behind these masks.

Spiritual Level: Brings about a better understanding of suffering (one's own and that of other people). Beneficial for all relationship problems. Stimulates a deeper level of awareness, both in general and during meditation.

Mental Level: Helps cope with the results of possible mental abuse (mental abuse means, for example, that parents or teachers constantly tell a child that he/she is clumsy, stupid, and so on).

Emotional Level: Clears deep fears and other threatening feelings. Helps let go of injuries and grief of the past, even of the distant past.

Physical Level: Useful for (chronic) skin diseases, as well as problems with nerves—for example, Parkinson's and Alzheimer's disease. Helps come to a greater acceptance of the illness.

Where to Apply the Substance: Around the entire abdomen.

Affirmation: I learn and grow through the difficulties of life.

Distinctive Qualities: Part of the Master Set. In past-life therapy, this substance can establish contact with the mystical traditions in Ancient Egypt, Ancient Greece, and the times before. This substance relates to the energy of Venus. (Regarding abuse, see the "Distinctive Qualities" of Bottle #5.)

 # 62

Name of Bottle: Maha Chohan
Color: Pale Turquoise/Pale Turquoise
Shakes Together As: Pale Turquoise
Chakra: Heart, Ananda-Khanda Center, and Throat
Tarot Card: Three of Swords
I Ching Sign: Thunder above, mountain below, No. 62, "Preponderance of the Small"
Main Theme: Connection between intellect and spirituality

Positive Personality Aspects: A very inspired and intuitive person who can express creatively that which concerns the heart (through dance, singing, writing, etc.). Is modest and humble, loves people, and knows him/herself. Follows own path and inner guidance, which comes from "above." Helps others as a result. Has a strong connection with crystals and minerals, especially with quartz. Is very much in contact with the subconscious. Possesses talents for speaking and for work with computers, as well as for working in the mass media.

Personality Aspects That Could Be Worked On: Tendency to punish and condemn him/herself for all kinds of reasons. Is afraid to express feelings, which leads to physical complaints. Loves the wrong people. Probably, this person's heart has been broken and has never healed. Has difficulties with modern tools—for example, with computers (technophobia).

Spiritual Level: Helps to get on the "level above," from where one can see more clearly. Brings freedom from fear and the possibility of releasing old patterns. Facilitates communication with inner and outer space. Inspires humility, and trust in the "flow." Helps let go of unconscious pressure.

Mental Level: Releases creative blockages. Strengthens people who are prone to shocks, and supports them. Encourages the individual to suppress the tendency to punish him/herself.

Emotional Level: Helps heal a broken heart and aids in processing the past. This substance is beneficial to people who have loved someone who was not good for them to come to terms with the resulting pain. Reduces feelings of isolation.

Physical Level: Balances the thymus gland. Soothes the heart. Helps with asthma, bronchitis, and speech impediments.

Where to Apply the Substance: Around the entire chest area and around the throat/neck.

Affirmation: I go with the flow of life.

Distinctive Qualities: Part of the Master Set. Relates to the Uranus principle.

63
Name of Bottle: Djwal Khul & Hilarion
Color: Emerald Green/Pale Green
Shakes Together As: Green
Chakra: Heart
Tarot Card: Two of Swords
I Ching Sign: Water above, fire below, No. 63, "After Completion"
Main Theme: Learning to understand the purpose of life

Positive Personality Aspects: A very open person who has the courage to speak the truth. Is always in the right place at the right time. Is assured of his/her own success, even if it will be success that occurs later in life. Is ready for any situation. A good referee, who is in tune with other people's needs. A practical idealist who believes in tomorrow and who has understood his/her life's purpose. Is selfless and understands the worries of those he/she is in contact with. Has great perseverance. A Good Samaritan in the best sense of the term. Possibly works for charities. Possesses the ability to make new discoveries in science.

Personality Aspects That Could Be Worked On: Indulges in negative feelings and has great difficulties seeing the positive side of things. Arrogance can hinder this person's success. Keeps him/herself imprisoned in fear and narrow belief systems. This kind of behavior is in the way, especially when he/she wants to see the truth. Has not used youth well. Cannot handle time.

Spiritual Level: Brings about a sense of peace and a feeling of renewal.

Establishes a connection with the real purpose of life, as well as own true ideals.

Mental Level: Encourages the release of phobias, especially agoraphobia and claustrophobia. This substance balances people who tend to give too much.

Emotional Level: Opens up to deep joy. Helps overcome fears and boundary problems.

Physical Level: Useful for chest problems and pain in the upper back.

Where to Apply the Substance: Around the entire chest area.

Affirmation: I am in the right place, at the right time, doing the right thing.

Distinctive Qualities: Part of the extended Master Set. In past-life therapy, this substance can establish contact with incarnations in the time of persecution (for example, witch hunts), and can help to process the trauma that resulted.

64

Name of Bottle: Djwal Khul
Color: Emerald Green/Clear
Shakes Together As: Green
Chakra: Heart
Tarot Card: Ace of Swords
I Ching Sign: Flame above, water below, No. 64, "Before Completion"
Main Theme: The only constant in life is change

Positive Personality Aspects: A seeker of truth who explores truth through his/her feelings. Has understood that life is about learning. Loves to investigate the patterns that work in nature. Always strives for balance. Uses the mind as a tool. A very determined person who feels drawn to high emotions (love, compassion, etc.). A crusader and fighter, who does the right things at the right time. Is in control of his/her thoughts and fate (this is meant in a positive way).

Personality Aspects That Could Be Worked On: Is very easily disappointed and possessed by fear. Holds on to material things. For emotional reasons, often compromises, which damages the integrity. Holds on to grief instead of going deeper to explore the reasons behind it and working with it, even though this person would have the potential and opportunities to do so. Indulges in false modesty. Does not want to look at the difficulties in life because is unsure where his/her path leads. If this person would turn to the light, he/she would very easily see what the true goals are.

Spiritual Level: Facilitates an understanding of the cycles of life and death. Helps gain wisdom from life's experiences. Inspires joy. A bottle for a new beginning, which helps to bring the individual's own destiny into a new direction.

Mental Level: Supports the search for truth. Injects clarity into the subconscious in order to find out which tendencies rule this person's behavior.

Emotional Level: Helps release feelings that have not been let out. Also brings balance and clarity into the emotional life. Encourages the person to adapt to emotional change. Brings about a deep relationship with nature.

Physical Level: Beneficial for all problems of the chest and heart. Aids detoxification, especially where fear and anger have built up in the body and have, thereby, stored up poison.

Where to Apply the Substance: Around the entire chest area.

Affirmation: May the spirit of truth come to earth so I can find the inner light.

Distinctive Qualities: Part of the Master Set. Useful for people who are searching for hidden patterns in life—for example, astrologers.

65
Name of Bottle: Head in Heaven and Feet on Earth
Color: Violet/Red
Shakes Together As: Dark Red
Chakra: Base and Crown
Tarot Card: King of Pentacles

I Ching Sign: None (ends with #64)
Main Theme: Identical to the name of the bottle

Positive Personality Aspects: Is very interested in transformation on a psychological, emotional, and physical level. Is in contact with the "inner child." Has "the head in heaven and the feet on earth." Knows where he/she is and what his/her destination is. Dreams are fulfilled because this person knows what needs to be done to fulfill them. Has progressive ideas and a very positive, passionate side. Loves freedom, morale (in the positive sense), and strength. Is very strong and able to awaken him/herself and others. Is clairvoyant. Has no problems with material matters.

Personality Aspects That Could Be Worked On: Gets caught up in feelings such as anger, rage, and resentment. Broods too much, which results predominantly in difficulties with material matters. Holds on to frustrations, out of which all kinds of mental and physical problems arise. Feels more important than he/she actually is.

Spiritual Level: Brings spirituality to earth. "Grounds" generally, but leads the user into very "high" dimensions at the same time. Stimulates the energy that is needed to provide the service to the world to which one is called. Supports people who feel exhausted by their leadership duties.

Mental Level: Encourages fulfillment, productivity, and renewed energy. Improves the self-image. Injects clarity into thoughts; helps to better distribute mental energies when one's head is "full."

Emotional Level: Assists in tackling anger and transforming it into something constructive—for example, into discipline. Brings about a sense of distance so that reaction can be transformed into action.

Physical Level: Frees the energy flow in the body, especially when thinking has hindered it. Is especially suitable for stimulating a flow of energy to the legs and feet. Helpful with problems in the lower back area.

Where to Apply the Substance: Around the lower abdomen and along the hairline.

Affirmation: I know where I am, and I know where I am going.

Distinctive Qualities: Shows whether somebody is putting his/her energies into people or situations where they get abused or where they get lost. Useful in guiding frequent sexual fantasies into a direction where the passion that is in the background can express itself differently and more constructively.

66

Name of Bottle: The Actress
Color: Pale Violet/Pale Pink
Shakes Together As: Pale Violet (Lilac)
Chakra: Base and Crown
Tarot Card: Queen of Pentacles
I Ching Sign: None
Main Theme: To surround oneself with beauty

Positive Personality Aspects: A brave, peaceloving, and cheerful person. Steps back in order to let others have a turn. Is intelligent and has a strong sense of responsibility. Supports others, is loyal and affectionate. Works intensively on finding the true self. Has a lot of motherly energy (in the positive sense). Uses feminine intuition to help others. Knows that life requests that one play different parts, and this person plays these parts supremely well without identifying with them too much.

Personality Aspects That Could Be Worked On: Is extremely sensitive and easily hurt. Steps back too often. Has difficulty in deciding what is important. Had various difficulties in childhood, mainly with the parents. Possibly, does not want to be here (that is, does not want to be incarnated). Tends to be too idealistic.

Spiritual Level: Helps people who are very concerned about external beauty to find internal beauty as well. Connects the user to the true duty of service, which has to be fulfilled in this lifetime, and then gives the strength to pursue it.

Mental Level: Assists in detaching from possessions and obsessions and to use the energy, which had flowed into these things, generally and constructively.

Emotional Level: Makes it easier to accept love. This substance inspires a realistic view of people, especially of someone's parents, leads to liberation from them, and thereby brings about the possibility of integration.

Physical Level: Helps with gynecological problems, insomnia, and nervous headaches.

Where to Apply the Substance: Around the entire abdomen and along the hairline.

Affirmation: I pay attention to who is on the stage of my life.

Distinctive Qualities: Brings actors in contact with the essence of the parts they have to play.

67

Name of Bottle: Divine Love, Love in the Little Things
Color: Magenta/Magenta
Shakes Together As: Magenta
Chakra: All chakras, also the "Eighth"
Tarot Card: Knight of Pentacles
I Ching Sign: None
Main Theme: Spirituality in action

Positive Personality Aspects: A very creative person who serves others. Acts for the cause, not for acceptance by others. Has understood how important and valuable the small things in life are. Lives spirituality in everyday life. Has deep understanding and affinity with the earth. This person's love is great and expands beyond the personal. Knows of the immortality of the soul and that the only guarantee in life is change.

Personality Aspects That Could Be Worked On: A tendency toward overexertion and overwork. Is easily disappointed. Perceives life as very difficult. Searches desperately for Divine love, because the love he/she receives from other people "is not enough." Wishes life would present all answers.

Spiritual Level: Helps to bring love into the little everyday things. Connects with the inner teacher. Stimulates awareness. Brings practical connections into spirituality. Dissolves spiritual disillusionment.

Mental Level: Increases concentration, as well as the ability to be silent and patient. Helpful with depression, especially when related to a lack of love.

Emotional Level: Frees from the exaggerated need to compare oneself with others. Lets the user see him/herself as he/she really is. Brings tenderness into passionate emotions.

Physical Level: Beneficial for all heart conditions. Stimulates adrenal production. Acts as a mild diuretic.

Where to Apply the Substance: Everywhere on the body (also excellent for use as a body oil).

Affirmation: I wait patiently for the Divine to reveal itself in my life.

Distinctive Qualities: Helps all chakras to function better. Useful in rebirthing, and also in other therapies, when a higher level has been attained and something new is to begin. Generally supportive when a new chapter in life begins.

68

Name of Bottle: Gabriel
Color: Blue/Violet
Shakes Together As: Royal Blue
Chakra: Throat, Third Eye, and Crown
Tarot Card: Page of Pentacles
I Ching Sign: None
Main Theme: Peace and spiritual understanding

Positive Personality Aspects: An artist who brings ideals into the material world. May be working as a healer, therapist, social worker, or spiritual teacher. A good organizer who can get along with other people extremely well. Can concentrate well and is patient. A very warm person who helps others with their transformation. Is able to express him/herself well. Lives a new spiritual philosophy in which psychic abilities and spirituality combine. This person's relationships are very dynamic and unconventional, which also applies to friendships and relationships formed at work. A bringer of peace.

Personality Aspects That Could Be Worked On: Talks without thinking. Does not reveal feelings. A loner who does not know how to get along with other people. Even as an adult, this person behaves like an adolescent. Has difficulties with the father and the authority principle. Cannot express spirituality. Feels guilty, as if there are debts to pay, possibly karmic debts. Pretends to be brave even when very afraid.

Spiritual Level: Supports transformation processes. Brings concentration and peace into spiritual problems. Helps gain clarity about ideals, and then brings about the ability to express them better.

Mental Level: Gives structure to thought before it is expressed. Assists in breaking free of conventions and in the formulation of a personal philosophy. Promotes the ability to plan and organize and to make ideas acceptable in groups.

Emotional Level: Connects to a more realistic view in the emotional area. Helps to integrate the male role model (the father).

Physical Level: Calms in all contexts, especially with throat problems.

Where to Apply the Substance: Around the throat and along the hairline.

Affirmation: I finish that which needs finishing so that a new beginning is possible.

Distinctive Qualities: If the bottle appears in the third position, it can mean that something new and unexpected lies ahead.

This substance stimulates the ability to grow in relationships and to see them as challenges.

69
Name of Bottle: Sounding Bell
Color: Magenta/Clear
Shakes Together As: Magenta

Chakra: All chakras, also the "Eighth"
Tarot Card: Ten of Pentacles
I Ching Sign: None
Main Theme: The power of love

Positive Personality Aspects: A successful person who is happy when working creatively. Has found his/her life purpose and understands life. Lives passions in a constructive and healthy way. Has gained material success and emotional satisfaction, often as a result of having a family and feeling content within this family unit. What this person has learned, he/she can pass on very well. Is interested in the well-being of the people that he/she interacts with. Is very concerned about peace. Often invests money in projects such as Amnesty International.

Personality Aspects That Could Be Worked On: Thinks he/she does not need to learn any more. Has many extreme personality streaks. Does not believe that he/she is getting the love that is needed and, therefore, carries a lot of frustration within. Strives for success in an intense way. Is unable to step back and view his/her own situation in a neutral way.

Spiritual Level: Encourages the user to follow a discipline, especially if the ideals behind it are seen as meaningful. Brings about breakthroughs. Enables the individual to contact the universal consciousness. Opens up to the perception of beauty in the material dimension.

Mental Level: Helps keep the connection when too many things are happening in life. Rebuilds the self-image after a breakdown.

Emotional Level: Fills the void after too much passion has been expressed. Lets suppressed tears flow. After these tears, the user does not feel fatigued but rather, refreshed.

Physical Level: Helps with impotence and frigidity, as well as with certain eye conditions—for example, with extreme short-sightedness or farsightedness. (In these cases, apply the substance to the temples and the neck.)

Where to Apply the Substance: Everywhere on the body (excellent as a body oil).

Affirmation: Between extremes, I find balance in my life.

Distinctive Qualities: None.

70
Name of Bottle: Vision of Splendor
Color: Yellow/Clear
Shakes Together As: Yellow
Chakra: Solar Plexus
Tarot Card: Nine of Pentacles
I Ching Sign: None
Main Theme: To gain greater clarity

Positive Personality Aspects: A sincere person who possesses a strong intellect, combined with empathy. Has knowledge from the past and is interested in philosophy. Finds joy in meditation. Knows him/herself very well. Is patient, active, and loves to be in nature. Can talk about inner experiences very well.

Personality Aspects That Could Be Worked On: This person is afraid to reveal him/herself, so there is a tendency to stay out of life. An inactive loner. Hides his/her talents, acts in an overintellectual manner (meaning that this person exaggerates self-portrayal to the extent that he/she makes a repulsive or suspicious impression on others).

Spiritual Level: Connects to the astral world and can remove confusion that occurred in connection with that aspect. Provides protection. Helps to overcome lethargy. Aids in gaining insights, especially into the nature of consciousness.

Mental Level: Removes mental confusion and intellectual self-satisfaction. Brings joy, especially in and of one's own thought processes. Connects with inner wisdom. Facilitates integration of newly acquired knowledge (does not apply to children, only to adults).

Emotional Level: Awakens ambition (in the positive sense). Helps to cope with loneliness and to find contentment.

Physical Level: Calming if somebody has the feeling of being trapped in the body. Eases certain skin complaints. Useful with compulsive eating and anorexia and with difficulties of assimilation.

Where to Apply the Substance: Around the entire solar plexus area.

Affirmation: By opening myself to joy, I gain clarity.

Distinctive Qualities: Can facilitate "automatic writing."

71

Name of Bottle: Essene Bottle II/The Jewel in the Lotus
Color: Pink/Clear
Shakes Together As: Pink
Chakra: Base
Tarot Card: Eight of Pentacles
I Ching Sign: None
Main Theme: Self-acceptance

Positive Personality Aspects: Has a lot of love, empathy, intuition, and creativity. Is gifted in dealing with the sick. Behaves in a very tender, caring, and selfless way. Understands that we create the reality around us, both the "positive" and the "negative." Is able to love from a distance without expecting anything in return. The same applies for healing—often without the other person knowing where the healing energy comes from. Interestingly enough, this person also possesses a great talent for advertising and public relations. Has overcome many fears because he/she has learned to care for and love him/herself.

Personality Aspects That Could Be Worked On: Feels unloved. Does not want to look within. Believes that he/she is always being tested. Repeats the same mistakes without learning from them. Has no discernment, especially not for where his/her care is appropriate and appreciated and where it falls flat. Finds it especially difficult to care of one's own needs.

Spiritual Level: Expands sensuality. Brings discernment and the ability to give care and love to oneself. Supports development of healing powers. Helps recognize that all life circumstances are self-created.

Mental Level: Assists in overcoming irrational fears. Brings female qualities into the mind—for example, intuition, empathy, and receptivity.

Emotional Level: Encourages the person to look within and to cope with
what one finds there, in a loving, nonjudgmental way. Releases fears, especially those related to the feeling of not being loved.

Physical Level: Beneficial for all gynecological complaints, especially
with irregular bleeding. Brings tenderness into sexuality.

Where to Apply the Substance: Around the lower abdomen. Additionally, a
drop may be applied to the vertebrae at the top of the head.

Affirmation: "Be still, and know, I am God."

Distinctive Qualities: In past-life therapy, this substance can connect with
Essene incarnations (see description of Bottle #11), as well as with the
Christ Consciousness (see Chapter 10).

72

Name of Bottle: The Clown (Pagliacci)
Color: Blue/Orange
Shakes Together As: Violet flecked with Gold
Chakra: "Second Chakra" and Throat
Tarot Card: Seven of Pentacles
I Ching Sign: None
Main Theme: To free the "sad clown"

Positive Personality Aspects: A person who has a lot of self-respect, without being arrogant. Knows his/her emotional needs, whereby a sense of
independence has been reached. Speaks from the depth of his/her own
experience, thereby touching others. Insights and instincts truly come from
deep within and can also materialize, for example, in art. A person who is
devoted to his/her work. Often this person works as an artist, gardener, or
as a therapist to those with sexual problems. Can give and receive well. Is
able to give up his/her "little ego" for something greater. Has a lot of
humor, radiates harmony and humility. Is able to step aside repeatedly and,
thus, constantly view things anew.

Personality Aspects That Could Be Worked On: Has had a deep shock, about which he/she can hardly speak. Leans towards relationships in which there is a sense of dependency. Tends toward addiction. Has difficulty letting in and expressing feelings. A childish, defiant person who needs recognition and appreciation to the extreme.

Spiritual Level: Stimulates insight and deep happiness. Aids the user in expressing his/her inner truth. Brings peace after a deep spiritual shock. Connects the individual with true humility.

Mental Level: Allows for an understanding of mental processes. Makes it easier to differentiate whether the "little ego" or the higher self is speaking.

Emotional Level: Helps realize which personality aspect is speaking now. Enables the user to care for his/her own emotional needs.

Physical Level: Useful with sexual problems, especially frigidity and impotence, and after sexual or physical abuse. (For abuse, see also "Distinctive Qualities" of Bottle #5.)

Where to Apply the Substance: Around the entire trunk.

Affirmation: "I assure you that whoever does not receive the Kingdom of God like a child will never enter it."

Distinctive Qualities: This substance is said to be able to change cellular structure and, thus prevent possible hereditary diseases and genetically caused illnesses. Helps attain harmony with one's own instincts.

 # 73
Name of Bottle: Chang Tsu
Color: Gold/Clear
Shakes Together As: Gold
Chakra: Solar Plexus
Tarot Card: Six of Pentacles
I Ching Sign: None
Main Theme: To transmit deep insights

Positive Personality Aspects: An independent thinker who has developed consciousness to a great extent. Can express the knowledge that is within very well. Possesses teaching talents. Has the capacity to overcome many fears. Truly wants to get to know him/herself because he/she comprehends that this is necessary. Is able to develop an excellent discernment in all areas of life. Can see common ground with others, and is, therefore, able to create a positive atmosphere. Understands that one is all the richer the more one gives.

Personality Aspects That Could Be Worked On: Expects that things "just happen" without the need to take action. As a child, was probably burdened with too much responsibility. Has problems sharing and giving. A person who secretly suffers with fears. Pursues the search for perfection with intensity, but without love. Strives for gold outside, thereby losing contact with the light within.

Spiritual Level: Brings recognition of what the user truly knows. Connects with the inner light. Brings awareness of the fact that a person attracts and brings into his/her life that which relates to him or her. Instills discrimination into spiritual matters.

Mental Level: Shows how thought processes work and in which patterns one keeps getting caught up. Thus, the contents of this bottle stimulate independent thinking. Brings about discernment, especially with respect to whether or not, in certain processes, the ego wants to assert itself or not.

Emotional Level: Assists in coping with deep fears. Releases the feeling of always having to look cheerful. Helps the person accept his/her own strength and authority.

Physical Level: Useful with digestion, elimination, and assimilation problems. Promotes acceptance of one's own body.

Where to Apply the Substance: Around the entire belly.

Affirmation: Happy is the person who can laugh at oneself.

Distinctive Qualities: The contents of this bottle represent a deeper version of Bottle #70.

 # 74

Name of Bottle: Triumph
Color: Pale Yellow/Pale Green
Shakes Together As: Pale Green
Chakra: Solar Plexus and Heart
Tarot Card: Five of Pentacles
I Ching Sign: None
Main Theme: To bring clarity into difficult emotional situations

Positive Personality Aspects: A happy, cheerful, kind person who is concerned about harmony and balance, as well as about finding the meaning of life. Speaks the truth even if this could get him/her into trouble. Has no prejudices and, therefore, gives a lot of warmth to other people. Believes love to be the elixir of life. Learns from mistakes. Is generous with everything, especially with time. Is connected and in harmony with personal feelings.

Personality Aspects That Could Be Worked On: This person often says: "You don't take me seriously!" Needs a great deal of attention and recognition. Finds the emotional side of life disappointing. Feels his/her shortcomings acutely. Does not want to share time or experiences with other people. Doesn't understand him/herself or others. Cannot express feelings. Tends to judge and condemn others.

Spiritual Level: Connects the user with deepest knowledge and with what is true for him/her. Helps truly recognize him/herself. As such, this person comes to know what can be done regarding progression on the spiritual path (for example, practice Yoga, connect more with nature, etc.). Promotes spiritual generosity—for example, helps understand that there are many different ways that lead to God.

Mental Level: Stimulates increased self-understanding and a reduction of self-criticism, but nevertheless, allows the user to see what needs to be changed. Helps to be more discriminating.

Emotional Level: Clears past emotional patterns (also from past lives). Shines a light on them so that they can be worked on. Assists in overcoming disappointment, as well as anticipation fears, especially in matters of the heart.

Physical Level: Beneficial for varicose veins, cramps, skin problems, and all emotionally caused illnesses. Supports digestion; strengthens the nerves.

Where to Apply the Substance: Around the heart and solar plexus area.

Affirmation: The way is the goal.

Distinctive Qualities: This bottle has a lot to do with emotions. It is especially useful for emotional problems and is highly recommended, for example, at the beginning of a new relationship.

75
Name of Bottle: Go with the Flow
Color: Magenta/Turquoise
Shakes Together As: Magenta
Chakra: All chakras; can be used on the whole body; especially effective above the chest
Tarot Card: Four of Pentacles
I Ching Sign: None
Main Theme: Identical to the name of the bottle

Positive Personality Aspects: Can see things from an unusual perspective and can impart this perspective to others. Has great creativity, as well as an eye for detail. At the same time, this person is cognizant of the overall view of a situation. Knows that one often has to work hard for the things that are important. What this individual does, he/she does well. Is very energetic, strong, and courageous. Supports others with love. Is interested in spiritual and philosophical matters and likes to talk about them. Has a connection with a depth within, which only very few attain. Shares this wisdom with others.

Personality Aspects That Could Be Worked On: He/she always asks: "Why me? Why is this happening to me?" Feels like a victim. Wants to become free from his/her own life; does not know how to change his/her life. Can reach a high degree of despair, similar to that of the Dutch painter, van Gogh, who cut off his ear. Tends to see the painful and negative aspects of a situation instead of concentrating on the growth opportunities. Carries a lot of anger and resentment within, which overshadows the love that is present.

Spiritual Level: Helps the user optimize talents and overcome illusions. Opens to an acceptance of fate. Clears the way to recognize what he/she truly wants to do for him/herself spiritually, and then to realize it.

Mental Level: Allows the user feel less victimized. Brings information from the subconscious into the conscious. Calms the intellect and brings emotions to the surface.

Emotional Level: Connects the consciousness with anger and resentment; supports coping with, or working on, love issues. Helps the user talk about emotions.

Physical Level: Beneficial for all chronic illnesses, neck problems, pains, especially with arthritis and rheumatism.

Where to Apply the Substance: Everywhere on the body.

Affirmation: I aim to see love anew.

Distinctive Qualities: The contents of this bottle help to release the energy when it has built up and become blocked. Facilitates the ability to "go with the flow" again.

76
Name of Bottle: Trust
Color: Pink/Gold
Shakes Together As: Orange
Chakra: Base and Solar Plexus
Tarot Card: Three of Pentacles
I Ching Sign: None
Main Theme: To reach one's potential through self-love

Positive Personality Aspects: A tender, gentle person who gives way to life's difficulties and goes with the flow. Is successful but not arrogant. This person's success is based on consistency. Lets things grow by intuitive wisdom and then gives birth to them. Has powers of extreme concentration and dedication, especially in regard to this wisdom. A genius in his/her field. Can rely on him/herself and is self-determined. A self-made person. Can express feelings very clearly. Has the gift of moving forward and backward in time, also to enter past lives and to delve into them in order to attain knowledge and wisdom.

Personality Aspects That Could Be Worked On: A rigid, self-centered person who does not want to submit to the stress of life. Believes that he/she invests more in life than is received in turn. Thinks that he/she is not getting the love that is needed. Generally fearful, especially so with regard to expressing love. Difficulty in opening up to love. Tendency to work constantly, instead of taking a break at times just to "play."

Spiritual Level: Instills wisdom of the past into the present and makes it applicable. Opens to psychic abilities and deep memories.

Mental Level: Helps the intellect to open with deep wisdom. Releases confusion and fears from deep within the self by learning self-respect.

Emotional Level: Encourages the patience to hold back in certain situations, as well as the ability to care for and love oneself.

Physical Level: Balances the hormonal system. Brings clarity into thinking. Supports assimilation.

Where to Apply the Substance: Around the entire abdomen.

Affirmation: I love you so that I set you free.

Distinctive Qualities: It is possible that this person belongs to a secret group. In past-life therapy, it can help the individual enter previous lives more easily. Supports rebirthing work. Can point out that abuse has taken place, especially when this bottle is chosen by a woman (for more about this subject, see "Distinctive Qualities" of Bottle #5).

77

Name of Bottle: The Cup
Color: Clear/Magenta
Shakes Together As: Magenta
Chakra: All chakras; can be used all over the body
Tarot Card: Two of Pentacles
I Ching Sign: None
Main Theme: The power of the light becomes the power of life

Positive Personality Aspects: An athlete or sportsperson who is also interested in spiritual matters. Is able to question him/herself. Has a lot of charisma and persuasiveness; can bring clarity into unclear situations. Carries the Christ Consciousness within. Is in harmony with the cosmic laws and the Divine plan. Has access to love "from above."

Personality Aspects That Could Be Worked On: Needs love excessively. Does not change even though he/she knows it would be important to do so. Justifies whatever action is taken by him/herself. Cannot accept being loved. Manipulates others to get the love he/she wants and is not satisfied with what is received. This person's need for perfectionism is exaggerated in all areas of life. It is possible that he/she leans toward sexual extremes.

Spiritual Level: Brings Divine love down to earth. By stimulating the mental aspect, this substance helps spirituality to develop, which means that it promotes the power of discrimination. Helps to attain clear information from above.

Mental Level: Reveals the qualities of the person. Helps to distance the individual from personal interests and to place the interests of the group at the forefront.

Emotional Level: Releases the need for self-justification. Brings exaggerated ideals back to reality, especially when related to relationships. Stimulates the ability to laugh about oneself.

Physical Level: Balances the hormonal system. Relieves constipation and can help alleviate bad breath, which is caused by constipation.

Where to Apply the Substance: Everywhere on the body.

Affirmation: I let go of my illusions and see clearly.

Distinctive Qualities: In past-life therapy, can connect with Essene incarnations (see Bottle #11).

78

Name of Bottle: Crown Rescue
Color: Violet/Deep Magenta
Shakes Together As: Deep Magenta
Chakra: Crown
Tarot Card: Ace of Pentacles
I Ching Sign: None
Main Theme: The full power from above comes to earth to help humanity

Positive Personality Aspects: A truly psychic person who has recognized and accepted his/her life purpose and vocation. Has also recognized his/her own Divine aspect and accepted it. The body, mind, and soul are unified. Is always in the right place at the right time. Discovers and lives who he/she is. Has recognized that life is Divine and is the greatest teacher, especially regarding matters of the heart. As this person's greatest gift, he/she possesses an indestructible will; however, at the same time, this individual is humble, in the best sense.

Personality Aspects That Could Be Worked On: Carries deep grief inside, which calls for its release. Has difficulty looking at his/her own shadow. Cries crocodile tears because is of the opinion that fate is treating him/her unjustly. Has experienced extreme losses and gains in life. Feels very experienced and, therefore, has a lack of freshness. Is characterized by prejudices and dissatisfaction. Spiritual life is completely overshadowed by matters of the material world. Great desire for worldly pleasures.

Spiritual Level: Helps understand the laws of karma. Focuses and brings concentration in meditation and prayer. Enables the soul to understand that deepest satisfaction is attained through service. Opens the Third Eye.

Mental Level: Connects the person with ancient wisdom and with ideas of how this wisdom can be rephrased and made applicable to the present time. Brings realization of the conditions we create ourselves by the programming of our unconscious. Because of the dawning of consciousness, which this substance introduces, facilitates a letting go of unwanted patterns.

Emotional Level: Brings joy back into life after a period of grieving. Supports deep work with the "inner child." Helps with oversensitivity in all grief situations, as well as with transitions of all kind (death, birth, psychological traumas, loss of employment, etc.).

Physical Level: Has the same effects as Bottle #1 (Blue/Deep Magenta). Is especially effective with headaches and migraine.

Where to Apply the Substance: Along the hairline, possibly also around the throat and neck, on the Third Eye, and the vertebrae at the head.

Affirmation: I invite spirit into all areas of my life.

Distinctive Qualities: This bottle was the first to be born after Vicky Wall's death. It is also called "Divine Rescue." In psychotherapy, this substance helps to bring light into the past, thereby creating success in the present. Relates to the Pleiades, the "Big Bear," and Canopis. This substance can be helpful to those who want to see devas, angels, and so on.

79
Name of Bottle: The Ostrich Bottle
Color: Orange/Violet
Shakes Together As: Orange
Chakra: "Second Chakra" and Crown
Tarot Card: None
I Ching Sign: None
Main Theme: Spiritual shock

Positive Personality Aspects: A very happy person who has gained deep insights and uses them to serve others. Acts instead of reacting. Searches for spiritual truth. Very effectively supports people who are experiencing hardships. Has found a balance between spirituality and emotions. Is deeply involved in his/her own task and enjoys fulfilling it, even if it is difficult and costs him/her a lot.

Personality Aspects That Could Be Worked On: This person's thoughts are ruled by feelings. Does not want to surrender but wants to run away ("like an ostrich"). Carries old heartaches within. May have been disappointed by a spiritual teacher. Is in deep shock because he/she has lost somebody who meant a lot to him/her.

Spiritual Level: Releases spiritual shocks and brings through the information contained therein so it can be integrated, which can result in great inner growth.

Mental Level: Assists in releasing old patterns, thereby helping the individual reach his/her potential.

Emotional Level: Heals relationships that are dependency and co-dependency related. Promotes independence and self-love.

Physical Level: Useful with sexual problems, especially when caused by guilt feelings. Also helps with diarrhea and assimilation problems.

Where to Apply the Substance: Along the hairline and around the abdomen.

Affirmation: I gladly accept the challenges of life.

Distinctive Qualities: Can point out that someone is confronted by his/her own death or the death of a friend or relative.

Helps break free from addictions. In past-life therapy, it can connect with incarnations in Ancient Egypt.

 # 80
Name of Bottle: Artemis
Color: Red/Pink
Shakes Together As: Red
Chakra: Base
Tarot Card: None
I Ching Sign: None
Main Theme: Awakening to the power of love

Positive Personality Aspects: A very energetic person who knows how much energy, power, strength, and courage he/she possesses. Is successful in work and uses his/her intuition. Handles the material side of life very well. Is awakened very quickly to the spiritual. Has had a direct experience with the Christ Consciousness. Can share love and warmth with others. Is creative, artistically talented, and musical, as well as reliable and responsible. Can bring his/her vision to earth and realize it.

Personality Aspects That Could Be Worked On: Carries around a lot of anger in connection with the feminine aspect, perhaps resulting from bad experiences with the mother. Has sexual problems that he/she does not recognize; therefore, they cannot be resolved. Also has difficulty with survival issues. Trusts neither life nor other people nor him/herself. Believes that there is not enough love and is angry about it.

Spiritual Level: Opens the user to love. Shines a light on difficult facts in his/her own life. Changes the attitude that is behind a lack of self-love and compassion.

Mental Level: Supports the individual in coping with survival issues in connection with a letting go of aggression.

Emotional Level: Releases feelings of disconnection. Useful after separation or divorce; brings back self-love. Helps couples who want or expect a child to gain access to emotions such as responsibility and love.

Physical Level: Instills energy. Supports the hormonal system, especially the adrenal glands. Assists the user in overcoming physical problems that are based on frustration.

Where to Apply the Substance: Around the entire abdomen.

Affirmation: In this moment I am free.

Distinctive Qualities: People who work in caring professions can, with the help of this substance, reconnect with their resources of love and their physical strength.

 # 81

Name of Bottle: Unconditional Love
Color: Pink/Pink
Shakes Together As: Pink
Chakra: Base
Tarot Card: None
I Ching Sign: None
Main Theme: Self-acceptance

Positive Personality Aspects: A very intuitive and concentrated personality, which is evident in everything he/she does. Brings warmth, tenderness, and intuition into all activities. Has compassion and can also express it. Can give and receive love very easily. Has a very strong feminine side. Helps others to overcome their difficulties. Possesses a great talent for working therapeutically with couples. Is connected to his/her feelings and is open about them. A person with intense temperament and a lot of energy.

Personality Aspects That Could Be Worked On: Longs for love. Feels persecuted. Denies the feminine aspect. Feels no warmth for him/herself. Instead of action, there is only reaction. Always seems to be in a defensive position. Because this person does not follow his/her intuition, difficulties arise.

Spiritual Level: Opens the heart to unconditional love. Transfers intuitive information into everyday life.

Mental Level: Helps people who grew up without a mother find the maternal energy within themselves. Brings about possible solutions for people who have difficulties in relationships.

Emotional Level: Stimulates self-acceptance.

Physical Level: Useful with overweight that is related to hormonal problems, as well as with anorexia and bulimia.

Where to Apply the Substance: Around the abdomen.

Affirmation: I love myself the way I am.

Distinctive Qualities: Supports rebirthing sessions. Clears patterns relating to persecution that occurred in former incarnations.

82

Name of Bottle: Calypso
Color: Green/Orange
Shakes Together As: Olive Green
Chakra: "Second Chakra" and Heart
Tarot Card: None
I Ching Sign: None
Main Theme: Overcoming deep emotional shock

Positive Personality Aspects: Has accumulated a lot of wisdom from the past and can apply it to today's circumstances. Possesses a high level of emotional clarity. Receives deep insights and can speak about them. Is also connected to the flow of his/her own emotions. Knows where to go. Trusts the feeling of happiness and joy within. Loves nature and understands how it works.

Personality Aspects That Could Be Worked On: A disillusioned seeker who is still shaken by a profound emotional shock. Had a difficult childhood. An egocentric who acts against his/her own principles and who is dishonest with him/herself. Is afraid to express the truth. In general, is possessed by a deep, unspeakable fear.

Spiritual Level: Releases past spiritual conflicts. Creates space to attain new joy and insights. Promotes a new beginning that may result in a very profound change.

Mental Level: Recommended for difficulties with the father and the resultant shocks and fears. Releases depression, as well as addictions, especially when the person concerned is aware that these stem from emotional difficulties.

Emotional Level: Brings about emotional clarity, happiness, and joy. Frees the user from profound emotional shocks and trauma.

Physical Level: For heart conditions, bronchitis, asthma, liver conditions, and difficulties associated with the elimination of toxins.

Where to Apply the Substance: Around the entire trunk.

Affirmation: I open my heart for a new direction.

Distinctive Qualities: This bottle is similar to Bottle #7; much of the description also applies to #82. In past-life therapy, this substance can help to retrace emotions. As a result, useful insights can be gained.

 # 83
Name of Bottle: Open Sesame
Color: Turquoise/Gold
Shakes Together As: Pale Olive Green
Chakra: "Second Chakra," Solar Plexus and Heart, as well as Ananda-Khanda Center
Tarot Card: None
I Ching Sign: None
Main Theme: Old wine in new skins

Positive Personality Aspects: A leader who carries ancient wisdom within and formulates it for a New Aeon. This person has a strong vision for the future and possesses the resources to realize this vision. Likes to communicate with many, rather than a few, and is able to realize such communication. Shares knowledge. Understands in this context that the more (information) is given, the more (information) is received in return. Can pass on a deep feeling of happiness that enriches others. Begins to find true "inner gold" through creative expression.

Personality Aspects That Could Be Worked On: Has difficulty in being in the here and now because of the deep fears that he/she carries within from the past. Even when this person has coped with these fears, extreme anxiety may still be present. Has been persecuted in the past; therefore, suppresses his/her potential, or rather, life seems to suppress this potential. Tends to manipulate and exploit emotional and certain other situations to his/her own advantage, especially if they have to do with power.

Spiritual Level: Opens the door to ancient knowledge, which wants to be expressed through the heart, and which touches people. Releases the spiritual persecution from the past; therefore, the creative potential can be expressed.

Mental Level: Stimulates release of deep confusion, as well as an understanding of what this confusion is about. Artists who experience creative bursts alternating with depression can find an inner balance with this substance (joy within a normal life; a state between extremes that brings contentment).

Emotional Level: Aids the user in understanding his/her own fears. Helps to be less manipulative and to be clearer with him/herself.

Physical Level: Balances the solar plexus chakra. Useful with low and high blood sugar.

Where to Apply the Substance: Around the entire trunk.

Affirmation: I open myself to the deepest joy so that I can share it with others.

Distinctive Qualities: In past-life therapy, can connect the person with incarnations in Lemuria, Atlantis, Ancient Egypt, with the Aztecs and Incas, as well as with incarnations within the mystical traditions of Europe. Can bring a connection with crystals and an opening to the energies contained in them.

84
Name of Bottle: Candle in the Wind
Color: Pink/Red
Shakes Together As: Red
Chakra: Base
Tarot Card: None
I Ching Sign: None
Main Theme: Awakens the true power of love

Positive Personality Aspects: Is prepared to sacrifice his/her own needs for others. Possesses a dynamic and "grounded" intuition, which, for example, can be expressed in the business world. Has a lot of compassion for people and is full of an inexhaustible energy. Is connected with the Christ

Consciousness and carries it within, which is manifested through the feminine side. Likes to care for others and has the energy to do so. Is awakened enough to be able to live and work for the greater good. Carries a deep stillness within, and with it a charisma that touches others.

Personality Aspects That Could Be Worked On: Thinks that he/she has not received the love he/she needs, mainly with respect to the female role model. Therefore, holds resentment against the feminine. Possibly, this person was disappointed in the first love relationship. Carries a lot of suppressed anger.

Spiritual Level: Leads to empathy for oneself and others and to expressing and using this emotion. Awakens deep intuition. Connects with the Christ energy, and opens to sacrificial love.

Mental Level: Helps the individual perceive him/herself with more clarity. Stimulates feminine, creative energy.

Emotional Level: Promotes self-love and self-acceptance. Releases resentment and disappointment, especially if these feelings have been caused by frustrated love.

Physical Level: Helps with anemia, frigidity, and impotence. Balances the hormonal system.

Where to Apply the Substance: Around the entire abdomen.

Affirmation: I say goodbye to the past and open myself to love.

Distinctive Qualities: The substance supports tantric work, which means the transformation of sexual to spiritual energy.

85
Name of Bottle: Titania
Color: Turquoise/Clear
Shakes Together As: Turquoise
Chakra: Ananda-Khanda Center and Heart
Tarot Card: None

I Ching Sign: None
Main Theme: Expression of suppressed feelings

Positive Personality Aspects: An artist who truly expresses and lives creativity. Gives so much of what he/she's got into art, that he/she feels empty. ("Emptiness" in this context means that which is the important aim of some spiritual traditions.) Has the ability to speak before other people. Also is able to communicate in nonverbal ways—for example, through artistic expression or through massage. May work with computers, and in this field, always finds solutions. Is in touch with his/her inner teacher. A generous person, especially with time.

Negative Personality Aspects: Has not yet solved inner emotional conflicts. Had to suppress feelings in childhood. Has accumulated anger about various matters, also about the inability to express feelings. Because of emotional blocks, is unable to use his/her own rational mind. Is afraid of the male aspect, so badly that he/she is blocked by it at times.

Spiritual Level: Opens up to intuition. Enables this person to express his/her own light and to release deep blockages from the past, especially if they are related to the inability to speak about spiritual matters.

Mental Level: Reveals current emotional problems. Helps to express feelings and release blockages. Beneficial for stage fright, fear of technical equipment (technophobia), and difficulties with foreign languages.

Emotional Level: Releases problems with authority linked to fear. Can also help find the joy in situations that have previously led to anxiety. Enables the user to release stored tears.

Physical Level: Helps with all heart, lung, and chest problems. Is slightly antiseptic and can cool infections. Also recommended after heavy weight loss.

Where to Apply the Substance: Around the entire chest area.

Affirmation: Life is love. I love life.

Distinctive Qualities: Can aid those who have (had) problems with implants.

 # 86

Name of Bottle: Oberon
Color: Clear/Turquoise
Shakes Together As: Turquoise
Chakra: Ananda-Khanda Center and Heart
Tarot Card: None
I Ching Sign: None
Main Theme: To bring clarity into matters of the heart

Positive Personality Aspects: A very creative person who has a strong connection to the distant past. Can convey this wisdom in a precise and moving way (through writing, speaking, artistic expression, etc.). Has close contact with the subconscious and can deal very well with what stems from that area—for example, dreams. Wants to use his/her creativity to ease the suffering of the world. Is a good mirror for others, and possesses teaching abilities.

Personality Aspects That Could Be Worked On: Has difficulty asserting him/herself. Would like to communicate, but cannot change, and does not "get anything across." Had an extremely difficult life, which closed off his/her psychic abilities. The tears this person has not cried tend to block creativity, communication abilities, and all emotions.

Spiritual Level: Opens up to ancient knowledge. Enables the user to explain his/her spiritual values and truths.

Mental Level: Helps people who work with computers to maintain their creativity and to be open to simple solutions. Also helps with concentration. Makes the user aware that he/she should not only communicate with computers, but also with people (applies especially to children). This substance enables children to stay connected with emotions, to foster friendships, and also to enjoy normal, "old-fashioned" children's games.

Emotional Level: Connects with the emotions. Allows suppressed tears to flow so that blockages can be released. After shedding these tears, the person does not feel exhausted. Instead, the heart can open, and the emotional world comes into balance.

Physical Level: Beneficial for heart and skin problems, which are caused by stress. Has antiseptic qualities. Can relieve a mild sunburn, for example.

Where to Apply the Substance: Along the hairline when dealing with mental problems; otherwise, around the entire chest area.

Affirmation: I open myself so that creation can express itself through me.

Distinctive Qualities: Part of the extended New Aeon Child's Set.

Helps people who deal with genetic engineering. In past-life therapy, it can connect to incarnations in Atlantis and Lemuria.

87
Name of Bottle: The Wisdom of Love
Color: Coral/Coral
Shakes Together As: Coral
Chakra: "Second Chakra"
Tarot Card: None
I Ching Sign: None
Main Theme: Unrequited love

Positive Personality Aspects: A person who can impart deep insights to others and who is useful as a vehicle for love and wisdom. Always lends an ear to others. Is very efficient and often works in a position with a lot of responsibility. Knows how to beautify his/her surroundings. Enjoys aesthetics. Generally feels great joy. Loves nature. Understands new technology. Has talents for coordination and for counseling.

Personality Aspects That Could Be Worked On: Repeatedly falls in love with people who do not return love as they receive it (because they are already in a relationship, or some similar situation). If a relationship would be possible, then the love stays unrequited. Promises made to this person are constantly broken (also by parents, friends, etc.). Possibly this person was abused. He/she doesn't trust because there have been many unpleasant experiences to deal with.

Spiritual Level: Brings the Christ energy in its new grounded way into the user's life. Helps to gain spiritual insights and to connect with deep inner joy.

Mental Level: Increases efficiency. Enables the person to see clearly what needs to be done first.

Emotional Level: Eases the feeling that "nobody loves me." Brings self-love into life and opens to love coming in from outside. Assists in overcoming disappointments, as well as the fear of not being good enough. Helps ease shocks, especially if they are related to relationships.

Physical Level: Useful for circulation problems, assimilation, general problems with the digestive tract and gall bladder. Positively affects adrenal production.

Where to Apply the Substance: Around the entire lower abdomen, as well as along the right side of the body, from the right earlobe down to the right ankle.

Affirmation: I say goodbye to the past and hello to love.

Distinctive Qualities: Beneficial in cases of abuse (see the "Distinctive Qualities" of Bottle #5). Also helpful in past-life therapy when dealing with the subjects of shock, abuse, and unrequited love in past incarnations. Can establish a connection with past lives spent with the North American Indians.

Often people feel especially drawn to this bottle at first sight. In this case, it is recommended that they use this bottle first and then take a break for a few days in order to wait for its effects, and following that, to choose the favorite bottle(s) anew. This choice is likely to turn out in a completely different way because work has been done on the problem of "unrequited love," which overshadowed everything else.

88
Name of Bottle: Jade Emperor
Color: Green/Blue
Shakes Together As: Turquoise
Chakra: Heart and Throat
Tarot Card: None

I Ching Sign: None
Main Theme: Love of nature

Positive Personality Aspects: Carries deep peace within and wants to share this feeling with others. Is especially concerned with world harmony. A fighter for the truth with an infectious love of life and nature. Is in harmony with his/her feelings. A writer, poet, and painter who lives through creative expression. Has a sharp intellect, but also understands other people with the heart. Encourages others to grow and creates space for them to do so. Loves internal and external journeys. Follows the path of the heart and walks his/her (spiritual) way with clarity and determination.

Personality Aspects That Could Be Worked On: Has difficulties with the male role model (in him/herself and externally), as well as with the expression of truth and of emotions. Feels deceived, especially in matters of the heart. Holds high standards, and criticizes people who do not live up to their standards (this applies to all levels—spiritual, mental, emotional, and physical).

Spiritual Level: Provides contact with the infinite aspects of the inner being. Places own truth into focus and helps to find peace.

Mental Level: Releases creative blocks. Helps to overcome mental conflicts related to jealousy or envy (the person's own feelings, as well as those projected by others).

Emotional Level: Useful in solving relationship problems. Releases emotional blocks. Shows that which is emotionally true for the individual. Opens to love and understanding of nature. Helps to create the space necessary to regain balance.

Physical Level: Helps with bronchitis and heart conditions, problems in the upper back, and shoulder and chest area. Beneficial when changing eating habits.

Where to Apply the Substance: Around the entire chest area and around the throat and neck.

Affirmation: I open myself to my love of nature.

Distinctive Qualities: Assists people who feel that they do not belong on Earth. In past-life therapy, it can connect with incarnations in Atlantis, Lemuria, and with the Knights Templar.

#89

Name of Bottle: Energy Rescue
Color: Red/Deep Magenta
Shakes Together As: Deep Magenta
Chakra: Base
Tarot Card: None
I Ching Sign: None
Main Theme: To attain healing energy

Positive Personality Aspects: A person with a lot of energy; a determined person who injects others with energy. Someone who devotes his/her sexual energies to the growth of awareness. Has overcome sexual difficulties. Is able to heal with energy (Shiatsu, acupuncture, etc.). Is knowledgeable in money matters, and also in the use of time. Matters that are difficult for other people, this person manages with ease.

Personality Aspects That Could Be Worked On: Has great problems with sexuality. All other problems are connected to this area. Also has difficulties in managing everyday matters. Is inclined toward anger, as well as constant justification. If this person has hurt people through anger, he/she tends to justify these actions.

Spiritual Level: Awakens the kundalini energy, the true Self, the Logos, in oneself. Stimulates healing energies. Facilitates personal growth.

Mental Level: Helps with determination. Changes the way the user deals with anger that comes from external sources. Also changes behavior relating to money issues.

Emotional Level: Assists in coping with anger and frustration. Supports the healing of sexual difficulties. Releases resentment, especially if related to relationships. Helps with extreme lack of self-acceptance, especially if this lack is caused by an emotional problem.

Physical Level: Useful with sexual problems, especially frigidity and impotence. Beneficial after electrical shocks, even after electroshock therapy. Can re-energize in cases of extreme lethargy. Strengthens the immune system.

Where to Apply the Substance: Around the entire lower abdomen.

Affirmation: Energy follows the intent.

Distinctive Qualities: This bottle was born on July 26, 1992, when the calendar of the Mayans showed the end of an important cycle. Therefore, this bottle is also called the "Time Shift Bottle." Is suitable for tantric exercises. Helps people who work with earth energies. Protects from negative earth energy radiation (that does not mean, however, that solutions on the practical level are superfluous).

90

Name of Bottle: Wisdom Rescue
Color: Gold/Deep Magenta
Shakes Together As: Deep Magenta
Chakra: Solar Plexus and all other chakras
Tarot Card: None
I Ching Sign: None
Main Theme: To embrace one's own confusion

Positive Personality Aspects: A teacher (even if this person does not work in the educational field) who has solved the most profound problems related to confusion within. Radiates joy, even when he/she does not feel like it. Knows about the power of Divine love. It is as though this person has found the pot of gold at the end of the rainbow, which contains the ancient wisdom that can now flow into the world. The rainbow stands for the peace treaty between God and humans after the flood. This means that this person is someone who has made peace with God. He/she carries hope for the future within.

Personality Aspects That Could Be Worked On: Is possessed by all kinds of fears relating to self-worth. Wants to possess personal power and strives for it. Uses tactics of fear to influence and manipulate others. Is confused and does not know how to behave, but nevertheless, he/she pretends to have no problems. Denies the wisdom that arises because this person knows that he/she would have to act responsibly, as a consequence.

Spiritual Level: Helps to consciously express inner wisdom by bringing the love that is there into small, everyday matters. Brings about an understanding of alchemistic matters, which enhance the qualities of love.

Mental Level: Transforms fear that is related to abuse and power, into the wish for joy. Helps people who have to study a lot to retain information and utilize it in practical ways.

Emotional Level: Stimulates joy even if somebody has just encountered difficulties. Helps the individual accept the reasons for that which has provoked the greatest fears, and enables him/her to recognize that he/she already carries within that which will be of help.

Physical Level: Useful with problems of the liver, pancreas, stomach, nervous system, and the skin; helps with nervousness that manifests physically.

Where to Apply the Substance: Around the entire abdomen.

Affirmation: Out of my chaos rises a new order.

Distinctive Qualities: Aids people who have condemned themselves so much for their little mistakes that they cannot express their great strengths. In past-life therapy, it can connect people to incarnations with the Mayans.

91
Name of Bottle: Feminine Leadership
Color: Olive Green/Olive Green
Shakes Together As: Olive Green
Chakra: Solar Plexus and Heart
Tarot Card: None
I Ching Sign: None
Main Theme: Developing feminine leadership qualities

Positive Personality Aspects: A leader who truly acts from the heart. Brings spiritual matters to earth, making them accessible on a material level. An abstract thinker and scientific esoteric who is deeply connected with his/her emotional side. Is not afraid to show scars and vulnerability. This person's experiences are very broad. Loves the truth. Is optimistic and practical and concerned with creating a better world. Sacrifices his/her own interests for the good of all. Lives a simple and modest life, but very much from the heart. Some find this person too direct.

Personality Aspects That Could Be Worked On: Lives a very difficult emotional life. Fear disturbs this person's peace. He/she lacks joy and searches for his/her own reflection instead of looking within. Is often bitter and feels that he/she deserves better than that which life is offering. Is dissatisfied due to a lack of success. Envies anybody who seems to be getting along in life better than he/she is.

Spiritual Level: Enables the user to integrate knowledge and to remember things, to bring them to the practical level. Stimulates a deep understanding of natural laws, of the harmony in nature, and of the underlying patterns.

Mental Level: Helps maintain a clear direction. Promotes hope, as well as the possibility of making new decisions. Useful with certain phobias and hidden fears. Lessens the tendency to criticize people.

Emotional Level: Brings forth the space that is needed to find joy in life. Clears fears that are related to the emotional side, especially the fear of expressing oneself in this manner. Supports people who want to become more relaxed and who want to "loosen up."

Physical Level: Helps with cramps, pains in the middle back, heart ailments (especially angina pectoris), and with problems in the chest due to water retention caused by kidney failure.

Where to Apply the Substance: Around the entire chest and abdominal area.

Affirmation: Hope is my way. I trust the process of life.

Distinctive Qualities: People who are under the impression that they are aggravated by extraterrestrials will find clarity in their situation by using this substance.

92

Name of Bottle: Gretel (as in Hansel and Gretel)
Color: Coral/Olive Green
Shakes Together As: Olive Green spotted with Coral
Chakra: "Second," Heart, and Throat area
Tarot Card: None
I Ching Sign: None
Main Theme: To gain trust in one's own intuition

Positive Personality Aspects: A person who is able to trust his/her intuition and is able to express what has been recognized through intuition; someone who knows him/herself very well and has overcome many fears. Possesses the ability to make use of difficult external conditions for the inner growth process. Has many deep insights and speaks about them from the heart. Is in touch with whatever his/her real truth is and lives accordingly. Loves the way he/she is. Knows his/her mission is in life and therefore carries a deep joy inside. This joy is his/her greatest treasure.

Personality Aspects That Could Be Worked On: A very disappointed and disillusioned person who has opened the heart in deep trust. This person may have been abused by others, resulting in cutting him/herself off from intuition. There is a tendency to manipulate the truth in a way that fits personal needs.

Spiritual Level: Makes contact with intuition and the "inner teacher." Links with the energy of the Goddess. Leads to deep insights through practical (spiritual) experiences. Allows the user to recognize his/her own truth and overcome spiritual arrogance.

Mental Level: Helps to say farewell to fears and to look at difficulties in relationships.

Emotional Level: Soothing for someone who has been hurt in relationships. Clears emotional shocks. Helps let go of dependency and co-dependency issues. Also aids in releasing addictions, especially in the context of relationships. Makes it easier to say farewell to this type of relationship and pattern of behavior.

Physical Level: Beneficial for all kinds of heart conditions and difficulties in the intestinal tract (diarrhea and constipation) when the cause is an emotional issue.

Where to Apply the Substance: Around the belly and chest. In case of shock, also apply in a band on the whole right side of the body, from the earlobe down to the right ankle.

Affirmation: Before enlightenment: chop wood, carry water. After enlightenment: chop wood, carry water.

Distinctive Qualities: Hidden in this bottle is "Pallas Athena and Aeolus" (#57, Pale Pink/Pale Blue). The energy of this substance also has a lot to do with the energy of Zeus/Jupiter. It supports the work with the "inner child" and past-life therapy. It is also helpful in difficulties relating to finding the "right livelihood."

Bottles #92 and #93 were practically born at the same time. They are very similar to each other. They have been named Gretel and Hansel, respectively, because the *Hansel and Gretel* fairy tale demonstrates an aspect of these bottles very well: they stand for the female aspect of the "inner child" (Gretel) who trusts in her intuition and overcomes her fear, pushing the witch into the oven; and the male aspect of the "inner child" (Hansel) who places his trust in the female aspect. He is therefore released and finds joy and happiness.

93
Name of Bottle: Hansel (as in Hansel and Gretel)
Color: Coral/Turquoise
Shakes Together As: Deep Violet
Chakra: Second, Heart, and fourth-and-a-half Chakra (Ananda-Khanda Center)
Tarot Card: None
I Ching Sign: None

Main Theme: Communication of deepest joy

Positive Personality Aspects: Loves aesthetics and beauty. One who is in touch with his/her own creativity and is able to express feelings. A person full of warmth and love. An independent free thinker who has overcome many fears, found inner balance, and has opened up to be guided by his/her feminine, intuitive aspect. Someone who might be working in the mass media/communications field.

Personality Aspects That Could Be Worked On: An uncentered person who fears many things, two issues in particular. One fear is that what has been won in terms of inner peace will be lost again. The other fear is that he/she dares not acknowledge the female aspect within. Has difficulty expressing feelings and is, perhaps, abusing the feelings of others. Tends towards dependency, co-dependency, and addictions.

Spiritual Level: Helps the user get in touch with knowledge from the collective unconscious and from his/her own intuitive layers. Also supports the ability to make use of the insights that have been acquired by this, and express them.

Mental Level: What the substance is achieving on this level is identical to what it does on the spiritual level.

Emotional Level: Encourages the user to overcome great difficulties with issues of dependency, co-dependency, and addictions, and to gain independence. Inspires feelings of self-love. Helps integrate the male role model. Lessens stage fright, fear of flying, fear of water, and technophobia.

Physical Level: Counteracts nervous coughs, pains in the lower back, and congestion in the chest if caused by emotions. Balances the thymus gland.

Where to Apply the Substance: Around the entire trunk.

Affirmation: I open myself to the universal truth.

Distinctive Qualities: Identical to those of Bottle #92.

THE POMANDERS

We have already given you some information about the Pomanders in Chapter 3. We mentioned that they were originally used to clear the atmosphere in rooms and to protect people. We also told you how the Aura-Soma Pomanders came into being and what they contain. Now we would like to present you with the most important and practical information about the 14 Pomanders in relation to application and goals.

First of all, the Pomanders invite you to experiment. Countless therapists around the world are busy trying out all kinds of different strategies. Some place the Pomanders on acupressure points. Some apply a drop directly on a client's navel, and so on. Some people follow only their intuition, while still others use test methods such as kinesiology. Here, we are not describing expert tricks like these, but we offer basic information. We recommend that first off you follow this material until you find out what specific effects the different Pomanders have on you. (When you discover that, then you will no doubt think of some possible new methods of application yourself.)

For example, certain Pomanders have such a stimulating effect on some users that they can stand only one application in the morning. If these people take them during the day, they might experience difficulties in going to sleep. But this wake-up effect can also be used to their advantage.

The Pomanders are meant to balance the electromagnetic field of the individual. On the one hand, that leads to protection from negative influences; on the other hand, it can induce positive influences to enter the body.

While the oils directly affect the physical body, the chakras, and the subtle bodies, the Pomanders support and stimulate the effect of the oils and directly affect the electromagnetic field. For some, that can have a profound secondary impact on the physical body. (There's more about that in the descriptions.)

It's important to note that the color of the Pomanders need not necessarily correspond with that of the balance oil you are using. Since the Pomanders have contact only with the hands and the aura, the two substances cannot disturb one another.

Even if you are momentarily not using an oil, you can still work with the Pomanders. To be sure, Vicky Wall and her helpers from "beyond" had in mind that the Pomanders support the effect of the balance oils and give protection to the person who is presently in the process of opening up. Our everyday life does not give us the space for such a process of opening up. In order to function well on the material level, people often give up on their inner growth. That no longer needs to be the case, for the Pomanders provide protection.

These tiny plastic bottles with their contents of highly concentrated, alcohol-based, quickly evaporating substances, can be carried in the smallest handbag, in the tightest jeans. Their use is possible everywhere and at any time. The little bottles are practical, also, because they do not need to be shaken and to be individualized, and because of this, one single bottle can serve countless users. This advantage is evident not only in daily contact with people, but also, for instance, if someone is visiting a sick friend or relative. Just ask the ailing person's permission to do so, and if he or she agrees, spread the appropriate Pomander around his or her aura. Similarly, you can help people who are unconscious, little children, sick animals, and plants. What could happen as a result? In the worst case, nothing; in the best case, however, something very constructive could occur.

With the help of the Pomanders, you can also change negative energy in rooms or homes. For that purpose, put the proper substance on your hand and go through the room or through the home waving your hand into all areas, all corners and around all doors. But don't do so in a robotic manner. Positive imaging is important. See the negative energies being swept out. Open the windows and doors so these energies can really flee!

And now, we offer some information on the description system of this presentation of the Pomanders. Fragrance plays a large role here. For that reason, you will find two categories. The first describes the experience of fragrance. The second names herbs that dominate the fragrance. In addition, you will find the crystals listed that put their energies into the Pomander concerned.

This information is especially important for therapists who are using essential oils and crystals in their healing work. They may coordinate the oils and the stones that they wish to use for healing with the contents of the Pomanders.

Using the Pomanders

This is how you use the Pomanders: Stand or lie in a comfortable position. Place three drops of one of the Pomanders in the palm of your left hand. Rub in the substance with your right hand until the alcohol has evaporated, and spread out your arms, with palms upward. Imagine that the healing power of the Pomander is beneficial not only for you, but also for other beings on this planet and the planet itself.

Now with both hands, stroke your body, but from a distance of a few inches, beginning with the head. Spread the Pomander in this way from head to toe, all around your aura as much as possible, even around the back of your head and your back. At the end of this procedure, hold both of your hands in front of your nose, and breathe deeply three times. Take the breath deeply into your abdomen. Visualize that you are totally taking in the 49 herbs in the Pomander, and its color, also. Imagine that you wish to support the work of the balance oil that you are now using, that you want to protect or cleanse yourself, or whatever you intend by using this Pomander.

If you are in a public place and want to use a Pomander unobtrusively, this short procedure will be sufficient: Put the three drops in the palm of your left hand, rub them into your right palm, and move them at a few inches' distance over your hair. In order to move over your body discreetly, and to reach your feet, you might stoop and pretend to do something to your shoes. If you want to avoid attracting attention during your deep breathing, act as though you are whiffing some eau de cologne.

What follows is the text of a meditation you can use in conjunction with the Pomanders. You might wish to read this meditation into a cassette so you can play it back while you are using them. Or, you can read the text often enough to retain the content, and concentrate on your meditation.

PEACE TO ALL BEINGS

Just relax.

Sit comfortably where you are. With each out-breath, focus on the letting go, a letting go of all that has gone on before this moment. Everything that dies in this world, dies on an out-breath.

Everything that is born in this world is born upon an in-breath.

So, in the letting go on the out-breath, we die to what we have been.

And on the in-breath, we're born again into the new moment as a new being, with the influences of the being that we have been in the past and all the potential and the possibilities of what we are yet to be in the future.

Each out-breath, a letting go.

A letting go of all that has gone on before this moment.

A letting go of any tensions in any place that is tight, anywhere in the body.

Feel for an ease with the out-breath spreading through the back of the neck,

A letting go, that the eyeballs may settle into their sockets.

A letting go, that the breath may come and go freely in the belly.

A letting go of all the little muscles around the anus.

A letting go of the muscles underneath the soles of the feet and around the toes.

Each out-breath, a letting go.

A letting go into the thought and feeling of peace.

Each out-breath, feel for the possibility of a greater ease.

Let go of the tensions and stresses that are in the body-mind.

Let go with the out-breath.

Trust that out-breath.

Trust the possibility of letting go, of surrender, of offering up all that you are.

Each out-breath, a letting go, into the thought and feeling of peace.

Peace, as the color, radiant sapphire blue.

Blue like the sky without any clouds.

Blue, scintillating, radiating, energetic blue.

With the letting go, visualize that blue energy filling a transparent bubble or globe within which you are sitting.

Filling it with a radiant blue energy with each out-breath.

The tensions, the stresses, the extraneous thoughts, the thoughts that race across the surface of the mind.

Let go, into the peace, and trust in the out-breath.

Bring the attention to a point, to a place just above the navel and a little way inside, a point, like a diamond or a star at the center of your being.

And on each in-breath, visualize that star becoming brighter, more radiant, more full of light.

That the whole of the temple of the body may be filled with light.

That each cell may be radiated from the center, and the whole body may be illumined.

Each in-breath light expanding from the star in the center of the being, filling the whole of the body with light.

Each out-breath, peace.

Peace as the color, as the color radiant sapphire blue, gently filling the transparent bubble or globe within which we are sitting.

Let us go into the silence for a few moments with peace and letting go on the out-breath, and light expanding on the in-breath from the star in the center of your being.

(Pause.)

❦ ❦ ❦

Peace and letting go, on each in-breath light expanding in all directions.

Peace to all beings.

May all beings be well and happy and free from fear.

From the smallest cell to the largest galaxy in space.

May all beings be well and happy and free from fear.

Peace to all beings, whether known, or yet to be known.

In the world of ideas or the world of the imagination.

May all beings be well and happy and free from fear.

Peace to all beings, born or yet to be born, real or imagined.

May all beings be well and happy and free from fear.

Peace to all beings, near or far.

May all beings be well and happy and free from fear.

Peace to all beings that relate to all of the elements or their combinations.

May all beings be fulfilled in space.

May all beings be well and happy and free from fear.

Peace to all beings, particularly those beings that we have been in the past.

May they be well and happy and free from fear.

Peace to each being within each being here.

May they be well and happy and free from fear.

Peace to all the beings that are yet to be.

May they be well and happy and free from fear.

Peace to all beings in all directions, to the North, to the South, to the East, to the West, above and below.

May all beings be well and happy and free from fear.

May all beings come to comfort and ease throughout all time and space.

With the knowledge that the radiant blue sphere of perfect protection sur - rounds you, and that the light from the star in the center of your being glows a little brighter, that you may become the star you are.

❦ ❦ ❦

When you find an out-breath that feels good, open your eyes to a new moment.

❦ ❦ ❦

So ends the text of the meditation. By the way, the color of the Pomander that you use does not matter. The protective color blue that is vital in this meditation shall perform its function regardless. (Besides, there is a small sample set with mini-spray bottles. Every little bottle contains enough for three or more applications. This allows you to try the various Pomanders. In the course of two or three weeks, you can decide which Pomander suits you best.)

Of course, the meditation will be effective even if you don't use a Pomander. And certainly, you can, in connection with all of the Aura-Soma substances, pray or meditate in your own familiar and intimate way.

THE 14 POMANDERS

#1 — *The Original Pomander (The White Pomander)*
Color: White
Fragrance: Medicinal, warm, stimulating
Predominant Essential Oils: Kajeput, California laurel, laurel
Crystal Energies: Morganite, quartz, selenite
Physical Associations: Nose, throat, the entire body

Effects: Especially recommended for the nostrils. Closes wounds. Lessens local discomfort—for example, wasp bites. Protects all chakras and brings them into balance.

Distinctive Qualities: Contains the entire "rainbow." Protects the whole electromagnetic field and is good for everyday use. (All Pomanders protect the electromagnetic field, but this one is especially effective; also works in situations where there is no special concern.) Stops bleeding. (Apply it directly; it can be put onto the wound.) Protects against radiation. Helps people who suffer from allergies, those that stem from nature or from poisons originating outside the body. (This does not include food allergies or those caused by medication.) Cleanses crystals, if they are to be used for healing. Useful for animals with ear and mouth infections.

In Past-Life Therapy, Helpful for Access to: Incarnations in Turkey and the Middle East

#2 — *The Pink Pomander*
Color: Pink
Fragrance: Flowery and sweet
Predominant Essential Oils: Rose geranium
Crystal Energies: Rose quartz, rose tourmaline, morganite
Physical Associations: Hormone system, above all, pertaining to the production of adrenalin

Effects: Affects the whole uro-genital area. Harmonizes group energies, influences group processes positively. That means that this Pomander lends itself especially to community endeavors.

Distinctive Qualities: Protects when someone has opened him/herself up to love and warmth. At such times, this person can be very vulnerable. The substance prevents the person from being hurt. Protects against aggressiveness aimed at him/her. Helps to give and receive warmth and tenderness. Resolves stresses in the cranio-sacral region and can, therefore, be especially effective in cranio-sacral therapy. Brings about relaxation on all levels for individuals and groups. The effect of this substance is heightened if the user visualizes the color ("think pink").

In Past-Life Therapy, Helpful for Access to: Incarnations in the Mediterranean Sea area, especially Greece and Italy. This Pomander is suited to past-life therapy in general, also in resolving patterns in relationships and making connections with animals (even creatures of the sea), and with plants. Helpful as well with experiences that go beyond the domain of Mother Earth.

#3 — The Deep Red Pomander
Color: Deep red
Fragrance: Woody, earthy, spicy
Predominant Essential Oils: Cedar, laurel
Crystal Energies: Garnet, ruby, carnelite, strawberry-quartz, hematite, neptunite
Physical Associations: Skeletal structure of the body, the base chakra

Effects: Especially helpful in dealing with stress. Of all Aura-Soma products, this is the one that grounds most intensively, energizes, and provides the most effective protection. Its use after every meditation is recommended.

Distinctive Qualities: Protects against negative influences from earth energies. On the other hand, sensitizes for earth energies. Balances the electromagnetic polarities in the body. Harmonizes the base chakra. Protects at rituals and in connection with sacred dance. Protects persons who use crystals for healing and/or who handle crystals in other ways. Assists the user when there is the feeling that he/she is being sapped of energy. Helpful in cases of exhaustion from other reasons. Can have an aphrodisiac effect. Activates the right half of the brain and brings about profound feminine intuition. Removes fears regarding survival issues (for example, money). Lessens all types of fears. Causes poltergeist phenomena in teenagers to vanish.

In Past-Life Therapy, Helpful for Access to: Incarnations in North America (Native Americans), China, Russia, the Far East, and the Himalayas

#4 — The Red Pomander
Color: Red
Fragrance: Fruity, spicy, earthy
Predominant Essential Oils: Sandalwood, laurel, carnation
Crystal Energies: Garnet, ruby
Physical Associations: Circulation, base chakra

Effects: Stimulates the hormone system. Aside from the effects mentioned here, has the same functions as the deep red Pomander. The latter is especially helpful in extreme situations; the red, in more mundane cases.

Distinctive Qualities: Helps overcome negative effects from resentment or animosity (toward oneself as well as others). Restores harmony after too much sex, or after thinking about it too intensely. (The help of the red Pomanders relates more to the balance of energy than to the physical level.) Allows aggressive feelings to be overcome, especially in connection with a lack of groundedness. Reduces shyness in someone who does not dare to show affection to those he/she cares for.

In Past-Life Therapy, Helpful for Access to: Incarnations in Russia, China, Tibet, generally the Far East

#5 — The Orange Pomander
Color: Orange
Fragrance: Fruity, spicy, fresh
Predominant Essential Oils: Mandarin, cinnamon
Crystal Energies: Topaz, orange calcite, sunstone, tiger eye, jasper
Physical Associations: Uro-genital system, organs for elimination, and

second chakra

Effects: Stimulates the libido. Heals the etheric body. Helps all aspects of the personality—spiritual, mental, emotional, and physical—to overcome shocks from the past. Aids in the release of dependency and co-dependency issues and addictions.

Distinctive Qualities: This Pomander is most suitable for past-life therapy. Protects the user as well as the therapist and opens the gates to past knowledge. Through the application of this substance, the negative effects of the memory of earlier traumas is avoided. The information important for today, contained in these memories, will come up clearly in any case.

Can close the etheric rifts (see Chapter 4). Frees earthbound entities. Gives people who have difficulty in dealing with technical apparatus a relaxed way to approach them. Can help to overcome deep fears, especially if these fears manifest themselves in the stomach. It is recommended when the hormone system undergoes changes in the years of puberty or menopause. Beneficial for bedwetting problems (see Chapter 12). Stimulates objectivity and clarity if someone is inclined to hysteria. Weakens the tendency to become involved in everyone else's business.

In Past-Life Therapy, Helpful for Access to: Incarnations in India, the Middle East, and Egypt. Useful in connection with all shocks that could be significant in past-life therapy. Also helpful if in earlier incarnations, relationships existed that must be worked out now, and in which dependency and co-dependency played a role.

#6 — The Golden Pomander
Color: Gold
Fragrance: Flowery, fruity, like the forest
Predominant Essential Oils: Balm-mint
Crystal Energies: Amber, gold, zincite, citrine
Physical Associations: Skin and digestive system, influences the second and solar plexus chakras

Effects: Balances the metabolism. Positively influences the intake of nutrients and energy.

Distinctive Qualities: Allows inherent wisdom to come up. Inspires a deeper connection with one's own instincts and helps to contact the "inner teacher." Useful in bringing the wisdom of the past into consciousness, and to understand old lessons. Inspires spiritual humility.

In Past-Life Therapy, Helpful for Access to: Incarnations in Egypt, with the Aborigines in Australia, the Mayans, Aztecs, and Incas

#7 — The Yellow Pomander
Color: Yellow
Fragrance: Fruity, lemony, like the forest
Predominant Essential Oils: Citronella, sandalwood, lemon grass
Crystal Energies: Amber, fluorite, yellow quartz, topaz, citrine
Physical Associations: Nervous system, liver, kidneys, pancreas, and solar plexus chakra

Effects: Helpful with all problems in connection with nutrition and the intake of energy

Distinctive Qualities: Balances the solar plexus. Stimulates inherent knowledge. Helps to gain more energy through the breath and breathing. Brings sensual joy—that is, joy awakened through the sense organs (smell, touch, taste, etc.). Recommended for nervous depression and also seasonal depression (especially in winter). Allows overcoming of irrational fears and nervousness. Is supportive in the process of breaking habits such as smoking, drinking alcohol, coffee, eating sweets, etc.

In Past-Life Therapy, Helpful for Access to: Incarnations with the Aborigines in Australia, the Gnostics, and the Essenes, as well as incarnations in Ancient Egypt

#8 — The Olive Green Pomander
Color: Olive Green
Fragrance: Fresh, like herbs and woods
Predominant Essential Oils: Himalaya pine, lavender
Crystal Energies: Adamite, epidote, jade
Physical Associations: Lungs, diaphragm, solar plexus, heart chakra

Effects: Brings the immune system into balance and can stimulate it

Distinctive Qualities: Recommended for someone who stands at a cross-roads, but also for all decision-making processes. Stimulates self-knowledge; helps to find out what is right for oneself instead of living the truth of others. Brings out feminine leadership qualities and strengthens self-assertion, also in regard to feelings.

In Past-Life Therapy, Helpful for Access to: Incarnations in Atlantis and other prehistoric cultures, China, Israel, as well as countries of the Mediterranean area

#9 — The Emerald Green Pomander
Color: Emerald green
Fragrance: Medicinal, warm, like the woods
Predominant Essential Oils: Rosemary, Scotch pine
Crystal Energies: Malachite, Moldavide, emerald
Physical Associations: Immune system, heart, lungs, heart chakra

Effects: Claming, centering, balancing

Distinctive Qualities: Brings about the feeling that time and space are available, along with the feeling that this time and space is safe and is being respected. Supports decision-making processes. Encourages a new outlook. Makes it possible to look at aspects of the inner being that otherwise would be difficult to take responsibility for and bring into focus. Before a therapeutic session, it helps the therapist to concentrate on his/her own space so that the client does not come too close.

Supports every kind of breath work. Useful in cases of asthma and bronchitis. Brings about a strong contact with nature, mainly with trees.

In Past-Life Therapy, Helpful for Access to: Incarnations in China, Israel, Mediterranean countries, especially Greece and Spain

#10 — The Turquoise Pomander
Color: Turquoise
Fragrance: Sweet, spicy, fresh

Predominant Essential Oils: Cedar
Crystal Energies: Aquamarine
Physical Associations: Immune system, heart and crown chakra

Effects: Stimulates the immune system. Harmonizes the breath paths in severe cases (bronchitis and asthma, etc.). Brings about contact with feelings and helps make it possible to express them.

Distinctive Qualities: Stimulates the function of the ananda-khanda center (see Chapter 4). Is suitable for people working in or for the media, including those who work behind-the-scenes, such as technicians. Resolves creative blockages and is recommended for stage fright. Helps people learn a foreign language and encourages those who are too shy to use the knowledge of the foreign language(s) they already know. Supports the work with new technologies and thereby dissolves the feelings of inferiority that may have come up in connection with this work.

In Past-Life Therapy, Helpful for Access to: Incarnations in Atlantis, Lemuria, or other cultures from prehistoric times. Facilitates access to information about the future. Helps to make contact with the "inner guide."

#11 — The Sapphire Blue Pomander
Color: Sapphire Blue (sky-blue)
Fragrance: Sweet, like the woods
Predominant Essential Oils: Cedar, myrrh, lily of the valley
Crystal Energies: Aquamarine, blue agate, sapphire
Physical Associations: Neck, throat, thyroid, throat chakra

Effects: Protects, calms, fosters tolerance of oneself and others. Stimulates inspiration and trust in inner guidance. Strengthens resistance, physical and emotional (that is, it protects from damage to the body and the psyche).

Distinctive Qualities: This is the most suitable Pomander for the meditation of protection that is found at the beginning of this chapter. Helps with difficulties one might have with authority figures. Lessens extreme suffering, especially in times of transition. Protects psychic people.

In Past-Life Therapy, Helpful for Access to: Incarnations in Israel or wherever the person has grown up in a Jewish family.

#12 — The Royal Blue Pomander
Color: Royal Blue
Fragrance: Sweet, like the woods
Predominant Essential Oils: Lily of the valley, blue chamomile
Crystal Energies: Fluorite, lapis lazuli
Physical Associations: Pineal gland and third eye

Effects: Strengthens sensual perception (through the eyes, ears, etc.)

Distinctive Qualities: Helps to overcome feelings of extreme isolation. Opens up to powers of imagination and intuition, as well as the capacity for sympathy and empathy. Can stimulate emotional growth. Lessens ear problems (pain, being hard of hearing, tinnitus). Intensifies the enjoyment of music.

In Past-Life Therapy, Helpful for Access to: Incarnations in Israel. Opens up to the psychic domain, which generally refers to past lives. It helps people who have difficulty reaching a place where information about former incarnations is accessible.

#13 — The Violet Pomander
Color: Violet
Fragrance: Violets (an old-fashioned fragrance)
Predominant Essential Oils: Violet, rose, rose geranium, lavender
Crystal Energies: Amethyst, diamond, quartz
Physical Associations: Skull, nervous system, crown chakra

Effects: Frees thought processes. Leads to self-respect and respect for others. Brings about calmness. Lessens headaches and migraines.

Distinctive Qualities: Connects the first chakra with the crown chakra. Allows limits on all levels to be overcome and loosens that which binds. Heightens awareness. Allows overcoming of boredom and gives access to new experiences, as well as awareness of beauty and wonder in everyday life.

In Past-Life Therapy, Helpful for Access to: Experiences in past lives that have to do with the spiritual aspect of the soul

#14 — *The Deep Magenta Pomander*
Color: Deep Magenta
Fragrance: Fruity
Predominant Essential Oils: Lavender, frankincense
Crystal Energies: Garnet, ruby, sugilite
Physical Associations: Entire body, all chakras, including the "eighth chakra"

Effects: Leads to self-realization and to awareness of one's life task. (In the "eighth chakra," the chakra outside of the body above the head, is contained a kind of blueprint where the potential of every person is noted, telling what he/she can optimally realize. The deep magenta Pomander touches that area within the person.)

Distinctive Qualities: Brings the instinct and the intellect into unison. Stimulates focus and attention on small, everyday things and duties and helps to perform them with love. Points out that it is just as important *how* one does something, as what one does. Brings awareness of quality and understanding on all levels. Is restorative after a depression. Strengthens the positive energy that returns after a depression, and gives a protective influence. Helps to tune into nature. Facilitates reaching a deep meditative state. After meditation, this substance facilitates an integration of experiences that lie beyond words. Useful in gaining clarity about old family patterns and to develop new ways of conducting oneself.

In Past-Life Therapy, Helpful for Access to: Incarnations in the Philippines and Hawaii, South America, Japan, with the Aborigines in Australia, as well as the Hunzas

❦ ❦ ❦ ❦ ❦

THE MASTERS

To write about the Masters and the Master Quintessences is not a simple thing. The names alone could encourage joking or flippancy. They could also evoke a negative reaction or arouse suspicion. Here we have an alcohol solution, poured into tiny plastic bottles called "Quintessences" and given the name of a Master. Now, the word *quintessence* means "the very core of being," or "the most perfect manifestation of a quality." How can the "Quintessence," the core being of some "Master," be dissolved in alcohol, poured into little plastic bottles, and then be available to be fanned into your aura? Such questions have challenged many friends of Aura-Soma, causing them to be near despair.

Indeed, it is no mistake, especially in the spiritual aspect of life, to be critical and to use your mind. Today, there are too many "gurus" on the loose who desire financial gain and who manipulate innocent, trusting followers and clients who are hungry for "something more." It is understandable that you might have difficulty with the words *Master* and *Quintessence*. In this case, feel open to choosing a Quintessence simply from numbers or from colors. An example might be that you choose "Emerald Green" instead of "Djwal Khul," #9 instead of "Pallas Athena and Aeolus." But there is one thing you might surely avoid doing—that is to shy away from trying at least one or two of these substances.

We recommend that you allow yourself to pick them without thinking or analyzing. You might take the essence that appeals to you from its fragrance. (There are sets of mini-bottles available for just this purpose.) The effect is great, whether you like the name or not. The Quintessences enable you to open yourself to aspects of your life totally unfamiliar to you until now. They make great inner growth possible. It would be unfortunate if you deprived yourself of something so wonderful just because you are turned off by the idea of the Masters.

To those of you who feel that you would like to "come into contact" with the Masters via the little bottles, it needs to be said that such contact is not guaranteed. All that one can do in order to get in touch with the higher spheres is to open oneself. When the meeting occurs, there is always the factor of "grace" to be considered, which means that the "other side" needs to be willing. Besides, whoever uses a Quintessence is not "better" than others....

When Vicky Wall received the formulas, the main information was the following: that the substances of these colors, of these essential oils, minerals, and other energies, have something to do with personalities. The names that Vicky was "given" for them originated partly with the teachings of Madame Blavatsky (for example, "Kuthumi"), from the ancient Greek pantheon ("Pallas Athena"), and from history ("Lao Tsu"). The choices may seem to have originated from Vicky Wall, but they turn up in some other texts also received during meditation. These were received independently of Vicky Wall in time and space.

Instead of saying that the Quintessences had something to do with personalities, one could also say that the substances give way to the archetypes, the primal images of the human psyche. Pallas Athena, for example, is the Greek goddess of heroes, of the cities, of agriculture, of science, writing, and of the arts. She is said to have been born out of the head of her father, Zeus. Athena represents the primal image of a strong, intelligent woman, and can be very effective for men as well as women. If, for example, you were to plan a trip to Greece, you could take this Quintessence with you and use it there to get closer to the archetype Pallas Athena and to learn to know yourself better. On the other hand, you can gain closer access to the primal image of Athena at home. You can achieve it with the help of a specific and well-planned meditation supported by this substance. In this connection, we would like to repeat this about Aura-Soma: One of the most fascinating qualities is that it opens the possibility for the person to have access to the source of the primal knowledge of humankind directly and, consequently, to have some very personal experiences.

The first steps could be taken with Pallas Athena or Lao Tsu and Kwan

Yin. There is much information available about them. Later, it may be interesting to dare to approach El Morya or Maha Chohan. Because, as yet, there is not much information available about those two, you will need to rely on what your "inner guide" says. Or, you need to pay attention to what comes to you from "above," or from "out of the depths," and from what you might experience in energy, in memories, feelings, pictures, colors, and tones.

The "Masters" in Theosophy

The concept of the "Masters" turns up in esoteric literature. The explanation of their place in the scheme of our existence needs to be given a brief summary here. One fundamental belief in esoterics is evolution. It states that every being has its place in a hierarchical system in a chain of development. Life begins on a very low level and evolves from the domain of plants and animals to that of human beings. Above that level on a higher "rung of the ladder" is the domain of the Masters, which may be at some time attainable for human beings. That is, for example, the view of the Theosophists. According to their teachings, the Masters are highly evolved human beings who, out of love for humankind, have renounced their own further evolution so they could assist our planet. In order to be in contact with the inhabitants of Earth, they are to follow and master physical laws and are allowed to use a physical body to get in contact with us human beings.

For instance, Saint Germain is said to have appeared and reappeared within the course of a time frame of nearly 100 years. He is said to have met with persons from the 18th century and at these meetings to have appeared as a 40- to 50-year-old man. He is said to have spoken several languages, among them Sanskrit and Arabic, and also to have had knowledge about the occult, especially about alchemy. He is said to have traveled widely, to have been a confidant of Louis XV and Louis XVI. He was also seen in China and India. According to the Theosophists, Saint Germain was an embodiment of the Master of the Seventh Ray—that is, the violet ray.

Every Master is supposed to represent a certain domain, called the "Ray," which corresponds to a color. The Theosophists recognize seven rays, each reigned over by at least one Master.

Some assume that there are Masters living in the mountains of the Himalayas. Others say that they live on stars or in constellations that we can see from the earth. Another supposition expressed is that they try to influence humankind through certain groups, through movements such as the Knights Templar, Freemasons, the Rosicrucians, and the Theosophical Society. However, the Masters are absolutely supposed to respect the free will of human beings. Of course, that limits their direct influence.

Helena Blavatsky, a scintillating personality and founder of the Theosophical Society, declared that she was in contact with the Masters. She was born in 1831, the daughter of a German colonel serving in Russia. From childhood on, she lived on the border between the worlds by way of clairvoyance and other psychic abilities. At the age of 17, she married the Russian General Blavatsky. The marriage was short-lived, for after a few weeks, disguised as a man, she left him and fled. She obviously traveled all over the world and studied the spiritual traditions of that time. She is said to have experienced something significant in the valleys of the Himalayas. Here she is said to have met her secret Masters and to have been trained by them. In 1873, she came to New York, where she soon became the central focus of the occult circles. There she could shine with her talent as a medium. She was not above trickery, however. In such areas, she was even more deeply involved in later years, to the detriment of her reputation.

In 1875, Helena Blavatsky founded the *Theosophical Society*. At that time it was categorized as an alternative spirituality—that is, outside the more organized forms of religion. *Theosophy* (from the Greek) means "teaching of God's wisdom." Today the movement is usually spoken of only in connection with Madame Blavatsky and Alice Bailey. The latter developed the teaching further in the same vein of Blavatsky, but we'll discuss that more later on. The teaching of Theosophy is much older, anyway. All spiritual paths are labeled Theosophy if the believer is in meditative touch with God, desires to know the "why" of world events, and if on this path it is said that it is possible to have direct access to God without the mediation of a church, a priest, or any similar representative.

The German author, Rudolf Steiner, known worldwide by his alternative schools, also started out with the Theosophist Society with Blavatsky and Bailey, but left in 1913 to found Anthroposophy.

In 1878, Helena Blavatsky moved the headquarters of the Theosophical Society to India. In the same year, her book, *Isis Unveiled*, was published. In it she presented this theme: All religions and their related philosophies can be traced to a single ancient wisdom religion, which was carefully guarded. She stated that her Master had revealed that knowledge to her.

Blavatsky's second work was *The Secret Doctrine*. In that work, she also mentioned the Masters. Her books are very difficult to read and understand. It can be assumed that Helena Blavatsky did not necessarily want to be understood. For example, in the third volume of *The Secret Doctrine,* she said the following in connection with the Masters:

> The little that can here be said about the subject, may or may not help guide the psychic student into the right direction. Since the choice and responsibility are left up to the writer to recount the facts as she has personally understood them, therefore the criticism of causing possible misunderstandings must fall alone on her. The doctrine was given to her, but it was left to her own intuition—just as it is now left up to the discerning mind of the reader to sort out the secretive and confusing facts. The incomplete messages that are given herein are fragments of that which is contained in certain secret volumes. But there is no rule that these details need to be published.

Not a very satisfying thing, to comb through the "secret doctrine" in search of reliable and firm information about the Masters. The literature on the subject available since then leaves much to be desired in terms of actual informative content. And it was avoided or thought unnecessary to edit it and add reliable facts—an art which, up till now, only a few writers and journalists are able to perform.

Alice Bailey and Djwal Khul

Alice Bailey, another important figure in the Theosophical movement, was born in England in 1890 and grew up in a strictly Christian home. As a young adult, she worked on a voluntary basis as a helper in Ireland and India in homes where British soldiers lived.

After the break-up of her first marriage, she had a difficult time caring for her children. At that time, she lived in the USA. Through her acquaintance with two students, Alice Bailey came in contact with Madame

Blavatsky and the Theosophical Society. Her second husband, Foster Bailey, enthusiastically supported her interest in esoteric subjects. She began to write and teach in New York, and founded the "Arcane School," still in existence today, as well as some other organizations.

Alice Bailey was in contact with Djwal Khul, who at one time appeared to her as a living person. From a metaphysical plane, he declared himself to be an incarnation of a Tibetan Lama. What he dictated coincided only in part with the teachings of Tibetan Buddhism. Through Alice Bailey, Djwal Khul wrote 20 books. She herself wrote six.

The Theosophists did not appreciate what Alice Bailey did. Obviously, they believed that they alone had the privilege of contact with the Masters. As a result, Alice Bailey left the Society after some time.

To her, the hierarchy of the Masters was a reality. She, that is, Djwal Khul speaking through her, wrote that this was a group of beings both human and spiritual. They had taken over the responsibility for humankind and wished to help. There existed among them students, initiates, as well as Masters, who were subject to the Chohans and to the Kumaras, who in turn represented the highest conscious beings on our planetary sphere. The whole resembles a huge corporation. She wrote that the beings were not unlike angels and archangels in Western religions.

Djwal Khul let it be known through Alice Bailey that the hierarchy had taken on an assignment on the political level to bring about international cooperation and economic synthesis. In the realm of religion, they fostered spiritual consciousness and a kind of universal world religion. In the domains of science, education, and psychology, the aim was to expand human consciousness, knowledge, and human capabilities in general.

The members of the hierarchy sent out thoughts, ideals, activities, and projects in order to influence people, who worked in the political, economic, and scientific arenas. The plans may be idealistic, yet realizable. According to Djwal Khul, there now exists an example of such international cooperation—the Red Cross.

People who open themselves to a dedication to the "greatest good" through the Masters apparently sometimes receive "instruction" from the Masters during the night. Dreams could confirm this by their content pointing to school situations, libraries, and the like. One of the organizations in existence as a result of Alice Bailey's work recommends meditation at the time of the full moon and of the new moon. For at those times, contact with the higher levels is more easily attainable.

This kind of work should under no conditions have an ego trip as its goal; rather, it should be to subordinate oneself to a higher plan in partnership with others.

The professor of psychology, Arthur Hastings, in his book, *With the Tongues of Men and Angels*, a publication that he realized with the support of the renowned American Institute of Noetic Sciences, wrote the following:

> In metaphysical terms, the system described by A.A.B. is at the astral and subtle levels. These are the levels where there are auras, out-of-body states, psi functions, chakras, discarnate beings, personified deities, and other energy forms (Wilber, 1980). These realms are considered accessible to consciousness through meditation, visualization practices, altered states of consciousness, psychedelic substances, and shamanistic practices. Many spiritual traditions—Christianity, Islam, Buddhism, and Shamanism, for example—assume that, on these levels, there are higher beings or spirits that can relate to humans. However, these are not usually considered the highest spiritual levels of experience.

> The path of most traditional mystics, in or out of religions, is to move higher in the levels of spiritual consciousness toward unity with the Godhead or toward cessation of attachment in the Buddha nature. The Bailey writings emphasize putting oneself in service to humanity via the Plan, rather than continuing on the mystical path toward ultimate Being, which is seen as a much later stage involving many lifetimes. Also, they give little attention to personality level work. While D.K. is clear that the disciple must gain control over desires and thoughts, there is no discussion of how negative emotions, obstacles or physical desires are to be eliminated. Of course, these instructions were given at a time when there were few psychological tools for therapy; now the possibilities are somewhat wider. Transpersonal psychology suggests that spiritual work is likely to be handicapped by inner conflicts, negative emotional states, repressed issues, and similar problems (Vaughan, 1986). Those who study this system would be well advised to address emotional and psychological issues before or during their training.

Vicky Wall did not know about any of this. She had read neither Blavatsky nor Bailey. She did not even know anything of the existence of any kind of Master or hierarchy. In 1986, in connection with the "birth" of Bottle #50 (Pale Blue/Pale Blue), it became clear to her that a new chapter in time had begun. It is true that single pastel colors had surfaced, but she now sensed that a full pastel sequence would be forthcoming. She noticed a change in other ways. She was confident in her sense that it was not sufficient to call this bottle "Pale Blue/Pale Blue"—rather, that it had something to do with a name. As she tuned into the blue ray in her meditation and asked for the name, she was given "El Morya."

Vicky was very surprised and confused. For, as we said, she did not know what to do with the name. She was concerned most of all because she did not believe, with her Hasidic background, that she could bear the responsibility of placing Masters between God and human beings, something like demi-gods. She spoke of this problem again and again with Mike Booth. He, by the way, was familiar with Theosophy and knew about the Masters.

Vicky carried her problems about this issue within her for two years. Finally, she calmed herself. In her daily prayers and meditations, she always kept the goal in mind to be in direct contact with the "Source," with God, with "the Father," as she usually said. During the time when she was coming to terms with the Masters, she experienced the power and energy of God in an especially impressive, strong, and direct way—much too difficult to handle for us humans. She realized that God had set the Masters as transformers, so to speak, between Himself and human beings. This was for Him to be able to send down His power, His light over the "rays" to us.

In the course of time and in the course of experiences that Vicky had in her meditations, she was able to slowly accept the idea of the Masters. Yet, up until her death, she had certain reservations about presenting something to the world that, in her view, placed something between God and humans. She did not at any cost wish to convey that idea. If there are any doubts, she advised (and so does Aura-Soma), that one had better turn to the Highest Authority and not to one of the Masters. That would always be the safest way. Vicky Wall often quoted this passage of scripture in this connection: "Knock, and it shall be opened unto you."

During the time that the Master Oils were born (Bottles #50 to #64), Vicky Wall received the information that the formulas for a new kind of substance would come through. It would have to do with the energies of the Masters and the pastel colors. Their function would be similar to that of the Pomanders, but would relate to a different subtle body—the astral body. It was to be the substance that would be given the name,

Quintessence. Their individual names were designated as follows:

❦ ❦ ❦

THE MASTER QUINTESSENCES

#1 Pale Blue	El Morya
#2 Pale Gold	Kuthumi
#3 Pale Pink	Lady Nada
#4 Pale Green	Hilarion
#5 Clear	Serapis Bey
#6 Deep Red	The Christ
#7 Pale Violet (Lilac)	Saint Germain
#8 Pink	Orion and Angelica
#9 Rose Pink	Pallas Athena and Aeolus
#10 Gold	Lady Portia
#11 Pale Orange	Lao Tsu and Kwan Yin
#12 Pale Coral	Sanat Kumara
#13 Pale Turquoise	Maha Chohan
#14 Emerald Green	Djwal Khul

❦ ❦ ❦

In this case, the numerological meaning of the numbers is not relevant. It can be experienced with the numbers of the corresponding balance oils. (For the sake of accuracy, Aura-Soma would have had to renumber the Quintessences in this sequence: #50 = Pale Blue = El Morya; #51 = Pale Gold = Kuthumi, and so on. Since that would have led to confusion, the easiest way was chosen, and they were simply numbered 1, 2, 3, and so on.)

After the bottles from #50 to #64 came through, Vicky Wall had the feeling that this aspect of the system was complete and closed. She was often asked whether there would be more Master Oils or Quintessences.

Her answer was no; these 14 would be the sole representatives.

The first seven—El Morya, Kuthumi, Lady Nada, Hilarion, Serapis Bey, The Christ, and Saint Germain—she saw as "Ascended Masters." Obviously, she meant that these Masters once lived as men and had risen to higher domains.

The next five—Orion and Angelica, Pallas Athena and Aeolus, Lady Portia, Kwan Yin and Lao Tsu, and Sanat Kumara—she saw as "Cosmic Masters." (Each couple represents one Master energy.) By that she meant that these Masters stand on a yet higher step than the first seven, that they experienced a yet higher initiation, and that they have not ever lived as humans. However, she said that they are capable of disguising themselves and appearing in a body. The last two, Maha Chohan and Djwal Khul, she placed outside of the group. Maha Chohan she saw as "Master of the Masters." She saw Djwal Khul as "the youngest Master," as one always available to those who are truly and honestly seeking. The name, "the youngest" is in no way meant to be interpreted as being less worthy, however.

❦ ❦ ❦

At the beginning of this chapter, we asked how a Quintessence, meaning the core of a Master's being, can be held in a solution of alcohol and be filled into bottles. Here is the explanation, and Aura-Soma is not alone in holding this view. Alice Bailey also regarded it in this way: The rays, or, in other words, the vital energy of the Masters represented by the rays, pass over into the mineral kingdom and the plant kingdom. That happens in sunlight, which, after all, is composed of colors as well as pure energy. The energies of the rays—that is, those of the Masters, are absorbed by the minerals of the corresponding colors and by the plants of the corresponding colors. With the Pomanders, it is somewhat different. With them we focus only on the minerals and plants that are to affect the rather coarser electromagnetic fields of human beings. In contrast, the finer and more subtle energies of the Quintessences aim to affect the astral body. More light and more energy is contained in them—the direct energy of the rays. As with the high potencies in homeopathy, the Quintessences are finer than the Pomanders, therefore potentially more effective.

What Vicky Wall had done was to place at human beings' disposal energies that have an enhanced potential by a method never before known and that have been arranged in optimal combinations and in a form ready for direct application.

In closing, we would like to add something about "The Christ." For some, it may appear strange that this name turns up in this system. Actually, it was quite a shock for the Hasidic Vicky Wall, when she, tuning in to the red ray during her meditation, received the name of the Master as "Christ." For her, the historic Jesus was a great rabbi—nothing more, nothing less. It was confusing to her that he should belong to the Masters. Besides, she regarded Aura-Soma as a neutral system; and this point of view is as valid now as it was then with her. Yes, of course, it is related to the Kabbala, but it does not intend to persuade anyone to believe in Jewish mysticism, any more than in Christianity or other religions. The word *Christ* in Aura-Soma does not mean the historic Jesus, about whose identity there has lately been much speculation. The meaning is the Christ Energy, Christ Consciousness, the Christ Logos. *Logos* is an ancient Greek term that means "word, rational belief." Since the time of Heraclitus (550–480 b.c.), Logos has been a basic comprehensive term in Greek and Hellenic philosophy. For Heraclitus, the Logos is a rational, sacred belief pervading the universe. In the Jewish Alexandrian religion, Logos appears, meaning the creative power of God and Providence. In the New Testament in the Book of John, Jesus was named as the sacred Logos, having become man.

The sage, Daskalos, in his book, *Esoteric Teachings*, came up with this definition: "The Christ Logos is Absolute Being, expressed for us humans as self-realization, consciousness, and rationality." And he wrote further: "Whatever is part of Christ, is part of us. For each one has the Christ in himself, the very same way as we all live in Christ." And finally, "It is up to us to knock or to seek." And: "When our faith is but the size of a mustard seed, that which we seek, will be given us."

❦ ❦ ❦ ❦ ❦

THE MASTER QUINTESSENCES

H ere, we present the basic information for the application of the Quintessences. The situation is much the same as with the Pomanders. Many possibilities for their use have not been tried. They are calling you to develop your own ideas and to experiment, to see which method is best for you. We are really only introducing possibilities and ways that in the course of time have proven worthy of recommendation. In case of doubt, including the question of the choice of a Quintessence, always follow your own intuition and your guidance. You might wish to choose a Quintessence simply based on the color or scent. If you find that you have a positive experience with that Quintessence, that is wonderful! This, then, would be the right Quintessence for you.

As with the Pomanders, Aura-Soma offers the Quintessences in tiny sample bottles. The set of 14, enough for several applications each, gives you the opportunity to put all of the essences to the test. And you have the chance to pick out one or two with which you can have the best experiences. For a start, it would be best to allow yourself a period of several weeks to stay with one Quintessence. By then, you could really sense what effect the energies have on you.

There is another way to find the suitable Quintessence—the orthodox Aura-Soma way: Look at the lower half of your favorite balance bottle, representing your "soul ray." The Master in charge of that one is "your Master," and the Quintessence coordinated with that Master is "your Quintessence." Here is a list of the Masters with their corresponding colors:

BALANCE BOTTLE	MASTER
Color of Lower Half	*Name of Quintessence*
Deep Magenta and Magenta	Pallas Athena and Aeolus
Violet and Pale Violet (Lilac)	Saint Germain
Royal Blue, Blue, and Pale Blue	El Morya
Turquoise and Pale Turquoise	Maha Chohan
Green, Olive and Emerald Green	Djwal Khul
Pale Green	Hilarion
Yellow and Pale Yellow	Kuthumi
Gold	Lady Portia
Orange and Coral	Lao Tsu and Kwan Yin or Sanat Kumara
Red	The Christ
Pink and Pale Pink	Lady Nada or Orion and Angelica
Clear	Serapis Bey

❦ ❦ ❦

If, within the group of your four balance bottles, one of them is a Master Bottle (#50 - #64), then that one is yours.

If you find two Master Bottles, then it is the one nearest to your third bottle–namely, the one representing the here and now (in other words, position #2 or #3 or #4). Should you find three Master Bottles, then it is position 3.

But as we said, these suggestions are meant only to stimulate you. Vicky Wall used to say in her seminars, "The greatest teacher is in yourself. What we offer are just guidelines." We encourage you to listen to what your feelings tell you, and that applies, in general, to anything connected with Aura-Soma.

As with all substances, the Quintessences also contain energies of crystals. Each of these always correspond to the color of the substance. But you will find rose quartz energies in all of the Quintessences, and that explains this concept: "Through the use of one single Quintessence—whichever one—all Masters are contacted."

Rose quartz takes on the rose-colored ray easily (in the language of Aura-Soma—the pink ray), and it does not take into itself any negative energies. On the contrary, it actually cleanses other crystals of negative energies. The pink ray has to do with unconditional love, which should be stimulated by the use of the Quintessences. Unconditional love belongs to the things most difficult for us humans to attain. And how important it is for the development of true humanness! Unconditional does not mean unconditional love in the abstract. Rather, it is a love that includes disagreeable neighbors and the teacher who in the past has not treated you fairly, or the uncle who may have beaten you. Unconditional love begins in that place where it is most difficult to practice: in the intimate circle of family and friends, in the circle of those in your daily life. An excellent exercise in connection with the use of the Quintessences would be to visualize in your imagination the neighbor, the teacher, the uncle, the homeless person in the park, the unfair co-worker—whoever presents a problem to you—and open yourself to the core of that person. And know that this center core is worthy of love, for it carries within it the Divine spark. Or you might pray that in the course of time you will be able to know that. You might repeat that exercise as often as it takes for something inside of you to have really changed.

The spiritual teacher Gurdjieff often used pictures to bring home a certain point. For instance, he used this one:

> Someone is on a trip. He sits in a carriage drawn by a horse and steered by a coachman. The coachman stands for the mental, the intellectual part of humans, the horse for the emotions. The wagon is to represent the body. And inside sits the traveler who should be served by the system—he is the Master. He symbolizes the spiritual part. If the trip is to be successful—that is, the destination reached without complications, all parts must be in harmony with each other and must communicate with each other...If just one drops out, the whole undertaking breaks up.

What often happens is that horse, coachman, and coach are relatively well bonded, but the Master is not. One may move forward, but the goal is not definite. Therefore, one is apt to ride in circles or even in an entirely wrong direction. Because everything seems to function well on the outside, the person is not even aware of what that neglect means, the failure to establish contact with the center of his/her being.

Let us suppose, then, that the Masters do not spend their time only in some higher "other" world, but are also a part of ourselves. If we do, then the Quintessences could serve as instruments through which we can contact the Masters in us, and we could then find out more about the direction and the goal of our life's journey.

In order to make such communication as easy as possible for you, we have included in the descriptions of the Quintessences the heading, "Meditation." In it you will find suggestions for the optimal use of the energy of each substance. The suggestions are brief and succinct to allow ample room for your originality. Test them, try them out, and see how much you will discover!

The Quintessences are primarily meant to ease you into the meditative state and to effect the best possible experience. How they affect the subtle bodies is explained in Chapter 4. But the Quintessences prove themselves to be useful helpers in everyday life as well. "Orion and Angelica," for instance, helps cope with jet lag after a long airline flight—an unexpected practical function. Under the heading, "Possible Effects and Areas of Application," you will find "everyday functions." These you can and will enhance with your own experiences.

Another use for the Quintessences is the clearing of the atmosphere in houses or apartments. You can treat sick plants and animals and, of course, other people, also. If you treat others, it is best to follow the directions given here or your own intuition. Please do not ever try to persuade someone unduly. It would serve neither that person nor you and certainly would not produce the desired effect. Refrain from judging or condemning anyone from whom you sense rejection. Aura-Soma does not appeal to everyone, and that deserves to be respected.

❧ ❧ ❧

And now, this is how you apply a Quintessence:

Open the little bottle, and place three drops on the pulse of your left wrist. Close the bottle, and spread the substance with the pulse of the right wrist. Now, lift the arms with the palms facing outward over the head, and imagine you are giving the energy to the world. Then, distribute the Quintessence around your aura from head to toe. Be sure to include the back as far as possible. It is also advisable to cross your arms over the energy centers.

Finally, breathe in the fragrance and the other contents of the substance with three deep breaths. Then you may begin with your meditation.

THE 14 QUINTESSENCES

#1

Name of Quintessence: El Morya
Color: Pale Blue
Fragrance: Flowery
Basic Theme: "Thy will be done"

Possible Effects and Areas of Application: Quiets the subtle bodies and brings peace. Makes the information in your astral body available to your consciousness. Stimulates artistic capabilities. Protects the subtle bodies, but at the same time allows positive energies to enter. Helps people who are not on good terms with their parents to find clarity. It is especially helpful for fathers- and mothers-to-be, since the way for new positive patterns of conduct are opened. Supports work with the "archetypal mother and the archetypal father," who are beyond any role models. Allows the understanding of the "laws of the light" to deepen on every level, including the physical.

Distinctive Qualities: The use of this substance is especially recommended in connection with the meditation for protection that was introduced in Chapter 9.

Meditation: The person who has reached the point where he/she can say to God, inner guidance, Higher Self, "Thy will be done," or the person who consciously desires to reach that goal, will find the best possible support through El Morya. It would be good in your daily meditation to include an affirmation such as the one mentioned above: "Thy will be done," or a similar personal sentence or mantra that suits you.

#2

Name of Quintessence: Kuthumi
Color: Pale Gold
Fragrance: Flowery, sweet, spicy
Basic Theme: To establish the connection between angels and human beings

Possible Effects and Areas of Application: Every living being, every plant, every stone, has a consciousness. This consciousness was at one time, and is still today, perceived by some as beings such as spirits, devas, and elementals. Kuthumi supports people who desire contact with these beings, in regard to healing work, gardening, and so on. The substance aids the person in creating a bond, to build trust—and not only his/her own, but also that of the "spirits"—that have often been misused by humans.

Furthermore, Kuthumi helps people to establish a bond with angels, beings who, in ancient times, were closer to humans, and who know more about God's plan than we do. Kuthumi can support us in finding personal symbols such as a "power animal," certain plants with which we have a deep connection, or humanmade signs and symbols. All of these can help us access the power we have within. With it we can tune into energies that will enhance our creativity, our love life, and our feeling of connectedness.

With respect to all we have said here, we should not forget to give something back. The beings and the energies with which we want to build a connection rely as much on our love, our gratitude, our warmth, as we rely on theirs.

Kuthumi also helps to lessen fears in the spiritual realm, especially when they are related to our own subtle energies.

Meditation: This substance makes it possible to become aware of the consciousness of living beings whom we would normally consider very different from us humans. You could, for example, apply it out of doors and, with its help and in a meditative state, sense the essence of a tree, open yourself to what lies deep within rather than the materially obvious aspects of the tree. You can do the same with a flower, a rock, a mountain. The same can be done with a body of water—best with moving water, like a creek or a river. (Stagnant ponds, for instance, are not suitable.)

This kind of meditation, also suitable for practice in a park, harbors enormous potential. It can lead people who work indoors all day into finding an inner balance. It can also be experienced when children are included. In this instance, adults can learn from children—a healing experience for both.

#3

Name of Quintessence: Lady Nada
Color: Pale Pink
Fragrance: Like that of roses
Basic Theme: To diminish aggression

Possible Effects and Areas of Application: Changes negative energy into positive, and that applies to all areas of life. Protects the user and changes the conduct of a possible aggressor because a small amount of unconditional love becomes stimulated. This is the concept we mentioned in the introduction of this chapter. Of all of the Aura-Soma substances, Lady Nada works most anti-aggressively. It makes communication possible that has been blocked or is in danger of being blocked.

People who work with sounds, with music, with the voice (in the mass media, in industry, or as a teacher or therapist) will find out through this substance how the healing powers in this area can be of use. Furthermore, Lady Nada opens the door for one to experience sounds, music, or voices as light or color—and vice versa. Also enables one to see colors or experience inner music during a massage.

The sage, Daskalos, whom we mentioned in Chapter 10, wrote in his book *Esoteric Teachings,* that the language of angels has to do with color and sound. And that human beings can learn to understand this language, and even to speak it. Whoever would like to go so far as that will find encouragement from Lady Nada.

This Quintessence helps people who feel a negative influence from the rhythms of the moon. It also makes full-moon meditations more effective.

Meditation: Because this substance is so closely related to sound, music, and voice, it induces a deeper experience of these phenomena. If you wish to experience music in your meditation, at home by yourself, in a concert, or in the opera, Lady Nada is recommended.

An exercise that can be effective to gain balance inwardly and outwardly is this: Find a place where no one can hear you and where you will not disturb anyone—the best place would be out of doors. If you are used to this exercise, you can also do it while you are sitting alone in the car. Now, find a tone that expresses your innermost being. Sing that sound using the vowels or "Mmmm." Repeat it louder, softer, and then voice it inwardly without an audible sound. Lady Nada supports this work and facilitates finding the sound again. (This exercise should be repeated often in order to be effective.)

#4

Name of Quintessence: Hilarion
Color: Pale Green
Fragrance: Fresh, like the forest
Basic Theme: To pursue the Way, the Truth, and the Life

Possible Effects and Areas of Application: Helps to make space on the inner plane, for example, to get to know oneself better. And that applies not only to a meditative situation, but to every situation. Makes it possible to find rest and peace in the midst of stress. Provides access to one's own truth, one's own wisdom. Hilarion helps to gain understanding of things on an emotional level when they have already been understood on the mental level. So it fosters understanding on a holistic plane. Thus, a true integration is possible. Helps therapists to take time for themselves, which they need, between sessions.

Meditation: This substance lends itself particularly well to quiet meditations, focusing on finding one's own truth. It makes the access to truth possible even in a stress-loaded environment. That can be very helpful in professional life when decisions have to be made.

#5

Name of Quintessence: Serapis Bey
Color: Clear
Fragrance: Spicy and flowery

Basic Theme: Cleansing

Possible Effects and Areas of Application: Cleanses the room after a healing or therapy session. Helps the therapist to cleanse his/her aura very effectively, to bring it into balance, to close and protect it. Also, it makes it possible for the client to integrate his/her experience. Stretches the electromagnetic field. Helps people to focus on star energy, astronomically and astrologically, in order to tune into the energy of the stars. It is also possible by way of the substance to contact the cultures that have possibly influenced the earth via the stars: telepathically, mentally, or by actual visits. Is particularly well suited for work with quartz crystals, reputed to be the keys to the mineral kingdom. (If someone is interested in delving more intensively into rocks, precious stones, and crystals, it is best to begin with quartz crystals.) Serapis Bey helps to find the inner dimensions of crystals. It can also be used for energetic cleansing of all minerals.

Meditation: The following will lead you to establish contact with a crystal, preferably a quartz crystal. Find a place in your house or apartment where you are least likely to be disturbed, where you can be alone. Take the crystal in your hand. Apply Serapis Bey, as described, to yourself. Then spread a little of it with your finger on each side of the stone. That cleanses it from influences that may have reached it and gives it protection. Aside from that, a resonance between the two of you is created. Send to the stone the thought transference that it might speak to you. Some stones carry much information within them, which is easy for them to share, and that is transferred through meditation in some, even in many, sittings. On the other hand, others may keep silent. In this case, it is important while you are handling the stone to carefully take note of the changes that are stimulated within you. For, sometimes the signs given are so subtle that they can be detected only from very delicate internal reactions. After that, allow the stone to say whatever it wishes. Handle it with respect, like a friend. It should be made to feel like a welcome friend and never feel used or abused.

Perhaps later you will want to focus on its message more specifically.

Then there is a possibility that you can "program" it. That can happen in the following manner: after you and your crystal have become bonded with each other, you can ask it during a meditation if it is ready to take into itself a very important theme. For instance, it could be a specific spiritual energy you wish to get to know better, or an idea that you are involved in and that you, with its help, would like to clarify. Then try to sense whether it is ready. If you have the impression that it is not willing, don't do anything. Perhaps you will ask it later, or perhaps not. However, if it should be willing, transmit the idea mentally. Then when you focus on that idea in your meditation, or in your prayers, include the contribution of the crystal each time. Your stone has been growing on this earth for an unbelievably long time and has access to dimensions unavailable to our minds. Who knows—perhaps it derives pleasure from helping you as a friend.

#6
Name of Quintessence: The Christ
Color: Deep Red
Fragrance: Like the forest
Basic Theme: To develop sacrificial love

Possible Effects and Areas of Application: Helpful in the domain of speaking and writing, especially in relation to the Logos. The Christ is the essential substance that helps a person to acknowledge his/her life task and to realize that it very much relates to this earth, to this dimension in the physical realm. On the other hand, this task does not have to be something "sensational." It could consist of rearing children well, selling beautiful flowers, or serving as an excellent secretary. The use of this substance supports an energy field, one relating to the Christ-energy in every person. (Also see Chapter 10.)

Meditation: Because the name, Christ, has been so closely related with the Bible, which, for some people, is quite a problematic book, we recommend the following meditation in which you can experience what is really meant by "Christ-energy." (The substance may be highly energizing; therefore, do not use it too late in the afternoon.) Apply the Quintessence as described. Then get in touch with nature, perhaps in a quiet park, in order to take a meditative walk. Focus your full attention on the act of walking. Whenever the intellect begs for your attention, direct it back to this activity. This meditation might be called, "Walking in the footsteps of the Christ."

#7
Name of Quintessence: Saint Germain
Color: Pale Violet, or Lilac
Fragrance: Flowery
Basic Theme: Healing on all levels

Possible Effects and Areas of Application: Brings the masculine and feminine aspects of the self into balance. Calms the subtle bodies. (It is the most calming of all Quintessences.) Makes it possible for a person to empathize with others, for example, in connection with relationships, with therapy, and so on. Changes the inner energetic condition, for example, when someone is hyperactive, overly fearful, or overly sexually stimulated. It can transmute this kind of energy into spiritually usable energy. Helps with issues of survival (money, safety, etc.). Clears up unresolved emotional problems.

Meditation: Saint Germain is especially effective in helping with healing meditations. Here is an example of a sitting meditation, in which you ask your "inner Master" for healing for yourself. Begin, after applying the substance, to concentrate on the upper part of your head. Think that you desire to be free of pain, relaxed, and to be "connected," or whatever it is that you desire. Then, imagine violet light entering into the upper part of your head, and enfolding your entire physical body. Perhaps you can imagine the violet light as flames or large drops of light raining down on you. At the same time, be aware of the "Master in you" and thank him at the close of the meditation. You can dispel stress and anxieties in this way. You can also send this violet light to someone else for healing and calmness. You can effect this if the person sits across from you and faces you. Or, if he/she is not present, you can imagine him/her being present. It can also be someone who has recently made his/her transition from this life. Keep in mind the affirmation: "Thy will be done," as you go through this process, knowing that what you are doing is in tune with the Divine will.

#8

Name of Quintessence: Orion and Angelica
Color: Pink
Fragrance: Flowery, like lemon
Basic Theme: Inner and outer travel

Possible Effects and Areas of Application: Helps to tune into synchronicity and to be at the right place at the right time. Frees the person from the effects of jet lag—that is, the physical effects of time-zone changes after long flights. To be used at the beginning of every new time zone—for example, if the time change is five hours, you would apply it five times. Better to use it a couple of times too often than too few times. An "overdose" is not possible. The Aura-Soma explanation of jet lag: Because of the speed involved, the subtle bodies slightly drift apart. Orion and Angelica brings them together.

Helpful at the beginning and at the end of projects. The substance allows the energies needed for this project to flow in. At the end, then, the substance gives the feeling of completeness and of closure, and the realization that you can now let go. Supports methods of healing that penetrate the subtle bodies.

Meditation: Orion and Angelica is an excellent companion for inner journeys. Also good for all kinds of visualizations. For example, with the aid of this Quintessence, you could approach the meditation for protection given in Chapter 9 from a different point of view. You can agree to experience all details particularly intensively, and visualize them: the blue sphere that protects you, and later all beings that were present in your past. With this you can have some astounding experiences.

#9

Name of Quintessence: Pallas Athena and Aeolus
Color: Rose Pink
Fragrance: Flowery
Basic Theme: Dream work

Possible Effects and Areas of Application: Brings the dream life into consciousness. Helps with interpretation of a person's own dreams and those of others. Brings deep insight into one's own dream symbols. Facilitates lucid dreaming, meaning that one takes the initiative and takes control of the action in dreams. This can prove very helpful in overcoming old behavioral patterns. The substance also makes it easier to understand shamanic traditions, especially if one wishes to become acquainted with the relationship of ancient peoples of the earth. The person learns to sense what the earth needs (the planet as a whole, but also that piece where he/she lives). Brings a connection with Greek and Roman myths and pantheon, above all in the sense of the archetypes. That is, it helps to find out which of these archetypes can be found in one's own psyche.

Meditation: As we mentioned, this substance is especially suited to dream work. It should be applied as directed evenings before going to bed. We offer another suggestion for those of you who might have a bothersome question or an unresolved problem for which you desire help from your dreams. Apply the Quintessence just before lying down. Then imagine that you have written the basic thrust of the question or problem in one word or in a very short sentence on a piece of paper. Then, visualize a circle of white light around the written word or words, and ask for help. After this, go to sleep. Should you awaken during the night, again imagine seeing the same picture: the problem in written form surrounded by white light. In this way, the conscious mind, or rather, the conscious connected with the subconscious mind, is kept active. It is possible that you will awaken the next morning with an idea for the solution of your problem, or an answer to your question. Perhaps, in addition, you will receive more ideas later.

Do remember to give thanks. Don't be disappointed if you, not yet used to this kind of work, at first experience nothing at all. It doesn't matter. What you can do is to train yourself. Repeat this practice over a period of time.

#10
Name of Quintessence: Lady Portia
Color: Gold
Fragrance: Flowery and summery
Basic Theme: Giving up judgments; not condemning oneself or others

Possible Effects and Areas of Application: People who are constantly working, never taking a break, find out how they can be less self-critical. Those who are inclined to criticize and condemn others learn through Lady Portia to develop compassion. On the other hand, the necessity is also brought to mind that at times it is necessary to analyze oneself and certain issues. Only in this way can one attain perfection. So then, when criticism or self-criticism or a judgment is needed, Lady Portia can help you develop the ability to communicate this appropriately and politely. It gives support in rebirthing work and also in facing your own birth trauma and to lose fear in that regard. It allows clear formulation of thoughts, especially those relating to ancient wisdom and self-realization.

Meditation: Lady Portia assists with all kinds of breathing meditations, in yoga, for example. If you want to experience a simple breathing meditation, it is recommended that you concentrate on the out-breath and focus on the idea of letting go. For everything that passes away does so on an out-breath. A further recommendation would be to take the Quintessence along on a walk in nature and apply it before concentrating for a longer period of time on in-and-out breathing. Be sure to focus only on breath, air, and how wonderful they feel. Then your head and body will become free.

#11

Name of Quintessence: Lao Tsu and Kwan Yin
Color: Pale Orange
Fragrance: Like oranges, spicy
Basic Theme: To receive information from past times

Possible Effects and Areas of Application: Helps to receive information from earlier incarnations and, in general, from earlier times, without having to cope too much with the shock one might feel from knowing about what one might have experienced. The information transferred comes on an energy level rather than on an emotional one. Has a similar effect as Bottle #26 and the orange Pomander, whereby the balance oil goes out from the body and works itself into the subtle bodies. The orange Pomander is effective from the electromagnetic field on the physical and then on the subtle bodies. The Quintessence goes from the astral body inward. The Quintessence brings understanding and appreciation of the worth of what we have brought with us from earlier times and allows self-love to evolve. As a result, brings about a feeling of deep peace.

Meditation: This substance works well in all those contexts in which you wish to free yourself from "old programs"—in therapy, in dynamic meditation, in prayers in which you state such a request, or also in the context of a ritual with the same aim. For instance, you might write your problem on paper and then ritually burn this page in order to let the problem enter into a different dimension. Or, you might find a stone, tell it your problem, and ask it to take that worry on for you, and throw it into flowing water. It is very important in such rituals that you are really focused, and that you, after the closing, no longer think about it, nor worry, but rather give up all of it and let it go.

#12
Name of Quintessence: Sanat Kumara
Color: Pale Coral
Fragrance: Spicy
Basic Theme: Synthesis (Sanat Kumara fulfills the functions of all the Quintessences)

Possible Effects and Areas of Application: Helps to get to the bottom of things, to see behind the masks, behind the backdrop, behind the disguise. If abuse or something similar has happened in the past, this substance will open the possibility of developing a masculine or feminine role model within yourself. Builds bridges between this world and other parallel worlds.

Meditation: Is especially suited during meditation to receive information and impressions from other worlds. With this Quintessence, you can aid every meditation that you wish to practice, and every one we have recommended here. Sanat Kumara can bring you into simultaneous contact with all the Masters.

#13

Name of Quintessence: Maha Chohan
Color: Pale Turquoise
Fragrance: Sweet and deep
Basic Theme: To build up feelings of connectedness to yourself, to others, to nature—to everything

Possible Effects and Areas of Application: Helps with expression from the heart. Recommended for people who make ancient wisdom available through teaching or via the mass media, but in such a way that it is useful for the present time. Gives access to very deep contact with the "inner teacher" and with the "inner Master." Facilitates the building up of emotional ties with higher, that is, faster frequencies than human ones. Presents an invitation to the inner guide, to the inner Master, to become really involved in the life of the person. This is to be done not from a sense of need, but from a readiness to learn.

Meditation: After applying Maha Chohan, sit down comfortably and relax. Imagine that in the center of your being sits a tiny but powerful figure of light, your inner guide, your inner Master. Take as much time as you need to realize on all levels that this spark has always belonged to you, that it will always belong to you, and that you, starting today, will never forget it. Give thanks to the figure of light at the end of the meditation for showing itself to you. This suggestion can open many different avenues for you: For example, in your imagination, you can enlarge the figure and discover whom it resembles—does it look like you, like someone you know, or someone you have known? Does it look like a saint, a well-known personality, a spiritual teacher? Like a figure out of the Bible, out of another book of wisdom, or out of mythology? You need to remain totally relaxed during this exercise. Just wait and see what turns up before your eyes. It is also possible that you receive no information at all. Then simply repeat the process over a longer period of time. Or perhaps you will see or sense something entirely different from a person. It might be a symbol, which would be just as significant. But allow yourself to be open to whatever comes. Do not have any preconceptions of what should happen. Be prepared for surprises. It is also possible that today you could perceive another energy or person, another symbol than would be the case in one or two years. In the process of evolving, there will be changes. You could also ask your inner Master for advice about a problem you are facing. You can ask him to comfort you if you feel lonely, even perhaps desperate. It is important that you always keep in mind that this being, this spark within you, is not God Himself. It is important also that when you are in doubt, always turn to the "original," to the "Source," to God.

#14

Name of Quintessence: Djwal Khul
Color: Emerald Green
Fragrance: Fresh, like the forest
Basic Theme: Space (within oneself, but also directed outward; for instance, very good for astrologers)

Possible Effects and Areas of Application: People interested in astrology will have easier access to horoscopes (their personal one, that of others, and also of events). Brings balance to the subtle bodies, as well as a grounded point of view. You learn that not everything can be accomplished through intuition, but that the intellect is also a very useful tool. You also learn that both should be used together, or both at the same time. It helps prevent the information gained through intuition from being overwhelming. To people who are apt to be fearful, this substance stimulates clarity and self-love (especially in connection with claustrophobia or other phobias). Helps to create the time and space one needs. Shows you where you are going. Brings about an understanding of the rhythms, the laws, and the patterns in nature.

Meditation: Suitable for meditative dancing, especially when these dances are to open the heart (Sacred Dance, Sufi dance, ritual dance, improvised dances, also dances performed in nature). Suitable for meditations that have to do with the stars and specific qualities of time. For instance, if you are interested in astrology and you know that on a certain day a certain constellation will appear, Djwal Khul helps you to tune in to it meditatively. Another suggestion for a meditation, one meant for Mother Earth and one especially supported by Djwal Khul: Apply the Quintessence as described.

Sit down comfortably and relax. Imagine that you are filling up with light and that this light is expanding at the same time, so much that it encompasses your entire physical body. Then it grows even more until it fills the room, your town, the whole country, and, at last, the whole planet. And it progresses in this way with every out-breath. Now you are aware that everywhere on the planet are scattered points of light. You are one of them. All of them are connected with threads of light. Thus, a whole light net spans the earth, giving its strength to the planet and to the cosmos. At the close of the meditation, imagine that the earth, engulfed with this net of light, begins to shrink until it fits into you and that you are carrying the earth within you.

HOW TO CHOOSE A BASIC COLLECTION

Most likely after you have worked with the first four balance bottles, as we suggested, you have developed your own ideas about how you might continue your journey with Aura-Soma. And yet you might like to know if there are recommendations concerning specific situations, perhaps crisis situations—that is, you may be interested in a kind of basic selection.

Let's say that you'd like to get more involved with the energies of Aura-Soma but do not wish to buy all the bottles, but rather have access to a well-balanced representative assortment. In that case, we recommend the Chakra Set. It contains the bottles that directly relate to the energy centers.

The Chakra Set Contains the Following Balance Bottles

#1 Blue/Deep Magenta	Crown Chakra, Third Eye
#2 Blue/Blue	Throat Chakra
#3 Blue/Green	Heart Chakra
#4 Yellow/Gold	Solar Plexus Chakra
#5 Yellow/Red	Base Chakra
#26 Orange/Orange	"Second Chakra"

This is the basic Chakra Set. Usually Bottle #20 (Blue/Pink) is considered a part of it. It relates to the Crown Chakra.

This Chakra Set Is Expanded with the Following Balance Bottles

#6 Red/Red   Base Chakra (the most stimulating of the
                                      Aura-Soma oils)

#10 Green/Green   Heart Chakra (the most harmonizing oil)

#16 Violet/Violet   Crown Chakra (the most calming of the
                                      Aura-Soma oils)

#43 Turquoise/Turquoise   Heart Chakra, Ananda-Khanda Center

#0 Royal Blue/Deep Magenta   "Eighth Chakra"

(The fact that these bottles belong to an extended Chakra Set is not mentioned in the bottle descriptions.)

The following method of working with the Chakra Set is a very good one: Every morning after getting up, choose the bottle that appeals to you the most. Apply the oil as instructed, or let your partner or friend massage the relevant part of your body with the oil. The choice itself shows you which energy center you especially need to focus on that day. Be sure to notice any effects that you might sense.

The Children's Set Consists of the Following Balance Bottles

#11 Clear/Pink

#12 Clear/Blue

#13 Clear/Green

#14 Clear/Gold

#15 Clear/Violet

This is the original Children's Set.

The Children's Set Is Expanded by the Following Balance Bottles

#55 Clear/Red

#77 Clear/Magenta

#86 Clear/Turquoise

(The fact that these bottles belong to the expanded Children's Set is not mentioned in the bottle descriptions.)

#20 (Blue/Pink) is recommended for acute situations in the life of a child (or for work on the "inner child" of an adult) when healing is desired to be stimulated.

Using the Children's Set has the following aim: It is meant to accompany a child from birth and to support him/her until he/she becomes a responsible young adult. For this purpose, the sequence of the bottles in terms of rank is this:

- #11 is the first.
- #15 is the last.
- #11 is suitable for newborn children until the ninth month, when the fontanelles close.
- #12 is suitable until the end of the nursing period. If the child is not nursed, then until he/she can drink from a cup. The Clear/Blue Oil eases this transition.
- On you go with #13 until the close of the rebellious period. It will soften that phase.
- #14 is to be used until the beginning of school.
- #15 is to begin at age 7. At the age of 7, a very important phase of development is completed. That is explained in many traditions, for example, in Anthroposophy, which sees the entire human life running in seven-year phases.

Accordingly, the significant transitions occur at the ages of 14, 21, 28, 35, and so on. After the first seven-year period, the perception of color changes in the child, so says Rudolf Steiner, the founder of Anthrosophy. This view is very much in tune with Aura-Soma.

Between the 8th year and the beginning of puberty, Bottle #15 is recommended, and in a crisis, #20.

The expanded Children's Set—#55, #77, and #86—should not be used before the onset of puberty. Exactly if and when needs to be left up to the parents or the young person.

❦ ❦ ❦

In the work with the "inner child," the difficulty that the person encounters at the specific age in one's past determines the remedy, or the number of the bottle, to be used. Let's suppose that a little boy had a long stay in a hospital at age 4 and had incurred damage to his soul. In the integration of these painful memories, Bottle #14 would help this person so that his fear and sadness could come up in his consciousness. He would accept them so that he could "integrate" them. This process will make it easier for him to change his present situation or feelings in regard to an inner relationship with a partner, with his own children, or perhaps with his professional environment.

The Children's Set is also beneficial when it accompanies mother and child during pregnancy.

Bottle #11 might be used by a couple desiring a child. It supports a "conscious conception." The oil should be used until pregnancy is assured.

During pregnancy, then, you continue with Bottles #12, #13, and #14. Every bottle ought to be used for as many days, weeks, or months as the intuition of the mother-to-be indicates.

Bottle #15 should be used as soon as contractions begin. It is helpful in easing the birth process and in allowing the mother to experience it while conscious. The same effect is also achieved by Bottle #2. If the mother did not continue to apply the oils until the end of her pregnancy, she can use them on her child utilizing the time frame described above. This is not a crisis solution, but follows the concepts of the Children's Set system.

To rub or massage a child with an Aura-Soma oil or to enfold him/her in a Pomander or Quintessence can be something very special—for the child and for the mother or father. Children love the colorful bottles with the light shining through them. They love the delicate fragrances of the substances. They can surely sense that something good is happening when they are applied to their skin or wafted around them. In order to establish contact with a small baby, a massage is one of the first and best things to do. The older the child, the more individualized and the more imaginative the Aura-Soma ritual can be—with a song, with finger play, with a little story....

Now, let us give you two more recommendations for older children:

If children feel threatened by another person or a specific situation, Bottle #34 (Pink/Turquoise) is especially recommended.

When the problem of bedwetting arises, the orange Pomander has proven helpful. It is important in this case to remember that the parent uses the Pomander along with the child. Here, too, a little ritual is effective. The best time for this process is shortly before bedtime. Whether or not to tell the child the purpose of using the Pomander is left up to the adult to decide. Positive results may be noted after three or four days. The ritual should be continued regularly in any case.

The Master Set Consists of the Following Balance Bottles

#50 Pale Blue/Pale Blue	El Morya
#51 Pale Yellow/Pale Yellow	Kuthumi
#52 Pale Pink/Pale Pink	Lady Nada
#53 Pale Green/Pale Green	Hilarion
#54 Clear/Clear	Serapis Bey
#55 Clear/Red	The Christ
#56 Pale Violet/Pale Violet (Lilac/Lilac)	Saint Germain
#57 Pale Pink/Pale Blue	Pallas Athena & Aeolus
#58 Pale Blue/Pale Pink	Orion and Angelica
#59 Pale Yellow/Pale Pink	Lady Portia
#60 Blue/Clear	Lao Tsu and Kwan Yin
#61 Pale Pink/Pale Yellow	Sanat Kumara
#62 Pale Turquoise/Pale Turquoise	Maha Chohan
#63 Green/Pale Green	Djwal Khul and Hilarion
#64 Green/Clear	Djwal Khul

With the Master Set, the sequence of the bottles is not relevant.

The numbers on the bottles of the Master Set mean that they originated in that order and that specific energies are contained in them. (We have given you information about these energies and about the Quintessences in Chapters 10 and 11.)

❦ ❦ ❦

For crisis situations, it is recommended that the following bottles be kept on hand so that they will be available as soon as they are needed:

- #1 (Blue/Deep Magenta, Physical "Rescue") for injuries and pain;
- #20 (Blue/Pink, "Star Child") for all crisis situations with children; and
- #26 (Orange/Orange, Etheric "Rescue") for all situations involving shock.

In the descriptions of the bottles, you can read exactly what effects these oils have and see that they are available in plastic as well as in glass bottles. The oils in these plastic bottles can be used by anyone who needs them because they don't get individualized.

❦ ❦ ❦

During a convalescence phase, Bottle #25 (Violet/Magenta) brings back both physical and spiritual strength. The pink Pomander also enables the patient to get back on his or her feet.

Bottle #2 (Blue/Blue) can help a dying person to leave the planet in peace. But it can also help someone turn back to life long enough to put one's life in order—if that is the problem.

Bottle #11 (Clear/Pink) can help a dying person to a great extent, too. Just as it can aid in the decision to incarnate, it can also support the decision to let go of this incarnation in peace. Bottles #11 and #2 are to be applied on the dying person and not on the relative or those close to him/her. If it cannot be done according to instructions, then apply it to the hands or to the feet.

The violet Pomander brings a peaceful atmosphere into the room of a dying person. Its effect is positive for this person and for his/her loved ones.

If you have lost someone through death, we recommend #78 (Violet/Deep Magenta). If it is a case of sudden death, you would need #26 in addition—the Shock Bottle. It helps you to grieve and to finish grieving and to set the loved one free. Bottle #78 also has a positive influence on the one who died.

In the case of losing someone in a separation or divorce, the Robin Hood Bottle (#27, Red/Green) and the Maid Marion Bottle (#28, Green/Red) are especially helpful.

If you are in therapy, whatever bottle you have chosen for that purpose will be the right one. However, there are some substances that have proven very supportive in certain connections. You may want to know about them:

- #22 (Yellow/Pink) and #59 (Pale Yellow/Pale Pink), and the Lady Nada Quintessence are well suited for use before rebirthing sessions.
- #53 (Pale Green/Pale Green) and the Quintessence Hilarion are recommended especially for body work like Rolfing, Postural Integration, Alexander technique, Feldenkrais, etc.
- #20 (Blue/Pink), #58 (Pale Blue/Pale Pink), and the Quintessence Orion and Angelica are very well suited for work with the "inner child."
- Dream work is aided by the use of the Quintessence Pallas Athena and Aeolus.
- In general, it is strongly suggested that you use the green Pomander before a therapy session. It "creates space" for you as a client as well as for the therapist. The violet Pomander helps the client to perceive the therapeutic experience, in its depth and complexity, and to recall it later.
- In the case of physical suffering for which no real cause can be found, Bottle #35 (Pink/Violet) is advisable.
- For protection, we suggest using the sapphire blue Pomander, as well as the red and the deep red Pomander.

Before any type of travel, it is a good idea to have the following substances on hand:

- the Quintessence Orion and Angelica (prevents jet lag);
- the green Pomander helps if someone is inclined to feel claustrophobic in an airplane or other means of transportation; and
- the golden Pomander (prevents nausea).

Before examinations or in the case of stage fright, the pink Pomander offers strength and centering. The turquoise Pomander also helps prevent stage fright. The golden Pomander enables the person to access stored knowledge at times of exams. The red Pomander locks in the person's reservoir of strength, which can be very useful before engaging in any type of athletic activity.

❦ ❦ ❦

In closing, a few words about a problem that seems to be pervasive—the difficulty that many people have in summoning up the will and the perseverance to get help where it can truly be found. We have discovered that people who are interested in Aura-Soma and in the immense potential that is contained therein, find themselves at a fork in their path. They know and sense that they need to change something in their life; they know that they want to grow. During a counseling session, or through involvement with the bottles themselves, and by reading about their meaning, they have discovered the factors hindering their progress and also where their journey could possibly take them. They have already chosen their "medicine" in the form of their bottles, the ones that promise the best support for their present challenges—a positive step.

Yet, in most situations it is worthwhile to keep moving forward and not just stop there. It would be highly advisable (if you can relate to this situation) for you to seek out a professional who can give you help when trying to overcome problems—for example, a person who can quicken your progress, can help you avoid side roads, and who can point you to alternatives that you might not be aware of while focusing on your own seemingly complicated circumstances.

In large cities and in many middle-size communities around the world, there are places where in the safety zone of neutrality and objectivity professional counselors can advise you. In Munich, Germany, for example, there is the "Health Park." There, psychologists offer information about various therapies for group or individual sessions. There are counseling centers or departments in universities offering such services. Alcoholics Anonymous is one of the best sources of help for people with addictions, problems of dependency, and co-dependency—it's not solely an outlet for those dealing with alcoholism. There are also renowned seminar centers that have helpful information available. They normally are in contact with a network of physicians, healing practitioners, body workers, and psychotherapists who can be of help.

When you have found a therapist, it is advisable to include one, two, or even three trial sessions in your plans. For it is entirely possible that the first therapist is not "the one" for you. There is no reason to be discouraged. And there is certainly no reason to give up. No matter how long a person has already suffered from a physical, emotional, mental or a spiritual problem, there have been people, when the time was right, who have been healed within a short period of time—even after having suffered for decades with chronic ailments. The Aura-Soma substances can make the right point in time and the inner readiness possible, readiness to deal with "old programs," which may have been so tightly adhered to.

If not only on a personal level, but also on a professional level, new paths need to be investigated, then it is beneficial to seek professional help. You could elicit advice from experts at an employment agency, or from an educational institution such as a college, a technical school, or a city or county educational facility. You could take a course in a foreign language, hone up on your computer skills, or attend a seminar in public speaking. You could learn techniques in art, gardening, woodworking, or a sport. You can only benefit, for sometimes it is important in life to overcome the status of the dilettante.

※ ※ ※

Seek for yourself the best and most suitable support possible. And try not to bemoan the costs that you might incur. To invest money in wholeness, health, in personal inner growth, and in a satisfying professional path is the most rewarding of undertakings. Perhaps it is the only endeavor worth the toil involved in the earning of money and the paying out of same.

In conclusion, we wish you the very best on all the paths that you travel in this life!

※ ※ ※ ※ ※

A P P E N D I X

OTHER AURA-SOMA PRODUCTS

In addition to the products we have already mentioned in this book, we would like to direct your attention to several others:

• The balance oils, already familiar to you, are available in 50-ml bottles. Aside from that, Bottles #1, #20, and #26 are available in 25-ml plastic bottles. Not yet mentioned is that the balance oils are also available in 25-ml bottles. The smaller glass bottles weigh less, of course, and are more suitable for travel.

• The Pomanders and the Quintessences have also been made available in 25-ml plastic bottles. You can also purchase a gift set, which is often called a sample-set. The tinctures are in 30-ml glass bottles with a dropper for your convenience.

• Vicky Wall developed formulas for Aura-Soma cosmetic products such as creams, lotions, bath crystals, and so on. A list of these is available by request. See the addresses in the Aura-Soma Resources section.

• A stand for the bottles is also available. It is made of transparent acrylic.

• In the form of posters or postcards, you can obtain a symbolic representation of Aura-Soma, the Color Rose, and the Chakra Chart.

❦ ❦ ❦

• *Vortex.* Original tape of a lecture by Vicky Wall (1987).

• *The Rainbow Wheel / The Angel Renewal.* Meditation with Vicky Wall. Music by James Asher (1991).

• *Peace to All Beings/Dawn at Dev-Aura.* Meditation with Mike Booth. Music by James Asher (1993).

BIBLIOGRAPHY

Argüelles, José and Miriam: *Mandala*. Shambhala Publishers, Berkeley, 1978.

Baginski, Bodo, and Sharamon, Shalila*: The Chakra Handbook*. Lotus Light Publishers, Twin Lakes, WI, 1991.

Bailey, Alice A.: *A Treatise on the the Seven Rays*. Lucis Publishers, London, 1950.

Blavatsky, Helena Petrovna: *The Secret Doctrine*. (Originally published in 1959.) Reprinted by Theosophical Publishing Co., Wheaton, IL, 1993.

Braun, Lucien: *Paracelsus*. Schweizer Publishing House, Zurich, 1988.

Brunton, Paul: *Conscious Immortality: Conversations with Ramana Maharshi, Sri Ramanasramam*. Tiruvannamalai, S. India, 1984.

Burghardt, Marlies: *Tarot und Lebensbaum*. Knaur Publishers, Munich, 1993.

Burmester, Helen S.: *The Seven Rays Made Visual*. DeVorss Publishers, Marina del Rey, CA, 1986.

Chögyam, Ngakpa: *Rainbow of Liberated Energy*. Element Books Publishers, Longmead, NJ, 1986.

Chopich, Erica, and Paul, Margaret: *Healing Your Aloneness*. Harper San Francisco, 1990.

Dalichow, Irene: *Beziehung statt Erziehung*. Hermann Bauer Publishers, Freiburg, 1989.

_____: *Zurück zur weiblichen Weisheit*. Hermann Bauer Publishers, Freiburg, 1990.

_____: *Sanfte Massagen für Babys, Kinder und Eltern*. Rowohlt Publishers, Reinbek, 4th Printing, 1995.

_____: *Der Weg der Kabbala*. In: *esotera* 12/93. Hermann Bauer Publishers, Freiburg.

_____: *Die ideale Therapie*. In *esotera* 10/92. Hermann Bauer Publishers, Freiburg.

Daskalos: *The Esoteric Teachings*. Published by P. Theotoki, Cyprus (no year available).

Davis, Patricia: *Aromatherapy from A to Z*. C.W. Daniel Ltd., United Kingdom, 1988.

Drury, Nevill: *Dictionary of Mysticism and the Occult*. Avery Publishing Group, Garden City, NY, 1992.

Dürckheim, Karlfried, Graf von: *The Earth Center of Man*. Routledge Publishers, New York, 1985.

Fortune, Dion: *The Mystical Qabalah*. Samuel Weiser Publishers, New York, 1987.

Freemantle, Francesca, and Trungpa, Chögyam: *The Tibetan Book of the Dead*. Shambhala Publishers, Boston and London, 1987.

Gale Research Company, *Encyclopedia of Occultism and Parapsychology*. Detroit, 1984.

Gnosis Magazine: *Kabbala*. San Francisco, 1993.

_____: *The Body*. San Francisco, 1993.

Goethe, Johann Wolfgang von: *Goethe's Color Theory*. Translated and edited by Herb Aach.Van Nostrand Reinhold Publishers, New York, 1971.

Grof, Stanislav: *Books of the Dead: Manual for Living and Dying*. Thames and Hudson Publishers, London, 1994.

Guiley, Rosemary Ellen: *Encyclopedia of Mystical and Paranormal Experience*. Harper Collins Publishers, New York, 1991.

Halevi, Z'ev ben Shimon: *The Way of the Kabbala*. Samuel Weiser Publishers, New York, 1976.

Hastings, Arthur: *With the Tongues of Men and Angels*. Henry Rolfs Book Series of the Institute of Noetic Sciences, Orlando, FL, 1991.

Kornerup, A. and Wanscher, J.H.: *Taschenlexikon der Farben*. Muster-Schmidt Publishers, Zurich/Goettingen, 3rd Printing, 1981.

Lansdowne, Zachary F.: *The Rays and Esoteric Psychology*. Samuel Weiser Publishers, New York, 1989.

Leuenberger, Hans-Dieter: *Das ist Esoterik*. Hermann Bauer Publishers, Freiburg, 3rd Printing, 1987

_____: *Schule des Tarot*. 3 Volumes. Hermann Bauer Publishers, Freiburg, 1981-1984.

_____: *Das ist Esoterik heute*. In: *esotera* 7/87. Hermann Bauer Publishers, Freiburg.

_____: *Stammutter eines neuen Äons*. In *esotera* 12/91. Hermann Bauer Publishers, Freiburg.

Liberman, Jacob: *Light: Medicine of the Future.* Bear & Co., Santa Fe, 1993.

Melody: *Love Is in the Earth—Laying on of Stones.* Earth-Love Publishing Co., Lakewood, CO, 1992.

Ram Dass: *The Journey of Awakening: A Meditator's Guidebook.* Bantam Publishers, New York, 1990.

Ring, Kenneth: *Toward an Imaginal Interpretation of "UFO Abductions,"* in: *ReVision* Magazine. Spring, 1989.

Shreeve, Carolie M.: *The Alternative Dictionary of Symptoms and Cures.* Century Hutchinson Publishers, London, 1986.

Simonton, O. Carl: *Getting Well Again.* J.P. Tarcher, Los Angeles, 1978.

Steiner Rudolf: *Das Wesen der Farben.* Rudolf Steiner Publishers, Dornach, 2nd Printing, 1989.

Tansley, David V.: *Radionics and the Subtle Anatomy of Man.* Health Science Press, Saffron Walden, England, 4th Printing, 1980.

_____: *Energiekörper.* Kösel-Verlag Publishers, Munich, 1985.

Tart, Charles: *Waking Up.* Shambhala Publishers, Berkeley, 1986.

Trungpa, Chögyam: *Cutting Through Spiritual Materialism.* Shambhala Publishers, Berkeley, 1987.

Wall, Vicky: *The Miracle of Colour Healing.* Aquarian/Thorsons Press, London, 1990.

Whorf, Benjamin Lee, ed.: *Language, Thought, and Reality.* MIT Press, Cambridge, MA, 1956 (13th Printing, 1978).

Wilhelm, Richard (translator): *Lectures on the I Ching.* Princeton University Press, Princeton, NJ, 1986.

Wolff, Katja: *Der kabbalistische Baum.* Knaur, Munich, 1989.

❦ ❦ ❦

AURA-SOMA RESOURCES

To be referred to the Aura-Soma practitioner nearest you, or to order any of the products we have mentioned in this book, please call or write one of the following world centers. If you wish to have a list of products and Aura-Soma practitioners mailed to you, or if you wish information on Aura-Soma seminars, please enclose a self-addressed, stamped envelope with your correspondence. (When calling or faxing from the United States, dial 011 before the international numbers below.)

NORTH AMERICA:
Aura-Soma USA, Inc.
Trish and Will Hunter
P.O. Box 1688
Canyon Lake, TX 78130
USA
(210) 935-2355 (telephone)
(210) 935-2508 (fax)

UNITED KINGDOM:
Aura-Soma U.K.
Dev Aura
Little London, Tetford
Nr. Horncastle
Lincolnshire LN9 6QL
GREAT BRITAIN
44-1507-533-581 (telephone)
44-1507-533-412 (fax)

AUSTRALIA:
Aura-Soma Australia Pty Ltd.
10 Cygnet Place
NSW 2234
AUSTRALIA
61-254-11066 (telephone)
61-254-30240 (fax)

AUSTRIA:
Aura-Soma Austria
Hanni Reichlin-Meldegg
Silbergasse 45/1
A-1190 Vienna
AUSTRIA
43-1-368-8787 (telephone)
43-1-368-87874 (fax)

GERMANY:
Aura-Soma Germany
Iris Rebilas and Constance Straeter
Gohrstrasse 24
42579 Heiligenhaus
GERMANY
49-2056-93140 (telephone)
49-2056-93144 (fax)

SWITZERLAND:
Chruter-Drogerie Egger
Unterstadt 28
CH 8200 Schaffhausen
SWITZERLAND
41-532-45030 (telephone)
41-532-46457 (fax)

Aura-Soma Laden
Sylvia Elsener
Zurichstrasse 12
CH 8134 Adliswil
SWITZERLAND
41-1710-0232 (telephone and fax)

ABOUT THE AUTHORS

Irene Dalichow is a journalist with a degree in education. She has worked in the advanced training department of a large company, and has also written for various German magazines and television stations. Since 1986, she has been a reporter and editor for the magazine, *esotera,* which specializes in spiritual subjects. She did a feature story about Aura-Soma for *esotera*, and subsequently, along with Mike Booth, brought this book into existence. She is the author of three other books.

Mike Booth has a background in art and holds a degree in education. He lived in Scotland for a while where he worked as a potter and painter—his mandalas are known worldwide. Before his affiliation with Aura-Soma, he was involved in management training and worked as a healer. He met Vicky Wall, the founder of Aura-Soma, in 1984, and remained with her until her death in 1991 as her constant companion and confidant. They traveled and taught together, and she entrusted him with the secrets of the Aura-Soma substances and their creation. Today Mike Booth is the director of Aura-Soma; manages the entire coordination, organization, and production; and holds seminars throughout the world.

❦ ❦ ❦

We hope you enjoyed this Hay House book.
If you would like to receive a free catalog featuring additional
Hay House books and products, or if you would like information
about the Hay Foundation, please write to:

Hay House, Inc.
P.O. Box 5100
Carlsbad, CA 92018-5100

or call:

(800) 654-5126

❦ ❦ ❦ ❦ ❦